The Miegunyah Press
at
Melbourne University Press

The General Series
of the Miegunyah Volumes
was made possible by the
Miegunyah Fund
established by bequests
under the wills of
Sir Russell and Lady Grimwade

'Miegunyah' was the home of
Mab and Russell Grimwade
from 1911 to 1955

WALTER
AND MARY

WALTER
AND MARY

THE LETTERS OF
WALTER AND MARY RICHARDSON

Edited by
Elizabeth Webby and Gillian Sykes

THE MIEGUNYAH PRESS

MELBOURNE UNIVERSITY PRESS
PO Box 278, Carlton South, Victoria 3053, Australia
info@mup.unimelb.edu.au
www.mup.com.au

First published 2000

Introduction and editorial annotations © Elizabeth Webby 2000
Design and typography © Melbourne University Press 2000

Designed by Sandra Nobes
Typeset by Syarikat Seng Teik Sdn. Bhd., Malaysia, in 11.5 point Garamond 3
Printed in Australia by the Australian Print Group

National Library of Australia Cataloguing-in-Publication entry

Walter and Mary: the letters of Walter and Mary Richardson.
  Bibliography.
  Includes index.
  ISBN 0 522 84923 7.

  1. Richardson, Walter Lindesay. 2. Richardson, Mary. 3. Richardson,
  Henry Handel, 1870–1946. 4. Letters—History and criticism.
  I. Richardson, Henry Handel, 1870–1946. II. Richardson, Mary.
  III. Richardson, Walter Lindesay. IV. Webby, Elizabeth.
  V. Sykes, Gillian.

826.6009

CONTENTS

ILLUSTRATIONS

Reproduced by courtesy of the National Library of Australia, Canberra, unless otherwise stated

ACKNOWLEDGEMENTS

PERMISSION TO REPRODUCE these letters has kindly been given by Miss Angela Neustatter, the great-granddaughter of Walter and Mary Richardson; and by Miss Margaret Capon, Henry Handel Richardson's literary executor.

Originals of all the letters are held in the National Library of Australia. Graeme Powell and the staff of the Manuscripts Room have been unfailingly helpful in making both microfilm copies and the letters themselves available for transcription and checking.

Some of the material in the Introduction was published in a special Henry Handel Richardson issue of *Australian Literary Studies*, after being presented at a conference entitled 'The Fortunes of Henry Handel Richardson', held at the National Library in 1997, organised by Associate Professor Susan Lever and Dr Catherine Pratt of the English Department, Australian Defence Force Academy. I am grateful to them for inviting me to speak at the conference and to Teresa Pitt from Melbourne University Press who, on hearing my paper, asked me to edit Walter and Mary Richardson's letters for publication. Thanks also to Jean Dunn for her excellent editing of the book.

For information about Walter and Mary Richardson I have drawn heavily on the work of Dorothy Green, particularly her *Henry Handel Richardson and Her Fiction* (Allen & Unwin, 1986), and Axel Clark, *Henry Handel Richardson: Fiction in the Making* (Simon & Schuster/New Endeavour Press, 1990). Much of the biographical information in the notes comes from Paul de Serville, *Pounds and Pedigrees: The Upper Class in Victoria 1850–80* (Oxford University Press, 1991) and Lucy Frost, ed., *The Journal of Annie Baxter Dawbin:*

July 1858–May 1868 (University of Queensland Press/State Library NSW, 1998). Thank you also to Tiffany Urwin for information about Caroline Dexter.

Research was assisted by the award of an Australian Research Council Institutional Grant. As the funds ran out long before the research was completed, however, Gillian Sykes' major contribution is acknowledged in her joint editorship.

ELIZABETH WEBBY

A NOTE ON THE TEXT

LIKE MOST NINETEENTH-CENTURY letter writers, Walter and Mary Richardson were not overly concerned about punctuation. While their letters have been transcribed as accurately as possible, a minimal amount of punctuation has been added where necessary, to allow for easier reading. Some characteristic errors, such as Mary's use of unnecessary apostrophes and Walter's spelling of 'freinds', have also been silently corrected. There has also been standardisation of date and place at the head of letters.

Underlining in the original is indicated by italics. Where a word or words have been underlined more than once for additional emphasis, italics and underlining have been used.

Anyone who has read the original letters in the National Library will have been aware of some inconsistencies in the ordering. Even so, the degree to which they were mixed up came as a surprise. As very few of Walter's letters were dated, attempting to arrange them in something like the right order has sometimes proved very difficult if not impossible. For ease of reference, letters have been renumbered, with the National Library number given at the bottom —in all cases these relate to MSS 133, Series 1 in the Henry Handel Richardson Papers. Wherever possible, dates have been added in square brackets.

Introduction

WALTER LINDESAY RICHARDSON arrived in Melbourne on the *Roxburgh Castle* on 28 August 1852. Although a qualified medical man, his first years in Australia, as with so many others attracted to Victoria at this period, were spent on the goldfields, initially as a digger, later as a storekeeper, and finally as doctor.

He had been born in Dublin in 1825 and named after an ancestral member of the aristocratic, and Protestant, Lindesay family. His father, Lieutenant Colonel Alexander Richardson, was in his seventies at the time and died nine months later. His mother Lucinda was Colonel Richardson's second wife; Walter had two sisters, Caroline and Lucinda, and a brother, Henry, besides half-brothers and sisters from the earlier marriage. Lucinda Richardson later married a Scottish doctor, Bayne Cheyne, and had at least one more child, John. No doubt influenced by his step-father, in November 1845 Walter Richardson began a four-year medical course at Edinburgh University. While at Edinburgh he studied obstetrics under Professor James Young Simpson, pioneer of the use of anaesthesia in childbirth, as well as homoeopathy under the Professor of Pathology, William Henderson.

After graduating in 1849, he spent terms of three months each as Assistant Pathologist in the Edinburgh Infirmary, Home Surgeon at the Maternity Hospital and Resident Physician at the Cholera Hospital. He subsequently worked in general practice in London and Wales, and from July 1850 until his departure for Australia was employed at St Mary Cray near Bromley in Kent, as assistant to Thomas Heckstall Smith. Smith's son, Alexander Brooke Smith,[1] who also emigrated to Australia, was later to introduce Walter to Mary Bailey.

Mary had been born ten years after Walter, on 28 December 1835 in Leicester, England, one of ten surviving children of John and Elizabeth Bailey. After her husband, a solicitor, died relatively young, Elizabeth Bailey ran a small school but poverty obliged most of her children to emigrate. Five besides Mary went to Australia and are frequently mentioned in her and Walter's letters: Sarah, John, William, Harold (usually called Ned) and Sam. Mary, Sarah and William arrived in Melbourne on 24 May 1853. John, the eldest, was already established in business in Geelong, and Mary went to work as a governess with the Bradshaw family, proprietors of the Family Hotel at Bell Post Hill near Geelong. Besides Mr and Mrs Bradshaw, who took on something of a parental role for the 17-year-old Mary (Mary refers to Mrs Bradshaw as 'Mother'), other members of this family mentioned in early letters are their daughters Polly and Matilda, often called Tilly, and their sons William and Edward.

Some six or so months after Mary Bailey arrived at Geelong she met Walter Richardson, who visited the Family Hotel with his friend Alexander Brooke Smith, then engaged to Polly Bradshaw. Early letters suggest that Walter was immediately smitten by Mary and that she fairly soon began to return his love. Certainly their marriage remained a strong and mutually passionate one at least until after the belated births of their two daughters in 1870 and 1871. And, while no letters from Mary survive from the 1870s, Walter's concern and love for her and the children are still clearly apparent in his later letters from Chiltern and Queenscliff, even as his health and professional livelihood collapse.

This collection of letters is therefore unusual in presenting, for the first fifteen or so of its almost twenty-four years, both sides of the correspondence between a husband and wife who shared a close emotional and sexual relationship. When apart, they wrote to each other very frequently, often daily, and complained when letters were not sent as often as they felt they should have been. The letters include many references by both Walter and Mary to their inability to sleep when apart. And, while Walter sometimes comments that he moderates his language because Mary will insist on keeping his letters rather than burning them, there are many clear expressions of his sexual desire for her, and hers for him. Presumably after 1870 Walter did destroy all Mary's letters. But she, her daughters and their descendants carefully preserved Walter's letters and Mary's earlier letters until their acquisition by the National Library in 1971. As well as their interest and value as personal documents of a marriage, the letters of Walter and Mary Richardson also have considerable historical value in reflecting the differing life experiences of a man and a woman in various locations in Australia and England during the second half of the nineteenth century.

For those more concerned with literary matters, the letters have particular interest as the most significant source material for Henry Handel Richardson's Australian classic *The Fortunes of Richard Mahony*. Ethel Florence Lindesay Richardson, elder daughter of Walter and Mary Richardson, for many years denied just how closely she had followed family history in the basic narrative structure of the trilogy: *Australia Felix* (1917), *The Way Home* (1925) and *Ultima Thule* (1929). Yet evidently she had first read her parents' letters as a teenager, writing in her diary on 27 May 1887, 'Read a lot of Father's and Mother's letters. It is like reading a love story of 30 years ago. I wonder if anyone will ever be as fond of me as he was of her.'

When she wrote this, Richardson was still recovering from her own unhappy love for her school friend Connie Cochran, which had followed an earlier infatuation with a local vicar, Jack Stretch. Axel Clark notes in his biography that she still saw both of them occasionally in 1887, 'But by now these affections which had once sustained her brought her nothing but pain'. (pp. 158–9) Given her own stormy relationship with her mother at the time, one might perceive a note of jealousy as well as envy in Richardson's comment.

As she acknowledged in her autobiography, *Myself When Young* (1948), Richardson drew on her early affairs of the heart for both *Maurice Guest* (1908) and *The Getting of Wisdom* (1910). Both novels were, for their period, particularly frank in their treatment of love in its painful, and sexual, as well as romantic aspects. If one reads Richardson's novels through in the order of their composition, it is quite a surprise to discover that *The Fortunes of Richard Mahony* (1930) is so sexless. One might assume that this new-found reticence was part of Richardson's acknowledged passion for historical accuracy—

the Victorians did not discuss sex and so she decided, in writing about them, not to discuss sex either. But as Walter and Mary Richardson's letters demonstrate, some Victorians—female as well as male—were not all that reticent when it came to describing their feelings for each other. Clearly, that had been Richardson's own response on first reading her parents' letters in 1887. Yet, when she came some twenty-five years later to begin writing the story of Richard and Mary Mahony, sexual passion was strikingly absent.

It is true that the first letters Walter and Mary Richardson exchanged during their courtship were fairly restrained, though the first extant one, from Mary to Walter, written on 22 April 1854, is a good deal more than the 'prim little note' with its 'right shade of formal reserve' which Richard receives from Mary in *The Fortunes of Richard Mahony* (Heinemann, 1954, p. 58). Walter's letters are also much more playful and more passionate than those of his fictional counterpart, even though they often cover similar material. By July 1855, for example, he was reminiscing about their first meeting, 'You little puss didn't you suspect I loved you when our eyes first met? Why you refused to come into breakfast the morning after my first visit. I suppose when you received my note about the key you began to suspect I had some little affection of the heart.' While Mary's early letters remain a little more stilted than Richard's, they reveal her to be a much stronger character than the submissive child bride we are presented with in the trilogy.

Although Richardson continued to rely on Mary and Walter's letters for the basic outlines and much of the detail of the lives of Mary and Richard Mahony, in keeping with her cooler portrayal of their relationship she did not make her fictional characters such com-pulsive letter writers after marriage. After their courtship, Richard and Mary's letters are rarely used as a narrative device until the time of the move to Barambogie in *Ultima Thule*. Then Richardson did draw very heavily on a series of letters written by her father from the Star Hotel in June and July 1876, while attempting to decide whether or not to set up practice in Chiltern. Chapter 5 of Part I of *Ultima Thule* consists of six letters sent by Richard Mahony from the 'Sun Hotel, Barambogie' while wrestling with a similar decision. Like Mahony, Dr Richardson waxed alternately pessimistic and optimistic over the prospects offered by the town. Richardson did, however, add much not found in her father's letters, especially the petulant, bitter tone. This is only found much later in some of Walter's last letters from Queenscliff when he, too, finally seems to have seen his wife as his biggest obstacle, someone determined to oppose him almost on principle. Nowhere in Dr Richardson's letters is there any equivalent of this heavily ironic passage from the trilogy:

> *It doesn't mend matters to have you carping at the class of person we shall need to associate with. For goodness' sake, don't go putting ideas of that kind into the children's heads! We are all God's creatures; and the sooner we shake off the incubus of a false and snobbish pride, the better it will be for us. There are good and worthy people to be found in every walk of life.* (pp. 628–9)

Nor is there any equivalent of the 'dissociation' described in Mahony's sixth letter, which foreshadows his coming mental collapse. Thus though they are clearly based on Walter Richardson's letters, the letters from Richard Mahony in this chapter have been carefully crafted by Richardson to provide a dramatic revelation of his mental and emotional state at this time, as well as ironic pointers to his past and future.

Some of the most moving letters in the Richardson correspondence relate to Walter's collapse in January/February 1877 while alone at Chiltern, with Mary and the children holidaying at the seaside. Even more than the earlier Chiltern letters, these were clearly the basis of Richardson's portrayal of Mahony at this period. Revealing as they do her father's increasing physical collapse and mental despair at the failure of his practice, they most likely provided the initial impetus for Richardson to tell Mahony's story, to construct some sort of pattern to which this was the necessary conclusion. Even here, however, Walter's love and concern for Mary and the children shine through much more strongly than in the letters of his fictional counterpart. A letter which has scrawled across its first page the cry, 'It will kill me if I don't get out of this soon. I would go away at once only I can't leave Mary [their servant]', nevertheless also includes:

> I feel very poorly again and hope it won't be long before you come back. I am very anxious & uneasy about you & the dear ones & am wretched *about the future*—I don't think I shall ever be an old man for I feel myself getting more feeble every year, and the worry & anxieties

of life make me very anxious to go . . . I am really very distressed at the idea of your having to move again & to
undergo the packing but there is nothing else for it apparently for this is done. (14 February 1877)

These letters from early 1877 demonstrate that the relationship
between Walter and Mary Richardson at this difficult stage of their
lives remained fundamentally different from that between Richard
and Mary Mahony in similar circumstances. Walter, despite his concern over his mental and physical state, was still capable of rational
thought and planning and did not attempt to conceal his financial
affairs from his wife. Hence she was not, like Mary Mahony on her
return to Barambogie, greeted with the news that eight hundred
pounds was still owing on their Hawthorn house. Thus although
Richardson composed the two letters written by Richard Mahony to
his wife while away on holidays (pp. 683, 696) almost entirely from
the series written by her father to his holidaying wife, she did so
both selectively and imaginatively. By rearrangement and compres-
sion she produced a more telling dramatic effect, emphasising those
aspects of Mahony's character that were most significant for this
phase of the novel. The letter on page 683, for example, concludes:

> *I do not see that we can incur the expense of another*
> *governess. The children will either have to attend the State*
> *School, or you must teach them yourself.*
> *I do not like your lined paper. I detest common notepaper. Go*
> *to Bradley's when you are in town, and order some good cream-*
> *laid. They have the die for the crest there.*

Mary Mahony is understandably exasperated by Richard's will-
ingness to spend money on luxuries such as expensive note-paper
while denying their children what she sees as an appropriate education. While references to both the expense of a new governess and
to buying new note-paper can also be found in Walter Richardson's
letters, they appear in separate letters and in very different contexts.
In a letter from early March 1877, Walter had written, 'I do not see
that we can incur expense of governess as my practice has quite gone'.
This was, however, in a letter mainly concerned with the fact that his
old friend Brooke Smith (the Purdy of *The Fortunes*) had left him
liable for a debt of sixty pounds. The next letter (4 March 1877)
acknowledges that:

I wrote in great annoyance in consequence of the rascality of that unprincipled fellow B.S. . . . If you like to venture on a governess you *can* try for 6 months to a year—I think you might buy a nice reading lamp or a drawing one like Mrs. Martin's. Also you had better get some paper & envelopes a[t] Purtons for I use a great deal . . .

An earlier letter, 12 February 1877, had included the comment, 'I do not like your lined paper. Go to Purtons. I am sure he will serve you better. I detest common paper & envelopes. You can see all kinds there & get them cheaper than any other shop.' By placing this complaint about 'common paper' alongside the earlier one about the expense of a governess, inventing the detail of the crest while leaving out the comment about cheapness, Richardson has created a very different letter, though one largely based on material from Walter's letters.

One possible explanation for the very different emotional tones of the Mahonys' and Richardsons' marriages may be because Richardson's depiction of the conflicts and differences between Richard and Mary Mahony was largely based on her own conflicts with her mother. From about the middle of *The Way Home* onwards, Mahony's attitude to his wife becomes increasingly bitter and resentful, a bitterness found only in Walter Richardson's very last letters from Queenscliff. On the other hand, as *Myself When Young* shows, the young Richardson felt that her mother did not understand her; they were in continual conflict until she left home for good (see pp. 47–8). Interestingly, the later relationship between Richard and Mary Mahony is depicted largely in terms of a mother-and-child one. As Richard's insanity increases, he transfers to Mary his childhood fear and resentment of his mother, while Mary comes to regard him as a wayward child who must be protected, and prevented from doing anything that might hurt himself or others. Richard's resentment of Mary's assumption of authority seems very like Richardson's own refusal to conform to her mother's 'ideas of what I ought to do and to be'. Mrs Richardson may have shared Mary Mahony's ambitions for her husband; she certainly had ambitions for her daughter which, like Mary's for Richard, were to remain unfulfilled.

If, as would seem likely, Richardson did base the relationship between Richard and Mary Mahony largely on her own with her mother, one can better understand the 'sexless' treatment of their marriage. Although a complete absence of sexual reference is in keeping with representations of Victorian propriety current at the time Richardson was writing the trilogy, it ignores the many signs of physical passion to be found in Walter and Mary Richardson's letters to each other. Much of the appeal of these letters comes, instead, from the fact that almost to the end they remain love letters.

[1] Alexander Brooke Smith (c.1834–82) arrived in Melbourne, 5 November 1852, and joined the police force as a cadet. From February 1876 to February 1878 he was officer in charge of the Ovens district. Later involved in the pursuit of the Kelly gang.

PART 1

Courtship

BALLARAT AND GEELONG
1854–1855

THE EARLIEST LETTER in the collection, a brief note from Mary, is dated 22 April 1854. Despite the formality of its opening and closing, it reveals a good deal more personality than the 'prim little note' invented by Henry Handel Richardson for Mary's fictional counterpart, Mary Turnham.

Both Walter Richardson and Richard Mahony, however, used the device of needing assistance with a new flag for his Ballarat store to continue the acquaintance (a later letter from Walter included a sketch of the store with a large flag flying in front of it). There is also a suggestion in his letter of 3 July 1855 that Walter may have deliberately left a key behind in order to begin a correspondence with Mary.

The remaining letters cover the period from Walter's proposal of marriage to Mary, early in June 1855, to their eventual marriage at Geelong on 27 August that year. Initially, Walter had hoped to be married in July, but Mrs Bradshaw, for reasons of her own, insisted on a longer engagement. Walter tells Mary about his family background and early life, urges her to drop her formal mode of addressing him, bemoans his bachelor establishment, and eagerly anticipates their married happiness. A practical man, he sends her money to buy a new dress and urges her to ensure she has warm clothes for their trip back to Ballarat. She complies, though again not without showing more spirit than is depicted in Richard Mahony's 'child-bride', little Polly. They exchange locks of hair and Mary complains that Brooke Smith's absence and silence are breaking Polly Bradshaw's heart.

[1]

Bell Post Hill
22 April 1854

Dear Mr Richardson

I received your kind note on Thursday & was very glad to hear that you received the key safely. I was rather afraid that it would slip out of the envelope but I endeavoured to fasten it as well as I could. Mr Candy called upon us on Tuesday as he was returning to Ballaraat so you see that he was not here to teaze us by hiding our thimbles & work. I am very happy to say that Matilda is very much better, but Mr Bradshaw has been very ill owing to a fall he had from the Hay loft he missed his footing & fell, & hurt his back very severely but I am pleased to say he is able to get about a little.

We are expecting Mr. Smith to see us next Saturday, & stay until Monday. I am sorry to hear that he is far from being well. Miss Jelfs desires to be kindly remembered to you. Her Father has returned so she will have to go on board on Tuesday & I think Matilda will go for a few days with her as change of air will do her good. I shall only be too happy to render you what assistance I can towards your new Flag if you will only send me word how it is to be done & I will do my best. We had a very pleasant walk before breakfast this morning to the cave to get some green boughs but had a great difficulty in getting up the Hill again & feel very tired from the efforts of it so you must please to excuse this hastily written letter. Mrs & Mr Bradshaw & Tilly & Polly join me in kindest regards to yourself—in haste

I remain
Your sincere friend
Mary Bailey

1/4

[2]

Ballaaratt
Thursday 2 p.m. {7 June 1855}

I was sorry to leave you my dearest sweet heart as I did the morn of my departure, but delay was dangerous.

The sun was just tipping the hills with gold as I ascended the steep of Bates Ford where I took a last look of that spot now so dear to me.

Anon I sat me down on a tuft of grass, and partook of the collation prepared by your dear self—then it rained and I thought of your prediction, true prophetess.

I have but this moment arrived and I haste to let you know that I arrived safely and that I shall expect you to keep your promise of answering this and enclosing *some thing* by return of post,

I trust your dear self and the family are well, remember me to them individually and kiss me dearest ✳ think on and get mother's consent to shorten the time for I need you *at home,*

Good bye sweet one.
I shall write by Monday's post again
Your fond lover
W. Lindesay Richardson

1/14b

✳ Here and elsewhere this symbol represents Walter's elaborate cross.

[3]

{Ballarat}
Thursday evening {7 June 1855}

D[ea]r and only sweetheart

Hurry mother and let us make the day in July instead of August, there's a love. What are you blushing about, and what are Tilly & Polly laughing about? My old place looked more comfortable than ever after my return, my little dog 'Fily' ran up to me and kissed me, crying like a child, and my other dog 'Brandy' evinced equal signs of pleasure; even my old cat came to greet me and I sighed as I thought that there was *one* want in my establishment. Business is very dull and as I am at a very great expense now, my hope is that you may come and help me to manage better, if you do, tell Mrs. Bradshaw, I promise that you shall spend some time with her (if we live so long) about the beginning of next year, but if she is heartless & cruel on this point she must expect other people to keep you when they get you—A thousand loves to your dear sisters, I hope you are well my darling, and have no cold; Remember what I told you, and treat yourself as if you were mine entirely.

Tell William I was sorry I could not wait for him on Wednesday morning but I knew that if I saw *your* face again I should postpone my departure another day, and as travelling and its et ceteras are very costly, I thought the more prudent plan was to tear myself from the neighbourhood and fly. I met two young men at a restaurant 5 miles beyond Meredith[1] & I directed them to Mr Bradshaw's for Thursday night, so you can tell them I did not forget business; The eight miles of floor upon which Miss Tilly purposes to come up for a gallop was very muddy when I passed up it, so much so indeed that I was glad enough to take the bush—

Friday. Very high winds indeed today, but the weather pleasant.

My neighbours all asking me why I did not bring Mrs. Richardson up—A patient who lived near William by the 'Prince Albert Hotel' and whom I left doing very well has had a relapse and is now again dangerously ill with Colonial fever.[2] We have had a nurse who has been paid 20/– a day for the last month & he is completely knocked up. I have been hunting all morning for somebody else, and altho' so many are out of work, have not got anyone, no one likes the situation.

I am afraid there will be hard times both here and in town this winter.

Sunday night.

I went today to the township to deliver your letter to William he asked me very politely to step in to dinner and I saw his lady and family. Little Charles your favourite is growing and is thin, Billy has a slight cold—Mr W. Bradshaw has a nice little estate and appears to be very comfortable.

Monday. Very stormy. At home all morning. Send this to the post [this] afternoon and expect a letter from you to be waiting there, you must excuse this, as my cat is in my lap purring furiously, insists on rubbing whiskers with me *doubtless suspecting my affections* are estranged! Ha! Ha!

> Good bye dearest. Kiss me ✳
> Love to family by the bye I saw <u>Mr Bannister</u> yesterday, tell <u>Tilly</u>; a
> very nice gentleman indeed[3]—
> Have you heard of my friend Brooke Smith?
> Good bye once more.
> Your fondly attached
> Walter

1/13

[1]   Half-way between Geelong and Ballarat.
[2]   This usually referred to typhus.
[3]   Henry Bannister, a suitor of Tilly Bradshaw.

[4]

Bell Post Hill
{10 June 1855}

My dearest Dr. Richardson

I was never so agreeably surprised as I was yesterday when I returned home from a long walk to the cave (where we had all been to gather mushrooms) to receive a letter from you dear. Mother gave it to me. I could not imagine for a moment who it could be from but the moment I looked at the address I knew it was from you dear. I was very glad to hear that you arrived at home safely. How very kind it was of you to write to me so soon for I know you must have been very tired after your long walk.

You were not quite out of sight when I came down stairs I could just see you going along the road. I thought I should have been in time to see you but I was doomed to disappointment. Mr. Bradshaw returned home that night but he could give us very little information about Mr. Smith, he only saw him for a few minutes. He said he had been out with the hounds on Tuesday but he could not find time to write to his old Friends at Bell P. Hill. I think he is acting rather unkindly to dear Little Polly do you not think so? I hope you will tell him of it when you write you will for my sake will you not dear? I am sorry to say that we did not yet get the pictures they were not ready, I am afraid they will be lost & that would be a great pity. Mr B thinks that he has left them at one of the Sergeant's houses but he has not written to tell us so we do not know what to do for the best. Mother has not answered Mrs Smith's letter yet I think she feels a little vexed at the neglect. William has gone over to see my Brother Harold today. I do not think he will be back tonight. I am very glad to tell you that William is very much better. I have enclosed you what I promised & I think it is nothing but right that I should ask for a piece of yours in return. I hope my dear you will not refuse me this but I do not think you will. I shall always answer your letters by return of post but I cannot always answer for their being in time for the post for the weather is often wet & then no one goes to town. I tell you this in case you should be uneasy at not receiving one. You left the piece of Poetry about 'John Brown' on your dressing table.[1] I have taken care of it. I think I may keep it until you come for it which will be in about three months. We must wait patiently until the time expires & then I will be ready to return *home* with *you*. I cannot get leave before that. I had to leave off writing my letter last night for my dear Harold came back with William. I was so pleased to see him & he is looking so well. I think my happiness is coming in so fast just now that I scarcely know what I shall do. There are some letters from dear Old England waiting to be sent for from Melbourne so I hope to get one from my own dearest Mother, I shall be so pleased. I wish you were coming down again soon. You cannot think how dull & lonely I felt the day you went *away*. I have again been interrupted in writing by the alarm of fire. I sat talking to Tilly about something when we saw some smoke from the drawing room fire place & there being no fire there made us call Mr B when it was discovered that there was some board on fire under-neath the Bricks & in the dining room as well. It appears to have been burning for a day or two but I am happy to say that it is quite safe now though we might have had the house on fire tonight if it had not been discovered in time. I think I have done all *you wished* me to do since you have been away and as I have nearly filled my paper I must begin to think of leaving off scribbling. Mother, Tilly & Polly send their kind love to you & with the same from Your ever loving & faithful

Mary

1/2

---

[1] Likely to be Charles Mackay's 'John Brown, or A Plain Man's Philosophy', *The Poetical Works of Charles Mackay* (London, 1876). Originally published *c.*1855.

[5]

{Ballarat}
Tuesday 11 June 1855[1]

Dear Love,

I wrote to you and Mrs Bradshaw yesterday, and I hope you received *all* safely. We have had very severe weather last night and today hail, rain, wind and snow, the last remaining on the ground some time, giving us the rare opportunity of a game at that hearty English pastime snow-balling. I hope you are all well. I am making *your room comfortable* been at it all day, sawing, nailing &c. My poor friend that I left doing so nicely has had a relapse, and is I am grieved to say gone to that bourne whence no traveller returns. I called in another medical man to give me the benefit of his advice but medicine is of little avail in that disease; Think my darling how short and uncertain life is and come and give me the benefit and the pleasure of your company thro' life—Good night dearest. Kiss me ✳.

I dreamt of you all last night and did not like to let the day pass without penning a line or two. Wednesday—I went to the Post Office today no letters from you, no lock of hair as you promised; I was at the Police Court all day as witness in the case of a dog that had been once mine, and was claimed by somebody who wished to appropriate her. Have not yet been able to go to the White Horse Gully[2] but hope to do so tomorrow. Am very cold so you must excuse my wretched scribble tonight. Good night, dearest love!

Friday. I went *yesterday* to the White Horse Hotel, White Horse Gully. Mr Ed. Bradshaw was not at home, but tho' disappointed in not seeing him I had a very pleasant walk, thro' beautiful scenery wh' I long to shew you—it resembles a gentleman's park in England more than anything else. I have caught a cold or rather a cold caught me while standing in the Police Court all day on Thursday but colds and Influenza are now quite 'a la mode'. How is William? Give him my compliments and ask him if he will be able to attend at our interesting ceremony? I suppose you have perused the service by this time! Ha! Ha! I can't write for laughing!—But joking apart, seriously, it is an impressive service—

'Wilt thou *love her, comfort her, honour,* and *keep her in sickness* and *in health,* and forsaking all other keep thee only unto her *as long as ye both shall live*'—Beautiful.

And equally so follows 'Then shall the priest say unto the woman'.

I gathered some lovely heath yesterday but tho' exquisite in appearance they want the perfume of English heaths, a great loss to the flowers of the Antipodes!—Good bye sweet one ✳

Sunday. Good morning dearest Mary. Many thanks for your kind letter and its enclosure which I received safely yesterday. I am confident your pleasure on receiving my letter was not equal to *my joy* as I had yours handed me and knowing by a squeeze what it contained hurried off to devour its contents in private. I suppose Mrs. B. doesn't see my letters to you dearest love for altho' there is no *harm* in *love*, still one hardly likes to write sweet nonsense for other eyes than the one next the heart. Well, I was going to say that I hurried off to devour it in private. I don't like '*My dearest Dr Richardson*', it's not kind of you to be afraid to say '*Walter*', is the name ugly?

And so you all went to the cave did you, pretty place that cave, Eh? I prefer the scenery a little further on, the wooded water course with the gentle slopes and steep precipices, with the track along the face of the hill, where you gently murmured *yes*! Of course had the ground been a little less rough and the season a little milder I should have *thrown myself* on my left knee and with one hand on my heart become pathetic but dearest I think we managed it very well, my feelings *prevented me* from saying all that I should have done and I fancied I felt you tremble on my arm; I had told Brooke the day before in Melbourne that I had a serious *duty to perform* and I certainly never expected to see him on the Sunday. With his usual exuberance of spirits he told me that altho' it undoubtedly was a serious matter he could not look upon any 'popping the question' otherwise than a most ludicrous affair & we both laughed heartily—

You ask *my opinion of his conduct to 'dear little Polly'*—Now darling I do not see anything so very unkind, consider my dear that he has a great deal to do, always knocking about, doubtless he has written before this, and besides 12 months is a long time and I think he felt rather hurt himself (*as I do*) at being treated somewhat cavalierly! put off for so long —Besides he knows he is safe in the heart of his little betrothed and surely a ride with the hounds was too tempting and perhaps he expected to be home in time for the post—I know he loves her dearly and she is his first and only love, and I would as soon doubt *my own constancy to you*, as his to his second self—Give the little dear my kind love and sympathise between you, sighing after two fond hearts that look upon each of you as part of their existence—

I think Brooke has very much improved and rejoice that he encountered the family for I think the mutual affection has been productive of much benefit to him. When we love, *and feel sure that we are beloved in return*, it does and must have *a beneficial influence* on *our conduct* —for as I would not like to have my body disfigured say by the loss of my fingers or eyes, so I consider now that *my mind should be* purer and the moral standard of my actions higher, is it not so? and is not this one of the good effects of love?, is not the state of love one designed for man by an allwise creator for his good! undoubtedly dearest! and altho' some are not so happy as to encounter a heart that can beat in unison with theirs every creature on earth loves some thing—I am not *poetical* on the contrary (you think rather *prosy*), plain matter of sense. I do not like poetry except perhaps on a fine Sunday morning, or late of a Saturday night; and I'll tell you why—*because I love it too much,* can you understand this apparent paradox? at one time of my life, I *was dosy* living in a land of dreams, of spirits, letting the realities of life glide past almost unheeded, that was when at college (when all young men go thro' a little studying and a great deal of what they fancy is *fun*). Late hours &c impaired my health and it was not until I gave up poetry and nonsense and took to hard work that I found myself able to cope with the combination of angel and devil in my fellow men's composition. I cannot read true poetry without feeling my heart beat stronger. I think you have poetry in your soul. I do not mean love that you can scribble verses any ass can do that, but I think *like myself* you look beyond *the hour, the day;* don't you? the *faculty* of *looking up* as it were, *looking to the source of things* I mean! Yes, I think we shall be happy. Of course dearest, every man and woman have faults, *blemishes, imperfections* of body and mind, but we must remember that there is *no perfect one*, and remembering this we must *forgive*—Are not the following verses pretty?

> The first dear thing that ever I loved
> Was a mother's beaming eye
> That smiled as I woke on my dreamy couch,
> That cradled my infancy
>
> I never forget the joyous thrill
> That smile in my spirit stirred,

Nor, how it could charm me against my will
Till I laughed like a joyous bird.

And the next dear thing that ever I loved
Was a bunch of summer flowers;
With odours and hues, & loveliness
Fresh as from Eden's bowers.

I never can find such times again
Nor smell such sweet perfume,
And if there be odours as sweet as them,
Tis I that have lost my bloom

And so it goes on until it comes to

And the next dear thing that ever I loved
Is tenderer far to tell,
Twas a voice, and a hand, was a gentle eye
That dazzled me with its spell

And the loveliest things I had loved before
Were but as the landscape now
On the canvass bright where I pictured her
In the glow of my early Vow

And so on finishing with old age—
like me as Mrs B. said! Ha Ha

Well this is a curious letter, but it is amusing and delightful to me
to talk to you and this sheet has occupied me as you see many days
proving to you that my morning thoughts and my evening sigh has
been dear Mary. I have got a little scheme *when you come to me;* you shall
write to *my mother* and *I to yours.* I have a dear old mother, that I love
dearly, if I were to say that she has been the *finest* & *the cleverest* woman
of her day I might offend you, sweet one, but she sang as I never heard
woman sing, played the piano, harp, flageolet,[3] accordion, danced in her
day, played whist and now poor old soul having become old is anxious
for me to return home, oh! *a letter from you will comfort her old age* and
shew her that her dear son is happy & does not forget the arms that
nursed him.

I am delighted that your happiness is *as you say* coming fast, I send you what *you ask* my darling but I am not accustomed to make bows with ribbon so you must take it as it is a token of my love—You say '*about three months*', now love let it be the *beginning of August* do there's a dear, I think it wrong, very wrong, to postpone it—as if you were afraid of me and as if Mr. B. was doubtful of my character—You will find a *humble home* and will have a poor man for your husband, but there's no queen will be more welcome if you can do without society *for a year or two* we will go to England & spend many a happy hour in the society of old friends. Kind love to Mrs B, Tilly & dear Polly and a thousand kisses from your dear and attached

Walter.

1/11–12

1   This is incorrect. Tuesday was 12 June.
2   On Ballarat East goldfield.
3   A small wind instrument.

[6]

Bell Post Hill
Sunday evening {24 June 1855}

My dearest Walter

I have only a little time before retiring for the night to write to you dearest for we have been so busy all day, a house full of company, that I have not had time to begin to write to you before. I received your dearly prized letter on Wednesday but was sorry to hear that you had caught a cold. You must take great care of *yourself* or you will be ill. I think it is my turn to talk to you now. I was thinking of you today when we went our walk to the cave. We had a very pleasant one indeed and we all climbed up those high rocks & stood & admired the scenery just where you & I stood but I think I looked more at the scenery today than when you were with me. I could not see that day but I blame you for it. I was sorry you did not see Ned when you went to White Horse Gully but am glad you enjoyed your walk. I am sure when you have time (when I come to Ballaraat) I shall only be too delighted to take the same walk with you & then we shall both be able to enjoy it together. Harry Bannister is down he is staying here. William will be up at the latter end of next week. I will send a short letter by him. I have not asked him what you told me at present about being down in August; perhaps I may but I don't much like saying it to him—do you not think it would be better for you to do it but I will if you wish me particularly.

You ask me if I have read the ceremony over, indeed dear Walter I have not neither shall I. Perhaps you will think me superstitious (well I think I am a little though I try to break myself of it) but they say you have 3 years bad luck so I *will* not read it for fear, so please do not ask me. I like those verses very much indeed they are very pretty. I am indeed very fond of poetry though as you say I cannot write that. I will indeed dearest Walter write to your dear Mother if you wish. I am sure nothing would give me greater pleasure if you think it would please her. I wish I could see her but I can fancy & I am sure I should love her. I would do anything to make her happy if she will but like me & *I will* do all I can to make you happy dear Walter but as you say we all have our faults & I am afraid mine are very numerous but I will do all I can to become better & *you* dear Walter must help me. I am afraid you will find me rather awkward at first but you must bear with me. You say that if I can do without society &c indeed & I can. I am one that cares very little about [it] & besides who shall I want when I am married but you dear? I am sure you will be enough. I know no one scarcely but Mrs Bradshaw's family for I have been here so long that I am known as Miss Bradshaw. So there will only be my brothers & sister Rebecca up at Ballaraat. We all feel very fatigued after our long walk this afternoon so you will excuse me writing this so badly & my head aches dreadful. I have not been well all the week. I have had an attack of Influenza so I do not feel very well just yet. I think it will go round the house. I think Mrs B. has it she seems very poorly. You made a very good excuse for 'Brooke' but I do not know what you will say when I tell you that he has not written yet. Now what excuse can you make for him? If you should see or hear from him first you ask him how he would like to see dear Polly wasted sallow and pale fretting about but he must expect it & to see her looks when anyone comes from town, the anxious have you any letters 'No Miss'. How would he like it I wonder? I am glad to say that Mr Jelfs have returned. Ellen has written & asks whether Mary has had any more letters from Dr R—& if she *answers* them if so to give her kind remembrance to him so I send it. I have not answered it yet but must tomorrow. Dear Polly & Tilly send their kind love, also Mother & hoping dearest that you will excuse this scrawl I must think of saying Good Bye but not before I return you many thanks for what I asked you for, the lock of hair. I prize it very much. I hope I shall hear from you on Wednesday & with very best love & kisses many ✳

> Believe me ever dear Walter to remain
> Your sincere & loving
> Mary

1/1

[7]

Bell Post Hill
Sunday afternoon {1 July 1855}

My dearest Walter

I received your welcome letter last Thursday & was very glad to hear that you were well. I am sorry that you would be disappointed in not getting a letter from me last Monday but it could not be for the weather was so wet that no one went to town but my Brother posted it for me on Tuesday. I do not know what days exactly the Mails leave Geelong & the weather being so unsettled Mrs Bradshaw does not go to town but I will write to you every week. William called here last Saturday & said he had seen Dr Richardson & he sent his love to Mrs Bradshaw & not to her alone but to the Misses Bradshaw—I must thank you for I think you meant some of your love for me at least I took some portion of it. Tilly went to town last Thursday to stay a few days with Miss Grundy. We are expecting her home this Afternoon for Polly has gone with her Father on horseback & she is to stay for a few days & Tilly to come back. I must thank you very kindly *dear* Walter for sending the money for my use. I hope some day I shall be able to make you some return for it but will you send me word how you wish me to lay it out? What I mean is how you wished me to be dressed when I am married, I wish you to send me word for I should like to have your opinion. I am afraid I am but a poor hand at writing letters but dear Walter you must take the will for the deed but rest assured I *feel* more than I can say. I often feel that I should say things & then again I do not like to. Perhaps *you* know how I feel but you must not laugh at me I shall get the better of it I hope. I am sure I shall when I have *one kind good* face looking at me. Mother is going to write a few lines to you I expect you will get a good scolding for she thinks you are too impatient & you might wait the three months but still I do not think she will be quite so strict as to wish to keep me so long however you will see by her letter what she thinks. I was sorry to hear of one of your patients being so ill again I hope he is better. The weather has been very fine the last day or two but it threatens to rain tonight. Polly & I had a little walk this morning & got a few mushrooms. Tilly sends her kind love to you & says that she will Galop up the 8 miles some day (when *we* are married) to see us. I think Alic is very unkind in not writing to any of us. We have never heard from him since he has been away. I hope nothing has happened to him. Poor fellow. I am afraid he is on a dangerous expedition, if you should hear from him first I hope you will let us know for Polly is getting very anxious about him. I cannot help thinking how disappointed you would be not to receive my letter before Friday I *hope* you will not be *angry* with me for I cannot help it if no one goes to the post. Tilly has come home & is pretty well. I shall be anxiously looking out for a letter next Wednesday I *hope* I shall not be disappointed. William has gone to stay with his Brother a few days, the change may do him good. I shall send a letter by him when he comes to Ballaraat which will be in a week or ten days. I am glad to say he is getting quite well again. I was sorry to hear my little favourite Charley was getting so thin if you should see his Father will you tell him I think that Bell Post Hill would do him good & to let him come down the next time Mr Wills returns. I have not received my English letters at present for Harold has not had time to go to Melbourne for them but I hope he will be able to go next week for I am so anxious to get my *own* dear Mother's letter it is so long since I heard from her. We have not heard from Mrs. Jelfs so I do not think they have arrived I hope nothing has happened to their vessel. Tilly is very busy hunting for a piece of poetry that would be suitable for you I do not know what it is for she has not shown it to me at present. I tell her that she ought to send it now. She has found it but I do not know whether she will or not yet. I have nearly scribbled my paper full. I am afraid it is an odd mixture but I do not think you will be tired of reading it will you dear? I know I am never tired of reading yours over & over again so I judge you by myself. You did not send me word how you liked Mrs W Bradshaw & Ted & all of them. Will you next time? I think I should make a pretty good hand at writing like you for I have been trying & I think a little practise would make perfect. I hope dear Walter that your business is improving since you last wrote. I can assure you that I will assist you all I can when I come to Ballaraat for I know your expenses must be very great just now. I shall be anxiously waiting for answer to this letter for you to tell me what you wish me to lay out the money in. I have filled my paper so I must leave off scribbling. They all send their kind love to you & hoping you will accept my *very very best love* & *kisses* many ✼ I remain dearest Walter

for ever your loving
Mary

1/3, 1/10

[8]

Ballaaratt
Tuesday {3 July 1855}

My dearest,

I posted a letter to you yesterday making the third since I left you, I trust they have all arrived safely, and that the contents pleased you. I have some hesitation about writing thro' 'Brown Brothers' altho' I suppose I can depend on none of my letters going astray. We have a splendid morn after a sharp frost and I feel well & happy, how are you love? I am like yourself looking anxiously for letters from my mother and trust the mail will not keep us much longer in suspense. My mother is, or was when I last heard, at Brighton. Where is yours? When did your father die? I lost mine when 9 months old—Where were you born? We have lots of questions to ask and answer each other, have we not? Of course I shall take more interest in you and yours than in any one else and all these little minutiae will possess vast importance when we come to hold dear converse, or to speak less a la Johnson,[1] our cosy chats by our snug fireside—Then I shall want to know what brought you out here, tell you where I was living at home, ask you to narrate your adventures since you came here, and tell you gossip about Smith's family &c &c &c &c and so on—

I hope darling you will adopt my plan of jotting down a few minutes converse *daily* it forms a good sized letter each week, and as you are occupied pretty busily it will not be a tax either upon your time or your love. Moreover you write a charming letter both in regard to penmanship and composition but letter writing improves our style of diction which is much noticed in life.

Thursday. Your last two letters have made me very happy, *my own* darling, & this last which I received yesterday at 12 o'clock commenced so nicely *'My dearest Walter'*, forgive any rude remarks in my last, love, but we men *are* rough sometimes—I'm so pleased to have a long letter from you as delighted to take it out to the top of a neighbouring hill, and seated on a fallen tree commence a perusal for the hundredth time of the whole series, commencing with 'Dear Sir' and ending with 'your sincere friend' to the last *'ever loving'*. You little puss didn't you suspect I loved you when our eyes first met? Why you refused to come into breakfast the morning after my first visit. I suppose when you received my note about the key you began to suspect I had some little affection of the heart.

I did send down *my love* but I sent it down to *every body* not liking to particularise to the bearer, altho' he was an intelligent man who had been 'butler & steward' in the late Duke of Newcastle's establishment, he said something about 'Mr Little's having been very sweet with the tall niece'. 'Ah!' said I 'he ought to have been sweeter';

I am happy to hear that Miss Matilda has been enjoying herself. Present my brotherly love and kind regards, how about the poetry that was *to suit me*, was it a reproof anent[2] my style of hat?

I am glad to hear that the cheque arrived safely. When you get the money love, lay it out as you best like. I hope it will be enough. I have known the want of money at *critical times* and I thought it *better* to let you have a little fund at *your own* disposal than to present you with something which tho' pretty might not be of real value—Moreover you ought now only to be dependant on *me*—I was very doubtful for a long time what I should do, for said I to myself 'if I do so, and so' she will *feel gratitude, not love*, however I resolved to do what I considered *right*, and I thought that *you would love me for doing so!*

As to *your dress darling*, my taste is simplicity, but do whatever *you like*, I am quite confident I shall *love you* in *any* guise, but remember 'Nature's dress is loveliness';[3] art only spoils—Mother *did* give rather a severe note on *impatience,* and *your value;* why tis the greatest compliment I could have paid *to me*, that *my future wife* is so much valued, that her friends absolutely will not let her go. However cross I may have appeared in my last, (and there is no doubt *sometimes* I do think it rather hard;) I am at this *present moment* quite reconciled to defer the happy day *until the first week in August.* Am I right? I know the ladies' privilege of choosing their own time. I have no doubt our worthy mother thinks that wooing time is the best time of matrimonial life, by her tendency to put it off till 1856 or 1857!

Friday evening I hope you will forgive me dearest Mary, but a sad mishap has occurred, I have lost *your lock of hair*. Oh! dear, Oh! dear; I always carried your letters and it, and on searching for it this evening I cannot find it! don't be cross, but cut off a *wee bit* more, do there's a love! and send me it next time—Tell your dear Polly that there is no reason to be uneasy about Brooke, he does not write for many reasons, he is busy, and <u>really</u> has now no time, sleeping perhaps one night in the bush, another night in some tent then he does not wish his letters to be seen passing thro' the post, perhaps, as his whereabouts is somewhat secret. I hope he will be able to attend in August, I think he will if *he possibly can*—I know he would like nothing better; I remember when he asked *me* to appear at *his* celebration of the event, we little fancied then that *ours* would be the first to come off. Time does slip by it is now more than a fortnight since I left you, three weeks next Sunday since our walk to the cave alone.

Mr. Wm. Bradshaw called yesterday and we had a long chat, he is really a *very sterling* common sense man; one that I like amazingly; I shall not tell you *all* we said, but this I may say he told me he had heard of *some event* that was coming off, and he congratulated me—Our conversation long as it was, was interrupted not however without his saying that he would see me again & resume the thread of our discourse. I gave him your message about your little favourite Charley and you will see him some day soon—He is one of the Committee for raising the Patriotic fund.

Business is dead, but I never lay my head on my pillow without thanking Providence for goodness shewn to me, and you may believe me when I say that I think I have <u>now</u> more reason to be thankful than ever I had before.

Hurrah! I've found it, the lost lock again. I couldn't rest until I had searched every where, Good night *dearest Mary*, my own dear love, kiss me ✳

Saturday morning, Glorious morn: up at six, have sent to the Post Office altho' I *do not* expect a letter from you dear but I think I shall have one next Wednesday.

Sunday morning.
Good morning dearest! We have a bit of a gale this morning. Going out to dinner today.

Monday.

I had been out yesterday afternoon, and on my return home was seated enjoying a pipe and a glass of sherry when fancy my surprise to hear a familiar voice and see the face of your dear Brooke—

He was accompanied by Mr. Bryce and it seems they *came a long distance,* and had a long ramble all day after me, the first operation was the preparing a hearty supper at which they distinguished themselves, secondly a little talking, laughing, telling stories, adventures, asking after absent friends, enquiring as to time past, present, and future, with many other little matters; after a reasonable time we adjourned and retired for the night, where of course there were many little private matters, scraps from letters to be read, locks of hair to be compared *and admired*, 'what a beautiful lock', how I 'shall blow Polly up'; Why said I, 'why for not giving me one like this' &c &c &c—

He says he has written—Tell Polly with my love, that he looks better than ever he did before in his life, is all spirits, and has an appetite like a hunter!! So I do not think there is any danger of a decline for *12 months*—And now dearest love farewell for the present. Brooke was very much pleased with my *little* place, and says there is only *one want*; There will *soon* be no need to make that remark I hope, for with your presence near me, I shall indeed be happy; I trust *you* will be so; if you can put up with the want of *many* comforts; that you may have been used to, if you can tolerate the rough style of a digger and his friends, and if you can do without *balls* for a year or so, you will find a fond heart and a little property at your disposal; farewell my darling, kiss me. ✳

Your fond lover
Walter.

The Vignette at the head of the chapter is a sketch of my place with the exception of the flag staff being 40 feet which it does not appear.

1/15

[1] Samuel Johnson (1709–84).

[2] Concerning.

[3] From Thomas Moore's poem, 'Lesbia Hath a Beaming Eye' in *The Poetical Works of Thomas Moore*, 'Collected by Himself. In Ten Volumes' (London: Longman, 1840–1841).

[9]

Bell Post Hill
Thursday morning {5 July 1855}

My dearest Walter

I have received your kind letter & was pleased to hear that you had recovered of your Cold. As William was starting today I thought I would send a few lines by him. I was very sorry that you kept dinner waiting for him last Monday he has been trying to get a seat in one of the coaches for several mornings but has always been disappointed owing to their being full. Ted came down last Monday evening he took us quite by surprise for we had never heard a word about his coming to see us. We have had some very wet weather this last week & it is so misty this morning that we can scarcely see five yards. I am afraid it will terminate in rain. I hope it will hold fine for a few days as we are busy washing & that must be my excuse for writing only a short note this morning. I am very glad to tell you that dear Polly is recovering her looks very rapidly since she received Alic's letter & she is anxiously looking out for another one. You would laugh to see me going about this morning I think for I have a bad foot I broke a needle in last Friday. I thought I had taken it all out but the last day or two it is so painful that Mother had made me put a large poultice on so my foot looks very funny this morning. I am very happy to say that Mr Bradshaw's arm is a little better though still far from well. We are very busy indeed this morning but I will write you a long letter on Sunday. I wish to write a few lines to Alic if I can possibly get time if I should not give my best love to him. Mother, Tilly & Polly all send their love to you & with *very best love* dearest & kisses many I remain

    as ever
    your loving
    Mary

I am very glad to say that Mr Jelfs have arrived safely in port. Ellen sends her love to you. You need not have asked me whether you might send your love to her for I like Ellen too well not to wish it but I think you are all getting alike for Polly just asked me whether she might send her love to Dr Richardson. I would say more dear but I really have not time. I have written a few lines to Alic he must excuse them for I have not time we are so busy

Good bye dear

1/9

[10]

Bell Post Hill
{8} July 1855

My dearest Walter

Sunday morning has again arrived. I have great pleasure dear in answering your last kind letter. I was almost ashamed to send that scrawl by William but as I had promised to write a few lines I sent them but we were so very busy I hardly knew how to spare the time for we had a large wash about at the time.

I was sorry to hear that you were so dull last Sunday dear. I hope that it did not last long.

I do not know whether you are the same as me when I feel dull it generally lasts a day or two. You say I did not tell you who my companion was when we went to the cave. Why if I must tell you it was Polly. We left Tilly to walk with the single young man, the rest were married & had their wives to walk with so Polly & I clambered up the High rocks we did not take the pathway until we got to the Brow of the Hill. Do you know Mr Parsons that kept the Queens Head in Geelong? He has met with a severe Accident he was thrown from his horse last Friday night & it is supposed the horse dragged him along & stamped on his chest & side he has five Ribs broken & his heart hurt. They hold out very little hope for his recovery. I think last week was nothing but a chapter of Accidents the[re] were two other Carriages upset but I do not know to whom they belong.

Business is dreadful dull nothing doing scarcely & such a quantity of poor men on the road begging for a bit of something to eat. I am afraid this place will soon get as bad as England. I was sorry you did not get any letters from England but I think dear we can condole with one another for I have not received mine yet & I know there are some waiting for me but Harold has not been for them yet. I have been expecting him up all the week but am disappointed. I intend to write to him if he does not come soon. Mother sends her love to you & says she will write to you next time but I think *dear* Walter we better let it be somewhere about the middle of August instead of the beginning do you not think so? I hope Brooke came to see you & cheer you up a little. You will bring him down with you when you come will you not dear? The weather has been nice & fine the last three days. I hope it will keep so for a short time for wet weather makes you feel so dull. Ted left us yesterday morning to return to the diggings.

I suppose you will have seen William before you receive this. Poor Boy he would have a wet walk but perhaps it might do him good & get some of his strength back ready for work. I daresay he would tell you that I had a bad Foot. I am very glad to say that I got a large piece of the needle out today but it still feels as though there was some left in it. I am going to have another poultice on tonight. I am going to have a plain White Muslin dress to be married in—I think that will look neater than anything. You have no objection to that have you? You said you liked anything neat so I thought that would please you best. They are all sitting round the table busy reading but they send their kind love to you dear Walter. We have not had an answer to the last letter that was written to Ellen Jelfs at present but I expect we shall soon for we expect her Sister Emma down to see us this week. I think I sent you word that she sent her kind regards to Dr Richardson—I hope dear that you have got quite well of your Cold dear. I am afraid you will put yourself to too much trouble about making your house comfortable for me for you know dear that I do not wish it for what will do for you will I am quite sure do for me. One thing I forgot to mention that is you told me if I ever felt too tired to write to you I was not to mind. I am sure you need not dearest be afraid of that for it is too great a pleasure to me to write to those I *love*. I must now say Good Bye & with kindest love & kisses believe me dearest Walter

Your true & loving
Mary

1/8

[11]

Ballaaratt
Tuesday 10 July {1855}

My dearest

William called last Sunday accompanied by Mr Edward Bradshaw, and handed me your last. I trust your foot is better and that Mrs B's treatment has been effectual. I suppose all lovers are more or less unreasonable for I confess, I felt when last Wednesday passed without any letter and that too the first time since I left.

However I am glad it was business that prevented you—William looked in during the morning and I am almost ashamed to say we were so much occupied that I had hardly time to say two words, the place moreover was in one vast heterogeneous confusion my man Friday not having the gift of *order;* I think if I remember rightly I was making a plum pudding in the intervals of business it *took me two hours,* but it was much relished in the evening and pronounced unequalled that day at least; in the afternoon of the same day we were visited by some 'coloured gentlemen' (who at some former period in the world's history may have been monkeys) I mean the natives or more properly aboriginals—They exhibited their performances which consisted of throwing the boomerang and asking for brandy—

Brooke has not made his appearance since and I now hardly expect him, *I half suspect* he is arranging matters so that he may [be] at *Bell Post Hill in August;* tell my little friend Polly with my love (if you will allow me) Ha! Ha! that she need not delude herself with any such hopes however as it is merely a vague suspicion of mine founded upon nothing—I hope I shall have a long letter from you tomorrow morning dear Mary.

Thursday: Tomorrow arrives my darling, and with it came your nice letter.

I did think the one by William was shorter than was absolutely necessary, but I know what a busy place you have of it sometimes— Mr Edward Bradshaw was telling me of some accident that happened to his father and your letter contains a very sad account of your own self going about with a needle in your foot, pon my word, my dear sweetheart, you must have a med[ical] man or Surgeon, to live at Bradshaws

Family Hotel and the house should either be called an Hospital, or *'The Accidental Hotel'*—What in the name of moron induced all the people in Geelong to upset their carriages in one week? Surely they might have arranged it better!

Your account of your ramble to the cave makes me fancy you must have spent rather a quiet walk a little different from the time my friend Brooke was cutting his antics and Polly was chastising him with her parasol!

Business is very quiet on Ballaaratt, and as you say this country is getting almost as bad as England for the poor man. People do not beg here. I am sorry to say they do worse, they steal—

You must not have any more low spirits now that you have fixed the day! or at least got so near it as to say the middle of August. You are not going to keep gradually putting off to next Xmas are you? Bravo, one says to another

Everything is ready here and her ladyship is anxiously looked for; I heard a gentleman the other night say *'So I hear the Dr. is going to be* [married]¹

'Somebody on the flat?' (meaning Ballaarat) [text missing] from Geelong.'

'Oh! who is she?' I [text missing]

No appearance of Mr Smith yet—I may be able to bring him down as you request but I fear Polly must not depend on it.

My kind regards and love to Mrs. Bradshaw, Tilly and Polly,

Remember me to the invalid Mr Bradshaw [and say that as it is] most probable I shall be down some [time] next month he had better defer his next accident until then.

Mrs Smith's address is
Rowlands
S. Mary Cray, Kent, England

Ask Mrs Bradshaw to remember me kindly to the family.

I am sure I shall admire you my dear Mary in your white muslin or any dress you may select, allow me to suggest the propriety of a travelling dress of good warmth, for we shall be a good many hours on the road and we must provide against either being wet or cold—

Tis a desperate morning on Ballaaratt, I don't know how you are down there. Ice last night. I have just been out sawing and splitting wood tis no use sitting over a fire!

This is not so long as my letters are generally but as I have got to go to the post office in the township a mile and a half off and as I have no more news to tell you and as you know very well that all I could tell would only amount to the three pretty little words that the birds say to one another, 'I love you' you can hardly blame me for saying farewell dearest, Take care of yourself, the last month that you are to be Miss Bailey, and oblige my dear Mary

. . . your fond Walter

1/21–2

¹   This letter is damaged, with part of the text missing.

[12]

Sunday evening {15 July 1855}

My dearest Walter

I received your kind but long expected letter yesterday afternoon. I think I never was so disappointed as last Wednesday as to receive no letter from you. I had written you a very long letter answering all your questions about my dear Mother and everything I could think of & was waiting very anxiously for an answer so much so, that although the roads were in a very bad state & the day very showery Polly & I per-suaded Mother to let us go into town for the letters for she expected one. She had written a short note to you & one for Alic enclosed in mine. I thought by my being somehow so over anxious I should be dis-appointed & indeed I was. It would be impossible to tell you all I imagined was the reason but the only one that had any hope in it was that you were coming down & intended surprising us. I cannot think how William could have forgotten it for he posted the letter on the Monday & he then started in the afternoon for Ballarat but meeting Ted & all of them he came back & did not start until Thursday & that was partly the reason that I wrote such a short note for I had scarcely any news left to tell but Mr Bradshaw is going to enquire at the Post office in Geelong about it & if it is not to be found there I will send you word next week & then you can enquire at the Ballarat Post Office. If it has been detained I should say it was because there was not enough postage paid for the letter I believe was over weight & when William came back I asked him if he had had it weighed & he said 'No' he put a sixpenny stamp on & he said he was sure it would be all right so I expected it would. If it should be laying at the Post Mr B. will pay the difference & send it to you. I think it was the longest letter I have written to you. I endeavoured to answer all your questions. I am sure I can always have plenty of time to write to you for Mother has sent in on purpose to have my letters posted & for me to get yours. I thought dearest of the first part of your letter that you were a *little bit cross* but you will see by my explanation I was not to blame but the latter part was kind I could [not] help laughing to think you were two hours making a pudding. You must have been interrupted or very busy—You tell me to provide against the cold thank you kindly dear for your thoughtful care of me. I shall attend to what you say but you have not as yet told me exactly what you mean to do. If it is not asking too much I should like to know your intentions & how we shall go to Ballarat. I should like to know dearest because I can then arrange things accordingly. I know you said we should go away after we were married but I think it would be such an expense dear to go to the Heads[1] but you know best so please yourself I have no right to interfere, but I was only giving you my humble *opinion*. Polly had a letter from Brooke on Friday she said he was quite well & is now on the Adelaide lead Maryboro.[2] He does not think he will be able to come but I mean to write & ask him & I know dear you will do the same. Many thanks for Mrs Smith's address Mother will remember you to her. The weather the last day or two has been very fine but looks tonight as though we should soon have rain. I should think the weather up at the diggings is more like the English Climate than it is down here for you have had snow & we have not. The destitution now pervading in Collingwood is distressing, there were thirteen cases in yesterday's *Argus* all respectable honest industrious people, that spoke of the people as actually starving, it is shocking to read them. I do not know whether I mentioned to you in my last letter that Mr Parsons of the Queens Head in Geelong was thrown from his horse & some of his ribs broken & his heart injured & that he was lying dangerously ill at the Separation. 'Poor Fellow' he has gone to his last home. He passed here on Friday in the hearse there was a Coroner's Inquest held over him the same day &

he was buried on Saturday. I am happy to say that Mr Bradshaw's arm is better though he is not able to move it at present. I told him what you said & he hopes he will not have the misfortune to meet with another accident. I have got one piece of needle out of my Foot but am afraid there is a piece still left in for whenever I attempt to walk or touch that side of my Foot it pricks me dreadfully. I have had poultices on ever since so I hope in time that it will be brought out. I think if the Hotel was called either of the names you mention that we should not have much custom for the house dear do you? I am wondering whether I shall have a letter on Wednesday I half expect I shall not till Saturday. You will be having this on Wednesday & poor me will have to go without. Ah if you had only felt half as disappointed as me I pity you. I was so struck that I could hardly believe Mr Brown for you had always been so regular before. I did not know what to think could be the reason. We have been very quiet today we had a run round the Paddock & Garden because the ground was too damp & cold for us to go to the cave. So you think ours must have been a very *quiet* walk that Sunday do you but then you must remember that we enjoyed it for most of our conversation was about *you* & Alic & they say talking about the one you *love best* is the best consolation to not having him with you. I very often get teazed & asked who it is that is going to be married & pretty well teazed where it is known but when people come & tell me that it is me I say *indeed* people seem to know my business better than they do their own & then I am away for I will not satisfy there curiosity. What a many things we shall have dearest to talk over when we are together so many questions to ask one another. I do not think we shall finish for a long time. Mother will write to you when she can answer your letter about different things. My letter love does not look so long perhaps as it generally is but I think it is only I have written it smaller & closer together. Mother, Tilly & Polly send their kind love & hoping my ever dear Walter that this may find you in good health, accept the best wishes with love & kisses many from your Ever true & loving

Mary
Good night & God bless & protect you dear Walter is my prayer.

1/7–8

---

[1]   Barwon Heads.

[2]   The site of a fresh gold discovery in Maryborough in 1854.

[13]

Mount Pleasant
Tuesday {17 July 1855}

My darling Mary,

It seems quite an age since I heard from you and as I trust there is a letter to me coming from you today I commenced to you—How is the foot, and how are all the family? Any news?

I have not heard of Mr Smith since I wrote last and your letter (and *its enclosure*!?) are quite safe; I suppose I had better bring them down when I come about *the end of the year*. Mr. Candy paid me a visit on Sunday last and enquired kindly after yourself and the family, he desired his kind remembrances—William paid me a visit last week. I expected to have seen him on Sunday again, but did not, he appeared in very low spirits: but I accounted for that by the fact of his not being employed at any definite work, as soon as he gets into a shaft he will doubtless be all right:

Tell Mr. Bradshaw that Mr. W. Bradshaw junior is now a *magistrate* and a *considerable man*.

I saw him on the hustings at the late election here—There has been a little more gold turned up at these mines lately and this is a very important point as it affects every one here directly and every one in the colony indirectly—I have not got my English letters but expect them by the next mail 'The Donald McKay' *due* since the 11th of this month—Have you heard from your friends yet?

Tis delightful weather, and reminds one of the joke of Curran's when asked by a friend if he 'had ever seen such a Winter' 'Yes' he replied 'last Summer' meaning thereby that Season equalled Summer[1] —Tis true our frosts remind us that it is not Summer and on that account perhaps, I often think it is as well *you* are not here until the mild warm weather comes!—

Thursday.

No letter from you yesterday! Business I suppose—

I was a little disappointed but don't want to be unreasonable. William came to see me last night, it was very wet and dark, and I insisted upon his staying until morning. I had had a splendid puppy given to me in the morning and was anxious to rear it if possible, the consequence was that we *got no sleep* as I had to get up two or three times to quiet the little rascal—

He insisted upon leaving before breakfast as he was in a great hurry to get to work.

Add to this that there was no supper cooked as my Assistant was out, and I fear he left us with a poor opinion of our hospitality!—

I am happy to tell you that his prospects now are very good, he has got into a party again who have one or two shafts as mines that are expected to do well!

I hope all are well? Remember me very kindly to all and to your little friend Miss Jelfs—

I shall not write a very long letter as I have to go up today to the Post Office, and tis a long dirty walk, so you will excuse this and taking the will for the deed imagine a thousand *loves and kisses*; ✳

I sent you Mrs Smith's address, when I wrote last, did you receive the letter?

I trust the foot is all right, and that you will be more cautious my dear in future.

I am sorry to hear poor Parsons whose accident you told me of in your last is dead, it is very sad to think of the number of persons who *kill themselves*.

Loves innumerable again my darling and believe me as ever

Your very affect lover
Walter

1/17–18

¹   The Irish judge, John Philpot Curran (1750–1817); known for his wit and eloquence as a speaker.

[14]

Sunday evening {22 July 1855}

My dearest Walter
     No letters all this week but I must not be impatient for you had to wait last week but do you not think that you ought to write two this next week to make up for it. I cannot write a long letter this time for several reasons first because I have not heard from you all the week.

Secondly I told you most of the news in my last & thirdly because it is getting very late. I have enclosed this in one to Mr William Bradshaw. I was really pleased last Thursday night to see my brother Harold walk in. He went to Melbourne next day to get a parcel that was laying there waiting to be fetched. I had a few lines from Mother saying they had not heard from me lately but letters had been sent to me at Melbourne but I have not received them at present. Ah is it not pleasant to receive letters from *those* that we *love* & particularly when we are so far separated. We are expecting Mr Bradshaw & his family all down next week so could you not contrive dear to write a few lines by him if you have time. We are expecting Ellen Jelfs down tomorrow to stay with us she sends her love to you. I have been busy reading all day it has been very dull all day & rains tonight although the last week has been very fine. We thought of going to Church this morning but forgot about it until it was too late so shall have to defer it until another Sunday. I have been reading a little of the 'Comic History of England'[1] tonight. I never thought of reading it before but happening to read a sentence or two was surprised to find how very amusing it was, there is something in almost every line. How do you like Ted Bradshaw—you did not tell me. We have not heard from Alic since I last wrote. I expect I shall get a letter from you dearest on Wednesday. Have you received the missing letter yet? I am so sorry you did not get it. There is nothing I dislike so much as my letters to be opened & particularly that one—I feel so vexed about it—you can't think. I must dear think of saying good night. Mother, Tilly & Polly send their love & hoping dearest that you will accept my best love & kisses Believe as ever—

Your loving
Mary

1/6

1   Gilbert Abbott a'Beckett, *The Comic History of England* (London: Bradbury, Evans and Co, 1848).

[15]

Ballaaratt
Monday 23 July {1855}

My *dearest love,*

Not getting any word from you last Wednesday, and not receiving your letter on Saturday altho' I sent (owing to the crowd) I determined to go *today myself*, and ascertain what was really the matter. To my *great joy* I received yours of *Sunday week* my darling; So that it could not have been posted to reach me last <u>Wednesday</u>, for I sent my assistant last Wednesday and he declares it was *not here*, altho' I got some business letters by that mail; I tell you all this because I see there *must* be one of *your letters to me* missing *somewhere*, as you yourself know; Now my dearest Mary, your last letter to me, was *the best*, *the longest* and *the kindest* and *the dearest* you have sent me, and I am going to write you a long and <u>*as Kind*</u> a one *if I can*—Firstly *my dear*, I must tell you that business has been *very good* lately, so that I am in good spirits; it is not very usual I suppose to talk about business in love letters, but still *you may* excuse this, as I look at it as much for the sake of the *future* Mrs Richardson, as for myself. The people around me are beginning to be civil, and altho' I have got an awful *riff raff set of Irish,* still there are one or two *decent* people that will be delighted to see <u>*you*</u>. Secondly my health is excellent, (and while I grieve to hear of your bad foot and wish I was there to advise you and to *take the needle out*) I am counting the days to the middle of next month, & this also puts me in good spirits!—

And so you and dear Polly actually walked into town to get no letter from me, now darling what shall I say by way of excuse or apology, let me see. I think the real fact is that the missing letter not reaching me by last Wednesday week's mail I waited and waited and now you will see that since I received the letter from you *before this*, I had written two *to you* without getting any at all *from* you. You say darling, you thought I was coming down, well it all rests with you to say when—

Tis strange about this letter of yours missing for only about a month ago a merchant in town sent me some goods to order, and the bill or invoice usually coming by the next mail, I was surprised not to get it, so when he came up soon after I began to blow him up about the unbusiness way of not letting me have the prices of the goods, he *declared* it had been sent, had been posted and yet it was not at Ballaaratt—Tis very kind of Mrs B. to take the trouble of endeavouring to get our letters transmitted punctually to one another; but you see with all the care all of us can take, as Burns says

'The best laid schemes of mice and men;
Gang oft agie.'[1]

And so you fancied the first part of one of my letters *was cross*, now I consider that *very* unkind Mary! and shall punish you for it when I see you! The reason why I was two hours making a plum pudding was because I was so busy, and moreover when you come to consider how it was admired! but I shall be happy to take a lesson from you in many little things; gentlemen who have lived in *the bush* are always more handy at any of the domestic part of life's drama! but I promise you, you shall have sole management of the cookery department; the great matter is to have *plenty to cook*, plenty of materials—

I think I will talk over our plans when we meet, I had intended going down to 'the heads' and don't know whether I shall not still, but as you say twill be costly! and perhaps the money might be better laid out—I know your aversion to *the conveyance* and will provide one *for ourselves*—

But all these matters can be arranged *next month*—

Time certainly does fly, tis but the other day since *I saw you* for the *first time;* I do trust my own dear darling that your foot is well, and do let me impress upon you the necessity of acting like *an old woman,* (I mean as regards care and prudence) for the remaining few weeks, not that I mean that you are not after that to take as much care of yourself, but then you know my dear you will have an *elderly medical gentleman* for *your adviser*! Love to Mrs. Bradshaw and Miss Tilly, not forgetting the future Mrs. Smith! Kind remembrances to Mr. B. no more accidents I hope—You ask me to write to Brooke how can I darling when I do not know his address, besides where he is today he may not be tomorrow;

Oh! I think we'll see him! Your little friend Ellen quite well? and happy? I suppose as the weather is so unfavourable and the walk so long that you have never been to the vineyard since; that was really a pleasant walk, and I enjoyed it very much, tho' not so much as our last, and which we are bound to bear in our memory.

I was much amused today, friend [text missing], sent me word he had a case or two of very [text missing] which he begged to recommend to *my* notice! This [text missing] the Post Office, *no letters*, so you see we are [text missing] turns—

Thursday morning

Good morning my dear, hope to receive a letter from you on Saturday. You must excuse the commencement of this epistle there was something amiss with the ink. I hear there is news from England and I hope a mail.

Good bye dearest love; and with every kind wish and prayer for your health and happiness believe me as ever, and for ever not only 'your sincere friend' but 'nearer and dearer' than that. Your ardent lover Walter.

I forgot to send you a kiss in my last. Accept a thousand this time and forgive me. ✸✸

1/19–20

[1] From Robert Burns' poem 'To a Mouse', 1785. ('The best laid schemes o' mice an' men / Gang aft a-gley').

[16]

{Ballarat}
Saturday evening {28 July 1855}

I have this moment *my own* darling received yours dated last Sunday, now do not blame me as you do! I have written constantly and regularly, you ought to have had one *today* and another *this day last week*.

I went to the Post office this morning and after waiting two long hours got nothing from the person I wished—However I make all allowance, I know there *must* be some little mistake now and then, and believing that I am *your own dear* Walter and that you love me as well as I do you, I fully believe we shall make it all right when we see one another—Cheer up, August is very near now! I have never heard any word of the missing letter, but am convinced it never came to Ballaaratt for two reasons 1stly Because there is no other Dr. R. here, and secondly because I am well known at the office—

Mr. B. looked very well today, your brother dropped in at the same moment and is looking very well tho' not in such good spirits as when I saw him last—

I hope all are well give my very kind love to all, to Mrs. B., Miss Tilly and Miss Polly as well as your charming little friend Miss Ellen Jelfs—

I suppose you will have such a nice walk tomorrow, how I wish I were there!

Be sure and enjoy yourself my darling Mary for this is the last week or two that you will have them around you, remember you will be in an awfully dismal place, no pretty faces around you! but in their stead a lot of grumbling Irish, and poor people with occasionally a tipsy man or two! Ha! Ha! Ha! a pretty picture I've drawn of the future Mrs Richardson's prospects! You must excuse this because I've been interrupted in almost every line until I forget how to spell and because I expect your brother William back every moment and he is to take it down to the White Horse to W.B.—

Now _do_ let me hear from you _dear sweetheart_ this coming week, and give me a good long letter; I know you will have _a house full_ and I suppose be very busy but do find time _my own_ love for a letter by next _Saturday_ if you have not written _by Wednesday_—I got your last kind nice letter on Monday and it consoled me during the week and I suppose this last note will have to this week. Ballaaratt is very dull weather fine, Brooke has not written to me since don't forget your promise to write and ask him to come down in August, Any more accidents? This _will_ make my second letter this week and redeem my character in your eyes. I wrote to your brother Harold when I came up last time but _I have never received any reply_;

And so you all forgot to go to Church did you?

I have never seen Ted Bradshaw! Oh! for I have I was thinking of Charles! They appear very nice, sensible, common sense young men— Make all enquiries about the missing letter my darling Mary, and believe me with every wish for your happiness, (until you join me a partner of my joys and sorrows in life)

Your very dear and fond and loving
Walter

1/111

[17]

{Ballarat}
Thursday afternoon {9 August 1855}

I wrote you _my darling,_ by Mr W. Bradshaw last Saturday, and altho' I have not much to say today I am anxious not to disappoint you of a letter next Saturday, as you seem like myself to look for one regularly.

Your last dear note told me by its tone that you were well and happy, altho' I fancy that *neither* of us will be sorry when the time expires that separates us: the days moreover are daily growing longer, and Spring that most delightful of our seasons in our adopted home approaches apace—Business I am glad to say continues good, and I am making preparations for my final trip—I have two very amusing incidents to relate which may *afford you* as hearty a laugh as they did me: I received yesterday along with yours of last Sunday a very suspicious letter addressed Mr Richardson and wh' the Post master *doubted* was for me; on opening it I found it a little account from a medical gentleman in Melbourne to wit

Mr Richardson
To—
For attendance on Mrs Richardson £20.0.0.

The second is that *I dream,* as of course everybody does and that I dream of her I think most of during the day is not to be wondered at, but I had a dream the other night when all around was still, that some how or other business had managed to go all wrong, and that *I was ruined* and compelled *to fly*; I remember distinctly saying to a friend for *I had one left* 'But my dear fellow, the worst of it is, that I was on the point of being married'—

I was much relieved when I awoke and found myself *all right*—I do get considerably quizzed at my being about to change my bachelor's life, everyone has to undergo these little matters, and I do not suppose we suffer more than others, in fact I rather enjoy it, for people seem to think me a *lucky fellow!*—

You must have waited a long time on Sunday evening if you sat up for your expected guests as I presume they did not arrive until Monday or Tuesday: Mr. W. Bradshaw is very full of some philanthropic schemes and I fear thinks rather indifferently of me because I don't join, the fact is I have been *so robbed* and have had so many *impositions* practised upon me, that I think more hardly of the diggers than I did—

William was not quite well when I saw him last Saturday but I invited him to pay me another visit soon and if I did not find some improvement I told him I should make him have some other medical man's opinion—

My little puppy is alive but sick, if I can rear it twill be a beauty.

I have no English letters, the May mail by which I expect letters from my mother and Smith's family has not arrived—

Strange to say altho' *I do not practise* I have now (just about when I am going down to see you again) a patient for *whose life* I have *great doubts*. His wife is *the nicest* person among all my neighbours and will be *so glad* of your company and society. *If he lives* we will have many a merry party—

I understand matters are very bad in town with the laboring classes, there is an influx of unemployed here which has the effect of reducing wages and making all grumble except the employers—

Mr. Hydes, & Mrs. Hydes, Mrs Young and the Geelong theatrical stars are coming here, also I believe Miss Catherine Hayes who I promise you we shall go and hear if spared, as well as Mr G. V. Brooke should he come here—[1]

Give my kind love to the family circle, I will attend to Miss Polly's request about the letter *I thought* there was an enclosure.

I am glad to hear that Miss Tilly contrives to make you laugh occasionally *I half guess* what it was about when you were writing *me last*!

I hope *the children* have afforded amusement and that now the fine weather has returned you enjoy many a nice walk, *I* shall expect to be shewn *all* the pretty spots in the neighbourhood.

No news from Brooke!

I shall not fail to remember all to Mr Candy who I am happy to say is *now* likely to be a *rich* man, having managed to get an interest in a rich claim—

Once more darling, adieu! a thousand kisses! and my best wishes, with every kind thought until we meet to part no more in life,

Your loving,
Walter

1/112–13

[1] John Proctor Hydes had initially performed in Sydney in the 1840s before moving to Victoria. The dancer and actor Jane Thomson married another actor, Charles Young, in 1845 and subsequently performed as Mrs Charles Young. The soprano Catherine Hayes made her debut in Australia on 26 September 1854 and gave a number of successful concert and operatic performances. G. V. Brooke (1818–66) was a British actor who arrived in Melbourne in 1855 and stayed until 1861, being especially well known for his Shakespearian roles.

[18]

Bell Post Hill
Sunday evening {12 August 1855}

My dearest Walter

    I am afraid you would think my last letter very short but I was so busy just at that time & Mr B going off that I could not write more so I will try and write a long one this time to make up for it. First thing, I must say, I was rather disappointed at not receiving any letter from you yesterday I quite expected one. How came you to forget to write? I was quite disappointed but the time is drawing so near that there will not be occasion to write many more. I suppose I must now make up my mind but you must not be angry at my not being quite ready to be married by the middle of the month but I think if you were to come down about Wednesday Week—that will be about the 22nd. I cannot possibly be ready before but you can come then & then you shall say when we shall be married but you must write again & tell me whether that will do. We had a nice walk to the cave again today the weather is beautiful. I hope it will continue so. We have had letters from Ellen Jelfs. I think it is very likely she may be down. I hope so. I begin almost to despair of seeing Brooke we have had no letters from him so we do not know where to write to. Poor fellow, I hope he is safe. I wish you knew where he was but you are like us left in the dark as regards his whereabouts.[1] I was sorry to hear from you dear such a poor account of William. I sincerely hope he is better, his strength is not equal I am afraid for the work he has to do. Give my kind love to him. I am sorry to say that Mrs Bradshaw's two youngest children have been very poorly all the week so we have had to nurse them, I think little Willie is very delicate. I sent you a letter Harold left here by Mr Wills. I daresay you have received it before this. I am very glad to hear that business is pretty good with you. Everything down here is very dull. Little or nothing doing. I hope that your friend will have quite recovered before you leave Ballaraat. I should think that you did have a very good laugh when you received the Doctor's Bill for attendance on Mrs Richardson & also at your dream. I did, it just amused me but perhaps not more than you. I hope dear that you are quite well & that you have received letters from home. I think I have been very fortunate lately. I was a long time without any & now I get them all at once. I received three more English letters on Thursday night. I have a great many to answer they are all angry with me because I had not written home for 12 months but I wrote a long one about three months back & another about a month since. So they will be getting them very soon. We have all got Bad Colds but I suppose we are only in the Fashion but it is one fashion we do not admire. I hope dearest that you are free from one. I am going to answer Ellen's letter tonight so shall have to be quick for it is getting late & we feel *tired* after our *long* walk—I shall hope to receive a letter from you on Wednesday & then the next I shall see you down but *do not* walk it is too far & the roads too bad.[2] Ellen desired her love to you & I shall send yours to her when I write tonight—I cannot find any more news to tell you dear so you must excuse more tonight—Mother, Tilly & Polly send their kind love to you & with best love & kisses dearest Walter

    as ever
    Your loving
    Mary

                                            1/5

[1]   Brooke Smith never did marry Polly Bradshaw.
[2]   A distance of approximately 50 miles.

PART 2
Early Marriage

BALLARAT 1855–1866

THIS SUBSTANTIAL BODY of letters covers the first eleven years of Mary and Walter Richardson's married life. All but a few relate to periods when Mary was absent from Ballarat, either recovering from illness, particularly one or more miscarriages, escaping the summer heat or attending to family matters. The Richardsons, as already noted, had a very close relationship and wrote to each other frequently when apart. During these years, Walter mainly remained at Ballarat, attending to the demands of his growing medical practice. While he had been looking after some patients before their marriage, after the Richardsons moved from the store to their new house in Webster Street, he returned to medical practice full time, registering with the Medical Board for the Colony of Victoria on 1 December 1856.

At the time of the first letters, Mary has returned to Geelong and Bradshaw's Family Hotel for the marriage of Tilly Bradshaw to Henry Bannister on 13 February 1856. Mrs Bradshaw evidently returned to Ballarat with her for a visit (Letter 21). The next major group relates to a visit by Mary in August 1858 to Melbourne and

Geelong, staying with her old friend Ellen Darling (the former Miss Jelfs)[1] and a Mr and Mrs Foster. Mary's brother Ned is now living with Walter; by this time relations with the Bradshaws have broken down and Walter refuses to allow William Bradshaw, his wife and children to stay during Mary's absence. In 1859, visiting Geelong while himself convalescing after an illness, Walter is able to tell Mary that the Bradshaws have now become bankrupt. On this trip he also stayed in Queenscliff and in Melbourne with Mary's uncle and aunt, the Turnhams. It was Mary, however, who had most of the illnesses and trips during these years.

In January 1860, Mary was convalescing in Melbourne, probably after a miscarriage or still-born child, staying at Heathville House in St Kilda with her friend Miss Cuthbert.[2] On 13 January, Mary had visited Parliament House, but did not enjoy it because of a severe pain in her womb and heavy bleeding (see Letter 43). Walter remained in Ballarat, now with his sister Lucinda as house guest and the added care of the small children, Harry, Trotty and Edith, of John Bailey, whose first wife Susannah, or Susan, had died on 13 August 1859. After moving to Ballarat in 1858, where he edited the *Ballarat Star*, Bailey had been elected to the Victorian parliament in 1859 as the member for Ballarat West, and was now living in Melbourne.[3]

In May/June 1860 Mary was in Melbourne once more, staying with a Mrs Patterson and then with her uncle John Turnham at Pentridge Stockade, where he was Assistant Superintendent. A year later she was again in Melbourne, this time staying at Bull Street, St Kilda with John Bailey and his new wife, Jeannie, whom he had married in April 1861. By this time Walter's practice had grown considerably—in 1861 he attended 130 confinements, for example —and he frequently complains of overwork, sending her lists of his patients as well as other local news. Walter's letters also reveal the beginnings of his interest in investing in goldmining companies. In Letter 39 he refers to North Clunes shares as having been sold for 7 pounds, adding 'It is a certain fortune'. As one sees from Letter 114, by 1869 shares in New North Clunes were now worth 159 pounds, allowing Walter and Mary to live very comfortably for a time.

Mary again visited Melbourne in November 1862, staying with Jeannie in St Kilda and admiring her new baby, though concerned about the looks and behaviour of Trotty and Harry. Later she also visited the Turnhams at Pentridge. Walter suffered from bad health during the summer, especially a 'Tic-douloureux', a type of neuralgia. Later letters are more difficult to date since in most cases we only have Walter's side of the correspondence, but at least two other visits appear to have taken place before the time of the last letter in this section, 22 February 1866, referring to the recent death of Jeannie Bailey.

1   Ellen Jelfs married John Darling in 1857.
2   Ann Cuthbert, sister of Henry Cuthbert (1829–1907), who became Postmaster-General in 1877. Henry arrived in Melbourne in 1854 with his brother Kingston and opened a legal practice at Ballarat. He was later joined by his sister, his father John and other brothers, Robert, John and Thomas. He married Emma Kirby in 1863.
3   John Robinson Bailey (1826–71), then Postmaster-General, resigned from politics in November 1860.

[19]

{Bell Post Hill}
Saturday Even{ing 9 February 1856}

My dear dear Walter

I thought you would like to hear from me by the Frenchman though I have no news to tell you. I do hope darling I shall soon hear from you. Yesterday Polly & I went into Town on horseback. I enjoyed it very much. I had Tilly's hat & habit we went quite early in the morning & staid all day so I saw all my old friends they enquired very kindly after you dear.

Today the Frenchman fetched us in a nice Spring Cart to the Vineyards from whence we have just returned. I am so sorry darling that I cannot send you any grapes but there are none ripe. I am so sorry. I met my Brother John yesterday he wanted Polly & I to go & have some dinner with him at Germans Town[1] but we were expecting Mother in Town but I said perhaps we would go another day. Give my love to Harold & tell him that John says his things are worth a great deal more than 20£ & he better pay it for Mr Marsh is going to leave & wishes to know what is to be done about them. Tomorrow evening we are expecting a few friends up to spend the evening so I suppose we shall be very merry. Ah I do so wish my own darling that you were here. I am afraid you will be very much worried whilst I am away but I must take the more care of you when I return.

I hope Sarah will arrive safely they all join me in kind love to her & not forgetting my dear Husband. Good bye darling with many kisses. Your ever loving wife

Mary
God bless you take care of yourself
MR

1/49

[1] Before moving to Ballarat in 1858, John Bailey lived near Geelong at Germantown (now Waurn Ponds) on a farm.

[20]

Thursday {14 February 1856}

My dear wife,

Sarah has I am sure told you of her hurried departure, and how I had no time to write a longer epistle, we had heard the night before that he was going to Ballaaratt & did not expect him. However Sarah was soon ready tho' she did not breakfast here nor wd she take a glass of wine, I did prevail on her to take half a doz biscuits of wh' I am sure she felt the benefit.

I was very sorry to part with her especially at such a time as the present, she behaved in such a lady-like way during the whole time she was here, that I do not for a moment wonder at Mr. Michaelson's feeling a blank in his household during her absence: I trust she will get comfortably settled as she deserves.

I am so glad to hear that you are enjoying yourself my dearest do not hurry to return on my account for I am sure this place will be so dull for you after the gaities of Bell Post Hill: I manage as best I can, and will get on pretty well, it is only a return to my old life, when I had no one to love & to cuddle me at night; I quite forgot to send you down the other £5 by Sarah, & indeed I had not got it. I send it now by Harry.

Mr. Norman told me he thought he saw you in town, William is all right again, I gave your message to Harold and am so glad that you are reconciled to your brother John: The weather upon which so much of our comfort here depends, has been very sultry since your departure, Thunder for 2 or 3 days with showers, today however the rain appears to have set in steadily and the atmosphere is delightfully cool & pleasant.

Had you a Thunder storm last Monday night I want to know this, because I saw sheet lightning in the South: Sarah awoke me in the night, saying (she had called me a doz[en] times) that she heard the creek rising, I got up & went out but *it was* the wind *this* time. I returned Alick's letter. I am sorry you sent it to me: especially as I had just had one from his father who poor man fancies he is earning a name & saving money & who actually sends him out £100 to commence house keeping! Don't you think it is about time the wedding day was fixed? I suppose it will be either the Thursday or the Monday. I hope you have given the bride the benefit of your experience—

Goodbye dear wife for today.

Friday

It had rained all day yesterday, & at dusk the water came tearing over the dam as it did before, making nearly as much noise all night, the creek rose three or four feet and very few slept soundly; Ellen says she was awake until daylight: I am rather glad Sarah & *you* were from home, altho' last night I did feel *lonely* at the prospect of having to get out at the back window again. Thank God nothing unusual occurred and this day the showers is bearable. The women miss you, and not a few have asked after you: we had everything off the floor, and all your things on the shelves, matting & carpets up, and we both slept in our clothes. Ballaaratt flat was under water but owing to the creek here being clear the water was not kept back: I shall I think move, as soon as you come back: You may give my love to all, I should so like to be present but I suppose matters will be managed just about as ours was.

You need not come up with Harry unless you like, that is if he asks you and if Tilly would like it.

He told me he would bring you up, without my asking it so do not be uneasy about doing it, unless you would like to stay longer and provided you have some other means of coming back. Do not come in the conveyance if you can avoid it. I have been compelled into reading Lucky[1] for want of something better & like it very much. Ellen is a good girl and manages very well.

Saturday

I do hope Harry will call for this. I have just been out splitting wood and cross cutting it with Ellen. I am going to have company tomorrow to dinner Mr. Reynolds & his brother. I trust you are still enjoying yourself and well. I dreamt of you last night also the night you first left: I am getting used to the big bed now altho' at first I did feel it a leetle strange.

The people are enquiring after Sarah, she promised one woman to cut out a *baby's dress*! I miss her very much—I suppose my dearest I may reckon on a letter from you on Monday. You must tell me when to expect you home, so that I may have things comfortable.

This is an awfully cold day: but I have got splendid fire: Business has been a little better since you left.

I drew a tooth this morning & charged 10/– I have no objection to as many patients as like to come at that rate.

I hope you have been well, & that you have not required the services of Dr. Gunn. Mr. Anderson from Malop St called here yesterday & Mr. Thom. I was saying that Miss Bradshaw was going to be united in the holy bonds of matrimony, when Mr Thom let out that he had once called there and they played the piano very nicely, & says he 'there was a governess there then'. Yes *I said that was my wife:*

Mr. Vineyards has just called; and as he is going down tomorrow I take the opportunity of sending this by him. He says something about a piano. I hope you have got your eye on one under a hundred pounds, you had better not purchase it or engage for its removal until we get removed. He gave me *a very sad account of Sarah on her journey*! She was nearly fainting by his account for want of food. This is not like her good sense.

Good bye dearest, God bless you, my love; I shall send Ellen up on Monday to the Post Office.

Your fond husband
W Lindesay Richardson

1/99–100

[1] Not possible to identify this with certainty.

[21]

Bell Post Hill
{16 February 1856}

My own darling Husband

I have just time to write a little to you before going into Town for Father is going to take Polly & I in on Horseback because I expect a letter from you in return to the one I wrote last Friday so I shall finish this in Town. The Wedding came off on Wednesday morning everything past off very nicely but they did not leave here until yesterday morning on account of the weather being rather inclined to be stormy. We had a very nice agreeable party in the evening & kept the Wedding up until 6 o'clock next morning. I did enjoy myself so much but all day we felt tired so I did not write to you. Next *Thursday* I & Mother are coming up in the four wheel carriage so you may look out for us love about Tea time for we shall start very early & get through in a day— please dear to tell Ellen to have everything tidy & comfortable for us but I need not say that for I know darling you will see to that.

We may be up on Wednesday but cannot say for certain but we shall be sure to be there on Thursday. The reason of my not coming sooner is because Mother couldn't leave sooner & she thought I should come up much more comfortable than if I came with anyone else. Many thanks love for the five pounds which I received safely by the Frenchman. I was sorry to hear about the heavy rain again but we did not have the Thunder here until the Tuesday night & then not much but it rained hard all Thursday & part of Friday.

All the news I have to tell dearest I shall leave until I see you. I hope I shall have a letter today. Mother, Father & Polly all send their love & with love & kisses to your own dear self I remain

Your truly loving wife
Mary

P.S. I shall finish this at Brown's if I get a letter & it wants answering. I shall not get my piano.

1/53

[22]

Wednesday

My darling Mary,

I have just been out taking a walk round; No xii have knocked off entirely, are not working, and have ceased washing up for want of water, they think it will be best to let the paddock remain until next winter!!!!!!

Harold's party are compelled to put their pipes in, which will take them a month at least before they can be at work again! Did you ever hear such confounded luck as our friends and relatives have on this hill —Vale's hole 'The 12 apostles' will turn out 4 lbs weight per man, I saw him this morning, digging puddling clay; he had heard from Mrs Vale, you can tell her he is looking very well—He has not paid me a 6d. of his account yet.

Yesterday was very sultry, a little rain in the night & this morning, rendering it pleasantly cool but there is every indication of a hot and dry summer.

I cannot sleep at nights, last night altho' my walk fatigued me so much that I went to bed at 8, I could not get to sleep until 12 o'clock; the night before I was just as bad. What is the cause I hardly know, but I can guess—I think I have made up my mind to follow my profession when we move; build a comfortable house for you, and confine myself entirely to that. Times are so altered now and store keeping so knocked up that I think it will be best to make a start; so when you come back we will choose a site and commence moving as soon as I can raise the money. You can ask Sarah to come up if you like, or we can advertise for a companion, or you might look out for *one now* as you are just on the spot to choose, also look out for a little parrott in a little cage to hang in your parlour.

You must write me longer letters for your last was very short, commencing with not having heard from me and ending as usual by saying somebody was waiting for you and therefore there was no time to devote to me!—Now independently of the pleasure your letters afford me, the occupation of letter writing is very improving altho' it may be a troublesome one—

Have you heard of Alick? or seen him? Did you go to Church last Sunday, I think Mr Vale get longer letters, and more news than I do, as he told me John took Mrs. Vale and Mrs. Whiteman to the Theatre on Tuesday, and set off on Wednesday last. I hope the poor fellow will be more successful in his new career!

I have packed up nearly all the goods, there are two cartloads, and think I have pretty well exhausted all topics of news. The piano is as bad as ever it was, the sultry weather of yesterday has had a ruinous effect on it! I am very sorry for I was getting on capitally, could play the two first pages! Umpelby has just passed poor little chap he complains fearfully of hard times.

Vale & Sheppard[1] do not come, they have taken to playing at a public house and formed a Whist Club so that our evenings are rather lonely. You know Allen, he was attacked one night lately while crossing the flat from the Whitehorse Hotel to the Punt by two men one of whom presented a pistol demanding his money—

No XII's shaft horses &c all to be sold by auction on Friday next—

With kind regards to Mr. & Mrs. Turnham love to Sarah. I remain my dearest wife with best love & a hundred thousand kisses and hugs for your darling self,

> Your fond husband
> Walter

1/14a

[1] Thomas Sheppard arrived in Melbourne in 1843 with his wife Harriet and settled at Buninyong. He was a brewer and magistrate who was actively involved in local affairs in Ballarat.

[23]

Friday evening

My dearest wife

I received yours of Tuesday this day and as you are so anxious to see me to take you home perhaps I may come next Monday if matters progress favourably.

There has been a Sale today at No. XII the proceeds came to upwards of £300.0.0 So that I shall have £20 to bring with me if that will suffice for our expenses. I purpose (God willing) setting out on Monday morning by the Geelong coach so you can meet the Geelong steamer wh' lands passengers I think at Sandridge. Should you be able to meet me at the wharf or at the railway station I shall be rejoiced to see your dear smiling pretty face once more for to tell you the truth I have been very lonely. I am anxious that this letter should be in time for Umpelby so you will I know excuse brevity; Kind love to Uncle & Aunt until I see them in person to thank them for their kindness to my dearest Mary,

> God bless you dearest love
> Your loving husband
> Walter

1/56

[24]

Webster St
Wednesday {11 August 1858}

My dearest Mary

I hope that you arrived safely and that Mr. Foster was waiting for you.

We had a terrific storm all Tuesday morning so I expect that you did not cross the water until this morning. I see the Cyclone arrived yesterday Tuesday.

You will doubtless have seen your cousin & your trip will thus be very 'apropos'. We have had wet weather ever since you left: we get on pretty well: Ned has given Eyre notice of his intention to leave:[1] Brooke called yesterday evening & stayed an hour and then Shanklin came in & played two games of chess—

I payed O'Connor £5. this morning for the deed & I enclose you all I have left. I will send more next week if spared.

Mr. Barry wrote me & said he could not pay—post the enclosed to him: I am doing nothing & no money coming in.

W. Bradshaw & wife left about noon on Monday.

Remember me kindly to Mrs. Darling & believe me my darling

Your loving husband
Walter

Put it in an envelope & address to Mr. Barry or leave it at Mr. Brown 59 Flinders St East.

1/84

---

[1]   The Eyre brothers owned a hardware business in Ballarat.

[25]

Webster St
Saturday {14 August 1858}

My dearest wife,

I received yours safely and sent the note accompanying it to Miss Cuthbert: I enclose you another £1. and will send another by the end of next week:

What very unpleasant weather you have had dear, it has rained daily here until today. Ned had a letter from Bennett Brothers & I think it very probable he will leave Eyre this month.

I was sitting quietly reading last night about half past seven when I heard a gentle knock at the front door, as Anne was laying tea. Ned not having come home I went myself and judge of *my surprise* to see W. Bradshaw & wife & horror to see the children. I was *too irritated* by what you said of the slanders of Mrs. B. senior, and too much in fear of a repetition of squalls from baby *all night* to submit to the infliction and altho' W.B said they had come to trespass on our hospitality I told them as quietly as I could that I had no accomodation & that you were from home, they went away I have no doubt highly indignant but I owe nothing to them & it is time they were taught manners! A piece of the grossest effrontery! And it all arises my dear wife from you turning me out of bed on Sunday night. They thought if we were silly enough to do that once I would be ass enough to do without any bed for a night.

I presume by this you have seen Turnham & your cousin.

Your letter was very nice and welcome. Anne is *improving* tho' *very* stupid, I have to see after everything. No sickness and no money coming in:

I went to poor McNee's funeral on Thursday saw Mackie & all the farmers from about Learmonth. Ned paid me £5. but as I have to pay £1. every Monday besides butcher & baker & Anne's wages I have not sent more. I have not expended 6d this week on myself. I will send you down £1. in each letter. I don't know whether it is safe to send them to the Hotel but as you have only put Melbourne on yours I am unable to send it to your house.

I have not had any letters this morning from home: The house has not been burnt down yet. I am glad to learn that Ellen welcomed you cordially in spite of the malignant & base slanders circulated by the Bradshaws.

I hope you will see poor Mrs. Croll if you stay in Geelong as you return, she knows such lies are false—The weather seems clearing up today, & I do hope we may have a fine week next for your sake—

Susan and all are much as usual.

Do you know where my old white knife is?—I enclose Miss Cuthbert's answer. I think she means that if both lustres & China exceed £8. she will send the balance: Have a *distinct bill* of what the Carriage is *to be* and say it will be paid on delivery. Take Sarah or Uncle with you as a witness or else your cousin—Susan says she would like her parcel sent up, if it is a large parcel send it by carrier if a small one by coach. Address it to J. R. Bailey Star Office.

With love dear wife & kisses oh! so many to yourself, as well as kind regards to your host & hostess. I am as you know

> Your devoted husband
> Walter.

1/85

[26]

Webster St
Monday {16 August 1858}

My ever dear wife

Two and three letters to your one! I don't know that I ought to write again this week, but as I have had a letter from your mother wh' contains enclosures for Sarah & William Henry, why I suppose I had better send them as soon as possible. I enclose you another £1 wh' with the other two makes three sent to the Sir C Hotham Hotel—

I hope you are enjoying yourself and that you went to Church yesterday, you have been away a week today & you have not said a word about your *Uncle, the Webbs, your cousin, the box:* I hope you have the likenesses of all the family. Are you still with Ellen or has Turnham invited you, or the Webbs, do you intend staying any time in Geelong? What wretched dreary weather you must have had if it has been similar to ours, rain & drizzle & mud.

I do not know that I have anything to tell.

I hope the contents of 'the box' have pleased you.

Was Uncle kind? Did you find out from Aunt what it was all about? I am very lonely and it is quite disagreable to go to bed in fact I think I shall sit up tonight—

Croll's foundry is taken: Ned dined at John's yesterday. I send down the two Umbrellas by the carrier Binney & somebody. I will tell you the address tomorrow: a miserably small attendance at Church last night—None of the three Accouchements off yet.

Your poor old mother is very anxious that Ned should go home, it will be a great pity if he does just as he is remaking a footing for himself: he has given Eyre notice in writing to leave next Monday: and

I think he will too: I have written today to Lucinda and to Bill—I had no letters from my mother, this mail—

I do not suppose she has sent anything in the box or they would have told us of it before this—

Monday

This day is a little fairer and promises to herald in a fine week which I sincerely hope for your sake my dear Mary.

I think I will postpone finishing this until tomorrow as it is too late for today's post and you would receive one today from me written on Saturday: You did not say how you got on going down *alone* in the Coach. Was the Jehu civil and did any of the passengers prove troublesome? I was glad to see you had a woman opposite you!—I returned home & awoke Anne & felt very lonely—Was it not cool impudence of W. Bradshaw to try the trick twice of turning me out of bed?

Mrs. Paul had no doctor, Paul intended to have had me if anything went wrong—Mrs Sheppard has had a son. I think I shall have the brewery man's wife & another a friend of his—

Wednesday. I did not get any letter from you yesterday but the nice long one this morning dispelled all my clouds & made me happy; it does indeed seem an age dear since that nasty dark morning that separated us—I am so pleased to hear of your enjoyments, Get out as much as possible my darling! Last night Ned & I went to bed about ten, and at $\frac{1}{2}$ past 12 I was awoke by John at the window asking for Ned: he came round to Ned's door, came in & told us that there had been a fire at Eyre's place, nearly burnt down, with difficulty saved, insured on the 5th August for £2000—

What a lovely morning, had my hair cut.

Your arrangement with poor Mrs. Barry is *the best* that could have been made she ought to have sent an order to her sister to pay £1 however I will send Anne tomorrow—My evenings are so lonely and I cannot go out as I [have] three ladies in daily expectation! it is very annoying that they are so long. I have sent the Umbrellas by Binney & Broadbent, office corner of Flinders Lane & Eliz St try & get the best one mended it will save £1—My darling wife, I will be so happy to see you again. God bless you and protect you and bring you safely home to me, for if anything were to happen to you it would kill me.

Your loving Walter—

1/98

[27]

Webster St
Thursday {19 August 1858}

My dear wife Mary
    You will be surprised at my writing another letter to you today
after posting one to you yesterday but I want you particularly to get
your cousin to find out from Cobb's offices where '*Luther*' is and where
he lives: Mr Cuthbert has not succeeded in getting the summons served,
he says his agent wrote to say he lived in Melbourne. Do this at once
like a dear.
    We had a lovely day yesterday and today & all night there has been
a continued pour—
    What a trip you must have had. It seems as if the heavens and the
stars conspired together to make it as unpleasant as possible. I am rather
glad of the *heavy rain* for I know it cannot last:
    There was an enquiry all yesterday in the fire at Eyre. A Coroner's
inquest. Ned was examined, *everybody* suspects Eyres of doing it and half
the people say so:
    I look forward with great delight to seeing you again altho' I am
getting used to sleep without you: do not think of returning until the
weather fines. If you return to Geelong ask Mr. Foster to enquire at
'Cobb's' or the mail office where Jerry *lives and when he can be found at*
home:
    I am so glad you have bought Hugh Miller's book. Brown asked
me 15/. for it—[1]
    Send me up word in your next about Luther.
    And good bye my own darling be careful of yourself until we
meet. I enclosed £1. in yesterday's letter and will send another on
Saturday so as to let you get it on Monday.

    Good bye ever dearest.
    Your devoted husband
    Walter.

    Susan has been in & says she received the parcel & two Bibles last
night but as usual there is something wrong. *Her mother* wrote to say she
had sent in the box something for her & she has not got anything from

her family: pray write particularly & let us know if there was any parcel or letter addressed to her—

Your sister Lizzie has sent her likeness to John you did not say if you had one from her, she is very like you indeed:[2]

1/86

[1] Hugh Miller was the author of several books during 1857 and 1858 and it is difficult to identify this particular one with certainty. It is likely to have been *Scenes and Legends of the North of Scotland* (Hamilton: 1857).

[2] This would seem to be the Lizzie, then married to Jack, with whom Mary was to stay in Plymouth during 1868.

[28]

Webster St
Monday 23 {August 1858}

My own darling Mary

Your kind letter of Saturday reached me this morning. I do not think Miss Cuthbert wishes anything done about the furniture. She has not sent over and we had better not appear too meddlesome:

I hope you will have a pleasant day today at Collingwood. It is fine here but a strong N[orth] wind as usual. Give them my kind love if you see them again:

I would rather that your cousin enquired about Luther:

It is astonishing that you have had such fine weather while we have had constant rain, so wet that nobody could get out except those compelled by business: I told Susan this morning that you said you had sent everything and read her your letter where you said so, she said '*well it is very strange that my mother in her* letter written *six weeks* after the *box started* says she sent me a parcel'—We must have the boxes sent separate in future. She has sent me in your mother's letter to read dated April 7 in wh' your mother says she sends a handkerchief for John wh' she has possessed for 40 years. 'Your own mother encloses a parcel, & has dropped a trifle in Harry's box'. This letter is dated 'April 7.' Very strange is it not and very unpleasant. You had better enclose a note to John in your next telling him that all came in the box and assure him that his were sent safely & take no notice of what Susan says but we won't have it happen again!—Ned & I dined there yesterday in consequence of a pressing invitation from *John himself*.

Eyre has been imprisoned all Friday night, all Saturday & night, & was only released yesterday on bail of £500. John & Burton going surety: Ned remains till Thursday. He has been paid in full—Imagine poor Mrs Eyre's state: Nothing new: I enclose another £1.0.0. I would like you to go to 'Robertson Bookseller' near, opposite I think, *Argus* office & *buy* me a copy of the last edition of *Taylor's Medical Jurisprudence* price about 15/. and ask him to write down the price of *Churchill's Midwifery, Ramsbotham's ditto*, and 'Pereira's *Materia Medica*'[1]—Write & let me know when you start for Geelong and I will send you another £1. You have been very economical my darling heart—It is a fortnight today and you may imagine how slowly the time has past it appears a month at least.

Give my kind regards to Mr & Mrs Darling & thank them for their kind treatment of you: assure Mrs. D how happy we will be to see her when she can come next Summer: I do not think it at all likely that Ned will go to Melbourne just now: But he appears to think of going to England next year: Your mother writes so anxiously for him, strange with other sons at home: Tis a pity as I tell him, to blight his rising prospects here. He is a good son: Susan, children, & John, have all had influenza colds: I hope dear that yours is better and that you take care of yourself. I look for your arrival now daily, and trust that nothing may befall you:

I went to Church myself yesterday morning alone: Ned went at night also Anne: she has given over picking & stealing, for I locked the safe when I caught her at it and she has the making of a good servant. She can make plain suet pudding herself now: Be sure to call on Mrs. Croll in Geelong. I shall expect another letter on Thursday at latest and my next will be addressed to Geelong: I fear you have already trespassed on Mrs Darling's hospitality but we can return it: I believe Mrs Potter has lost her baby: She was in deep mourning yesterday.

Remember me kindly to Sarah, find out her prospects and mention Curtayne's name:[2]

I expect Brooke tomorrow: and possibly Curtayne with him: Have got a few eggs for you when you come back altho' all have stopped again:

I am very pleased you have managed so well about the Cards—I was obliged to give Anne a good talking to this morning she will *not* do what I tell her, but will persist in having her own way—However you can see what you think of her and if she will do *what she is told* you can keep her, if not she must be told to go home: I pay her regularly—have paid off all debts to this day, and am better off than we have been since we came into the house: I have been bespoken today to attend a Mrs. Hudson next 'Tam o Shanter.'

Good bye, my love good bye.
Your affectionate Husband
Walter.

1/80

¹ A. S. Taylor, *Elements of Medical Jurisprudence* (Churchill, 1836); F. Churchill, *Researches on Operative Midwifery* (Longman, 1841); J. Ramsbotham, *Observations in Midwifery* (Churchill, 1842); and J. Pereira, *Elements of Materia Medica* (Longman, 1854–55).

² Possibly a reference to Thomas William R. Curtayne, a Ballarat doctor.

[29]

Webster St
Wednesday {25 August 1858}

My dear Mary

I received yours this morning & feel much surprised at your not having got a letter I wrote to you and *posted myself* last Monday it contained £1: I went at once on receipt of yours to the Post Office & found that it was not there so it *must* be in Melbourne: But I trust before this reaches you you have received it safely. I have sent £1. in every letter I have written to you and enclose one in this—You say you paid carriage on the umbrellas—now I told you distinctly in my letter of last Friday, that I had paid all demands 2/6 and I wrote across the address twice /*carriage paid in full* and it is too bad if they have *defrauded you*. I enclose the receipt from the office—also a note to Luther, send it to the office and get an answer next day: John has gone down to Geelong today and we thought you would be there as I understood you were going across today.

I am very lonely and dull and have no news. Ned is out all day and unfortunately I cannot go out on acc[oun]t of those precious labours wh' do not come off.

A. Brook Smith called in passing and handed me some letters to read among them was one from Mrs. Bradshaw in wh' amidst of lot of rubbish, she spits out *her venom* at me. God forgive her she has evidently maligned me before to some extent: Drop the acquaintance with the whole family—I wonder if she remembers the command 'thou shalt not bear false witness against thy neighbour'.

I certainly fear that you are trespassing upon Mrs. Darling's kindness. I never dreamt you intended staying *there* so long, you know my dear one must not render oneself obnoxious or a burden; especially as she appears to be a friend of the Bradshaws and I look now with suspicion upon all _associating_ with them.

Your devoted husband
Walter

Susan & the family are all ill. John is coming up again next Saturday he is staying at Skarratts Great Western. He would take you to a grand ball on the opening of the Railway works.[1]

Ask for Mrs Skarratt if you go over—

I do not know what to do for the best in sending this letter as there has always been a delay in your getting letters sent to the *Hotham Hotel.* As I suppose you have got my last by this I think it will be best to send it to Geelong where I hope you are—as if you sailed on Thursday morning you wd not get it and it would be left behind in Melbourne.

1/89

[1] The *Argus* reported the turning of the 'first sod of the Geelong and Ballaarat Railway' on 24 August 1858, p. 5.

[30]

Melbourne
26 August {1858}

My dear darling

You see by the commencement of this I have not yet left Melbourne but I have just finished writing to Mrs Foster to ask her to meet me tomorrow by the Steamer & I would stay a few days with her.

I am going this morning to get the book you mention I was not able to go yesterday. I have such a bad head*ache*. I did not go to the Webbs I must write to them when I come home. I have got the Cards they are very nicely done. Mr Harris has been several times to Sarah's enquiring for me but I cannot find him. I think I shall be obliged to make up a small box & send by the carrier for I have no one to carry the things backwards & forwards for me & they are too heavy for me so I shall take the things out of the Tin box from home & leave it with Sarah & put some of my things with them into a small box & send them by Binney & Broadbent. I will put inside of this how much it will cost you can send Anne & the money with it. Susan's parcel shall be at the top. It was not my fault the things were not in the box & I heard nothing about them until I went down there last week, also the Silk Pocket handkerchief wh' was forgotten but you will find it all right. I will try today if I can get any second hand medical books that you mention but I will be sure to bring the one you want particularly. I shall be so glad to see you again my dear. I feel so lonely sometimes. I am so glad you do not think I have been extravagant. I bought a trifle & gave to Ellen for her kindness. I could not afford much—money seems to fly in Melbourne.

I am delighted to hear you are doing so well. I hope it will continue. I have not felt quite well this last day or two but I can guess what is coming soon. I will write to you from Foster's & tell you when to meet me. Mr & Mrs Darling desire to be kindly remembered to you.

Sarah will go to Mrs Barry's every week. I have written out 4 receipts for her to give as she receives the money & then she will send it up. I must say good bye now sweetheart for I must go out. I do so long to see you again with all my love & kisses ever dear Walter

Your loving wife
Mary

P.S. I have been to Robertson the bookseller & bought you 'Taylor's Medical Jurisprudence' the price was 17/6, they had not either Ramsbotham or Churchill on Midwifery. I will try in Geelong.

Send Anne Monday or Tuesday to Binney's for a box addressed to you. Pay for it. They do not take the money until delivered—in haste. God bless you darling.

MR

1/48

[31]

Webster St
Friday 8½ a.m.{27 August 1858}

My darling,

As Ned will see you this day I send this by him. I sent one the day before yesterday to you at Mr Foster's Geelong. And as I fear you have not received my previous one or letter addressed to you at the Sir C. Hotham Hotel posted on Monday I enclosed a £1 in the last & one in this: I hope that letter has not gone astray but I did not get one from you yesterday. I fear it must have been lost owing to the carelessness of the Hotel people.

Lonely day: how I long to see you and kiss you again.

Have you seen John?

I was up all night so you must forgive this short scrawl but I cannot write well.

God bless you until I embrace you my dear dear wife.

John returns tomorrow and Ned on Monday. Good bye

Your loving husband
Walter

P.S. Kind regards to the Fosters

1/109

[32]

Geelong
28 August {1858}

My dearest husband

I write to tell you that I arrived here safely last night & found a letter waiting for me from you dear. Harold called to see me in the evening & told me he forgot to bring the letter you wrote to me. I am so glad to hear you are well darling. Ned went to Melbourne by the first train this morning. I sent the letter to Luther by him—he said he would find him, also to the Carriers they would not let me have them until I paid, for it was not entered paid in the book. I had to sign it so Ned said he would make it all right.

I did not send the box by them for they would not take it for less than 12 shillings & I would not pay them so I brought it in the Steamer with me & luckily Mr Foster was sending a dray load of things to there place on the Melbourne Road so sent my box free. So if you send Ann about Wednesday to carry it. I have not seen John. I suppose he has returned home by this. I hope to hear from you on Monday darling & send me word if there is anything you want. Mrs Darling was very sorry I would not stay longer she has taken her farewell of the Bradshaws they behaved so badly the last time she was there. I intend going to see Mrs Croll if I can find her out. I shall return home next Wednesday but I will send you word on Monday which Coach I come by & what time it will arrive. Yesterday darling was the anniversary of our third wedding day. I was thinking of you all day, I am afraid you will feel very lonely dear. Ned returns on Monday by the Melbourne Coach. Mr and Mrs Foster met me at the Steamer & Captain McLean was very kind in seeing after my things. It is very warm more like Summer weather it thundered last night. I shall be so glad to see you again dearest & with all love & kisses I remain

Your loving wife
Mary

1/52

[33]

Webster St
Monday {30 August 1858}

My own darling Wife,

I did not write on Saturday because you had not answered my last, & I did not know if you might go to Geelong after all: I got yours of Sat. this morning, and am delighted to hear you are coming back on Wednesday; I will meet you without fail, I suppose you will come by the 10 o'clock coach, so as not to inconvenience Mrs. Foster by getting up so early as six: I enclose another £1. as Harold forgot it—

I did not find the letter until Saturday night or I might have posted it.

John came home on Saturday; you missed a great treat in Geelong! John went to the Ball, and wanted to find you to take you: I am so sorry you were not there.

I too, thought of our wedding day, yet we do not look back with regret, for we are happier now than ever we were. I have been very lonely, but I felt it more the first week than I have done since, I suppose like everything the habit accustoms. I think you have enjoyed yourself, and will have many things to tell us all. Bill is staying at John's. I have a very bad case, was called out three times at night last week: Susan & children been very ill, and not well yet. Incessant rain all night, & yesterday & the night before—I shall be so glad to see you! how I long to kiss you! and to hear of your adventures:

Anne has very much improved, and does not do any of her bad tricks—but I have never enjoyed my meals since you left, consequently your return will be joyfully welcomed.

I went to Church yesterday for the third time by myself, a gentleman from St. Kilda preached, & a collection was made for the roof.

I sent Anne to Mrs Barry's sister & she said she had sent down the money to Miss Bailey.

I am afraid Anne cannot carry the box from Fosters but I will send her for it on Wednesday so as to have it by the time you come back—

And now my darling, as this is the last letter I will write, Good bye, and may God who has so providentially watched over you keep you for me until you return to my arms, is the prayer of your dear

Walter

1/31

[34]

Westbourne Terrace
Monday morning {30 August 1858}

My own darling Walter

I have just time to write & ask you to meet me on Wednesday evening. I leave Geelong by the 10 o'clock Coach on Wednesday morning & I suppose will arrive at Ballaraat about 5 or 6 o'clock.

We are going to Toorak this afternoon & I want to post this in Town. I am much obliged for the pound you enclosed. I leave Melbourne by the last train on Tuesday afternoon and sleep at Skarratts so as to get a good seat in the Coach. I need not write more as I can talk to you dear so much better.

I have seen nothing of Smith. I hope I shall find you quite well & with all love and kisses darling

I am Your loving wife
Mary.

1/50

[35]

Bennetts Hotel Geelong
Thursday evening {21 April 1859}

My dear M.

Seeing a nice covered waggon passing about 2 P.M. I sent Mary out & got in, starting at once. We got thro' the Main Road pretty well the only person I saw I knew was Robert Cuthbert: after passing thro' Buninyong the driver found it was getting late & put his horses into a trot on a very bad road, it was very bad at first until I got used to it. We arrived safely at the Corduroy Hotel 7. o'clock, where I was moved for the first time—had tea of ham & one egg, and a glass of Brandy; to bed at nine, twice up in the night & three times before starting, which we did at 6 AM., fancy my getting up at 6. and washing in cold water, then turning out and not getting breakfast for 6 miles—which however we did at 8. on liver & bacon & hash. *Moved again*: then drove on to the Clyde to dinner at 2 *moved again*: hearty dinner, soup, fish, roast mutton, potatoes, cheese, ale—then drove in to this by 7. to tea off curry & chops—

So you see my dear I am already getting better: *no pain whatever*: and I feel I may eat what I fancy.

Tomorrow Good Friday is a great day, crowds going down to Queenscliffe.

The Williamsons were very civil indeed. Gave me a letter of introduction to the officer of Customs at Queenscliffe—

And now I am going to astonish you! The Bradshaws of the Family Hotel were sold off yesterday, Furniture House Land & everything, by Nantes & Brown, the house bought, & when I passed today the blinds

[69]

all down. They are all going to live with Alexander—very sad is it not, but a punishment for defrauding their governess of her just due!

And now darling I think I have told you all about myself and my doings.

I hope you will let me have a letter soon from you, you had better draw money from savings bank, & pay John £4 *at once* on those shares of the Clunes—

Off this morning not quite so well—in some pain. Will write again tomorrow.

Good bye darling
WR

1/168

[36]

Queenscliffe
Wednesday evening {27 April 1859}

My darling Mary

I got your letter again tonight the 2d, and as I find it will cost me 15/- to get from this to Geelong I have resolved to run up to Melbourne until Monday next. So if you have written me to Geelong P.O. why it will only lie there until I get it that's all—the enclosure all right—pretty well today not moved from 10 to 3 and took a fine walk to gather shells & sea weed—My certy [*sic*] the bazaar will realise £500 or more!

Weather colder, difficulty in getting proper food here for me—and I am tired of the place—wish I had stayed at Geelong! I am so grieved for poor Susan give her my love tell her how I feel for her and caution her against solid food—she ought to have had medical advice a month ago.

I hope to God John won't allow them *to do to her what they did to me.* Dr. H. ought to be cautioned that she is like me *highly nervous temperament* with a pulse in health often 100. tell him this—

I am better this morning than I have been, got a better night no motion from $\frac{1}{2}$ past 11 till 6—

I spent last evening at one of the pilots where we had a game at whist, his lady taking a hand. I took a glass of burnt brandy wh' I think did me good—Remember me to Shanklin. I suppose Mrs. S. is home by this.

I wrote Lucinda a long letter addressed to Miss Thompson's Kyneton was that right?

I leave this tomorrow morning 8 A.M. for Melbourne getting there about 1. or $\frac{1}{2}$ past.

If you write by tomorrow's post I will get it Saturday—& I think of leaving Monday morning—

unless they are very pressing & then I may stay a day or two longer.

I am going out for a drive this afternoon 4 miles to Point Lonsdale which you will see on my map—I hope you enjoyed the ball? & that you went.

The clergyman called on me.

I hope dear the house is not burned down, have you got the garden done? I suppose not!

Rather unfortunate that Mrs Jeffreys shd be confined of a still born child—Will write again Saturday next—

Good bye loved one
Your own Walter

1/226

[37]

Collingwood
Saturday morning {30 April 1859}

I wrote you last my dearest from Queenscliffe Wednesday night, and I sailed to Melbourne yesterday morning at 8 o'clock—I had not been improving in *my worst respect*, altho' I found my legs stronger; I took leave of the place with no regret, for the monotony was rather engendering ennui. I advised Dod the P[ost] Master to telegraph the English news up to John provided it came *in any night before 12,* so that they might have it in the *next* morning's *issue, without waiting for an answer to his letter.* I do not know whether John will consider that I was overstepping my legitimate business at Queenscliffe, by making arrangements for the *Star,* but I take some credit for what I did, whether he accepts the terms or not—

You can read him that: well I took no breakfast before starting except bread & butter & cold milk & on board some biscuits & a bottle of porter, no disturbance from 7. to 2. Cab from Station to here found Uncle out at Randle's funeral & Aunt delighted to see me, & so kind.

I live on the plainest food: Kangaroo soup twice after coming here yesterday & not moved *all night*, for wh' I am very thankful, *the first time since the beginning of my illness*! so you see dear I began to improve as soon as I started for this really—Everything much improved about the house & so hospitable, all so sorry you are *not* with me, & so am I but we must learn to do what is right.

I am so anxious about you, no letter now since Tuesday last enclosing £2.00. How have you been, & Susan is she better & the bazaar & the ball & everybody?

Expect me back Monday night or Tuesday night as I suppose they will not let me start before Tuesday, & they really are so kind it is a pleasure & a happiness to be here. Willie appears to be a nice boy, pity he has not got the necessary qualification strict probity—Ned has written here, he has got a situation 15/- per day at Malmesbury, he say date 23d. he has written me—Have you got it?

We are going in today with Uncle & Willie to see the Museum & Dr. McKirdy—I breakfasted off two eggs & a cup of milk, they keep a cow & make their own butter—Lots of ducks, & turkeys, & fowls, & rabbits, we must really see if we can't do something of the sort or else have a jolly good garden to amuse us,

> Good bye dearest,
> I am in a hurry,
> Your loving husband
> Walter

Aunt & Uncle's kind love & pressing invitation to you for next summer promised.

1/169

[38]

Heathville House, Alma Road East

My dearest Walter

I cannot let the day pass without writing to you as well as Lucinda tho' you have not written to me as yet. I am glad to hear darling that you are so busy & that you are well tho' you miss me very much. We are very comfortably settled here & live remarkably well. Breakfast at $\frac{1}{2}$ past 8 o'clock Lunch at 1 dinner at six & Tea at 8. We generally walk over to South Yarra after dinner to Miss Cuthbert's Cousins she has a great number all living in nice houses—with pianos & we pass the evening very pleasantly—there are three of them widows & the finest & prettiest set of ladies I have seen since my arrival here—the oldest is only 27 years. John came to see us last evening & walked over with us. I never saw him so agreable & enjoy himself so much. Walked with Miss C—all the way chatting but I fancy was rather taken with the pretty widow—walked with me to make enquiries about her & whether she had any family. I told him one little girl but this is only imagination on my part so do not breathe a word. He is very kind & I fancy will take these lodgings when we leave them & have Harry with him. Yesterday we went to Pentridge saw them all very pleased to see me. Uncle apologised for not writing but his hand is not any better. It is very expensive to go there being such a distance. Cost me 7 shillings & so in proportion for every place you want to go to—

Will you send me down a prescription for some ointment for a place that looks vastly like ringworm this shape [drawing of shape of ringworm] very red like tiny blisters round the edge. Also for some blistering liquid as I suffered a deal of pain this last few days. Send some ointment that will take away the place quickly as it looks nasty. The weather is terrifickly hot. Not one cool day since here we've been. I am going into Melbourne to seek something for Lucinda. I am so glad darling to hear that you are quite well & that the children are good. I hope they do not teaze you too much. I hear that Mrs Bradley has a Son. How I wish it was mine. There's to be grand doings at the Christening. Go to Miss Henham's Wedding & send me all the news—do write to me darling. I long to see your handwriting though I cannot see your face.

God bless & protect you darling is the prayer of

Your loving Wife
Mary

Miss Cuthbert sends her love & so do I with plenty of kisses.
✳✳✳

1/61

[39]

Thursday

My dear Polly

I have been very ill with this confounded Influ: for two or three days—I had made up my mind to telegraph to you this morning if not better; but I am happy to say I am—

I had to refuse to go out to several cases yesterday evening & had to send Bunce[1] to a confinement in the night—I was just able to crawl down stairs with the shawl over my head—I had a letter from Ned this morning. He tells me you have had the same: I hope you went to bed and that you are now better also that you were not so bad as I was:

Tell John North Clunes were sold yesterday here at £7.0.0. Holthouse was offered 6.10.0[2]—It is a certain fortune: I have seen the stone & by no means the best specimen—There is ten years work to get out the stone between where we have struck it & the Victoria *without opening any more ground.* John might get *some cheap in Melb{ourne}:* to bring down the price of his: mine do not stand me more than £12.0.0 with this call paid—The old shaft is right over it—& where the Victoria are crushing from yields 10 cwts to the ton. No news to interest you—No sign of the Yorkshire 81 days from Plymouth on Sunday—I shall not be sorry to see the notice of her arrival.

I suppose I feel your absence more because I am so poorly. Nights are fearful.

If you were to see a nice small scarf necktie—

No home letters for you. Two for me—

A little better today: You had as bad an attack as I had.

Much love
Your affect Hubby
W.

1/96

---

[1]   Dr Richard Bunce migrated from Plymouth and set up practice in Melbourne in 1850. He moved to Ballarat in 1855.

[2]   Thomas Le Gay Holthouse arrived in Victoria in 1853 and also established a medical practice at Ballarat.

[40]

Heathville House, Alma Road East

My dear dear Walter

I did not get your letter until I returned home last night tho' I staid at home till eleven expecting to hear from you. The enclosure was all right. I went to Melbourne yesterday & posted a letter to you also to Lucinda. I went to Mrs Horn's & paid five shillings to have a name put down & Mrs Horn was to write to her about a Situation at St Kilda which I thought would suit her however I must now go & tell her that she is engaged.[1] John took me to see Mrs Patterson & Mrs Marsh at Richmond yesterday. I like them very well so grand Houses most magnificent. They drove me home in the evening. I have not been to Church. I felt very poorly but shall go this evening if I feel better. The weather has been most oppressive but last night we had a storm which has laid the dust & cooled the air.

I hope baby's quite well again. Trotty is a good girl only I am afraid she will be spoilt whilst here. I cannot get her to do what I tell her sometimes already.

John made me a present of a very handsome Table Cloth to match my furniture.

I shall have to buy another pair of boots, walking about so much soon wears them out. I have not been to see the Webbs yet people live such distances from one another that it requires a small fortune to go & see them. Miss Cuthbert will leave on Monday week. I think the change has done Robert good though he is very thin. I was weighed by Uncle & am 7 stone 10 lbs—Miss Cuthbert 7 stone 7 lbs. Not much difference & her dresses fit me better than my own. We are very comfortable, got in just for ourselves 8 bottles of Ale, 2 of Port wine & 2 of sherry, I pay a third of all expenses. We agree remarkably, very pleasant to live with.

I am glad darling you keep so busy & that you go to the Theatre it will cheer you up & do you good. You surprised me about Nicholson. You are getting on famously with Stewart & Heise.[2] It is as I have often thought that when you were well known you would be appreciated, there are not many so gentlemanly & upright as yourself.

I was glad to hear Lucinda has got the situation she wished so much for. Give my love to her & I will write when I return home. You would like this Sea bathing so much. I wish you could come & enjoy it, it would do you so much good—I will send the neck ties by Miss

Cuthbert. Send me word dear if there is anything else I can do for you any medical book or anything I can get. I long to get a real long letter from you. I have not had a whole one yet but hope I shall on Tuesday. I am afraid you will miss Lucy when she goes. How does Mary get on? I hope she does not leave the House. Servants seem to be just as scarce here as on Ballaraat.

Uncle & Aunt promised to come & see us this week & go down to Brighton with us. Have you heard from Ned? What a dreadful thing the loss of the Royal Charter is it seems to have thrown a complete sadness over Melbourne.[3] Be sure & send me my English letters that come to hand. I cannot think of any more news.

So with love & kisses many I am dear Walter

Your loving Wife
Mary

love to Lucy & children. Write soon.

1/62

[1]   Lucinda Richardson, Walter's sister, worked in Australia as a governess from the mid-1850s; at Kyneton in 1857 and at Daylesford with Mrs Dovelin in 1859. She returned to England in 1862, arriving 16 June.

[2]   Presumably a reference to the Ballarat doctors, George Nicholson, James Stewart and William Augustus Heise.

[3]   The *Royal Charter* was a passenger ship that sank on its way from Melbourne to Liverpool on 26 October 1859. Of the 500 people on board, only 41 survived.

[41]

Heathville House, Alma Road

My dear Walter

I have just received your dear dear letter. I was so disappointed yesterday. I was in bad spirits all day I fancied you were ill or at some bad case; I am glad you are well & doing such a good practise—I wish it would continue we could soon afford for you to take a Country trip with me.

I do hope this will do me good & that I shall not be any more trouble to you though I am thinner through bathing, than when I came down. Now I will answer a few of your questions.

First about our journey down there were no *gentlemen* in the Coach they would not assist us in the slightest degree only thought of making themselves comfortable but that did not trouble me much for I am too old a traveller to mind these things now. Mr. Rowe was very kind— when we got in the Railway Carriage at the Werribee got us Cakes & nice Hot Coffee & would insist upon paying for them himself. He keeps a Store on the Main Road, O'Connor's friend. It was bitter cold till we came to Batesford when the air seemed quite different & by the time we arrived in Melbourne we were in a perfect fever. I feel the weather much warmer than when on Ballaraat & yet I think it agrees with me. I have only the constant pain in my side.

Our weather must have been very like yours for we had a storm on Saturday & a wet Sunday. I am glad to hear that Lucy wears the Hoops.[1] I am obliged to get a new set for mine are all broken. I am having my silk dress made ready to go to the Houses of Parliament. 35 shillings for making & 10s for trimmings but I thought that such a good dress I had better have it made fashionably & then it would serve me for a pattern for the next year—I hope darling that I will please you when I come back. I will try & see all that lays within the power of my purse but the money goes so fast in going from one place to the other.

Miss Cuthbert leaves for Ballaraat on Monday. I hope you will go & see them. She takes her Cousin Mrs. Steadman up with her, her husband is a lawyer. She is only 18 & very much admired, by gentleman especially, so go & give me your opinion. She has been most kind & friendly with me; Spent nearly every evening at her house, in fact all Miss Cuthbert's relations have treated me like one of themselves, move in the best society.

I will give the letter to John. I have not seen him since Monday. Miss Cuthbert says you are to go & see them on Monday evening & she will bring you a letter from me & give you the latest intelligence respecting my health. I shall send your neck ties up by her—Tell Lucinda I will write her a long letter full of news as soon as I return home—give her my love & I hope she will be happy & comfortable—I enclose the cheque—Annie Maria sends her love & will be sure to have the dog tied up, go & see her she is so very kind. I expect Mr & Mrs Marsh to see me today. Tomorrow I intend going shopping in Melbourne to buy your neck ties & if I see anything else I will send it. I received the 2£s safely today do not be long before you write darling & now darling take care of yourself with love & kisses many ever your

loving wife Mary

I hope Harry will not be very bad how did he get the nasty pox?
Kiss baby for me, love to Lucy tell her to write & send me all the news—

God bless you

1/63

¹ A type of full-length petticoat introduced in the 1850s, with circular bands that
extended the skirt.

[42]

My dear Polly
I have been too busy to write before and have had nothing to say.
No news of any sort to interest you. All well. I have been so busy
with Influenza & I have had to perform Tracheotomy both yesterday &
today two different children diphtheria in the wind pipe
Kind regards to all—

Your affect
Husband
WLR
Tuesday evening—

I am a little better this morning but still very poorly
Wednesday morning.

1/97

[43]

Heathville House, Alma Road
Monday 16 January 1860

My darling Walter
I received your kind letter this morning. I thought you were never
going to write me any more & I fancied you were forgetting that you
had a wife who loved you in Melbourne. I might not have felt your
silence so much had I been well but being ill I felt very low-spirited.
When I last wrote to you I was feeling so much better but Wednesday

night the pain in my side got so bad that I had to send Robert out for a bottle of blistering liquid & which I applied to my side. Thursday I felt better & Friday morning I told Miss Cuthbert I had not felt so well for months. I thought I should enjoy the day so much for we had made a party to go into Melbourne & see the Library[1] & in the evening we were to go to the House of Parliament & hear them speak. About $\frac{1}{2}$ past 12 just as we were going into lunch I turned quite sick & faint but it passed off though I could not eat anything but while I was dressing I felt so ill I did not know what to do. A dull heavy pain in the (womb I imagine) left side low down with unwell pains came on. All the time I was in Melbourne it was misery to walk about but I did not like to miss the opportunity of going to the House because it was the only opportunity Miss C had of going. Well I went but was obliged to leave very soon.

John was watching me very anxiously for fear I would faint. I got safely home & to my horror was saturated with blood the pain still continuing. However lying on the bed eased me. Next morning I walked to Dr Evan's he said let Nature take its course there was nothing to be alarmed about. I have seen nothing since & the pain is going away, he says I am suffering from pure weakness. He was to come & see me today but has not done so as yet. I am anxious for this to be in time for the post so have not time to write a very long letter. Miss C started this morning. I could not get the neck ties in Melbourne they are not to be had. I will try St Kilda.

I sent you two Songs for you to have by the time I return. I am always thinking of you darling & what you are doing. I'm glad to hear you are still busy. I hope Poor Harry & Baby are better—do you think you will be able to come & fetch me home? the Sea would delight you, also the Public Library. I do hope at the end of the month you will commence to think about it. Anne Maria will take charge of Harry. Bye the bye she expects you up there tonight do go her friends have all shown me such kindness one of her Cousins a Mrs Fullerton is staying with me whilst I write this. She thought I would be lonely so came to take me a walk. John was down yesterday he is very attentive.

I intend going into Town tomorrow to try & find Mrs Darling & tell John about Harry—Write my dear as soon as you can. I feel low-spirited & your letters do cheer me so much. I know them by heart reading them so often. I called on the Webbs they want me to go & see Clara Agg—it is only 7s/6d a return ticket & I can go on a Saturday & return on the Monday.

I received the money all safely & was very glad of it for I wanted a pair of boots. I find the washing comes most expensive. I will send you a list of how the money goes in my next. God bless & prosper you is the nightly prayer of Your loving Wife

> With kisses many I am
> Your Mary

I was dreaming of you this morning. I scarcely sleep at all at nights—Good bye dearest.

1/59

[1] The State Library of Victoria was opened on 11 February 1856.

[44]

Tuesday morning {17 January 1860}

My own darling Walty

I have just received your dear kind, long letter. I really think it is the nicest you have written since I have been down. I am happy to say that I feel a little better since I last wrote & am trying all I can to get well. I take regularly the medicine Dr. Evans sends me & I think it is doing good he is very kind & I have changed my opinion of him. Mrs Evans could not be kinder if I was her own daughter makes me go there after bathing & gives me delightful hot Coffee & you know darling my partiality for that beverage—She has also offered me her riding habit & Pony if I can but get a Gentleman to take me out as she always rides alone. So last night I heard from Mr Harriman that Brooke Smith is at Richmond Barracks on sick leave. So I sent word for him to come & see me & then if you have no objection dear I will ask him to get a horse & take me a ride. I hope his being here will induce you to come down. You need not mind the expense for John told me when I left here he would pay me back what I had paid Mrs Hughes as he could afford to pay for my lodgings better than you could so if I stay here five weeks he will give me a cheque for 10£s—So you might draw the money from the Bank & I will pay it in when I come up. He is very kind—bought me two nets for my Hair & a fashionable Blue large parasol they are like small umbrellas only not so large or heavy as my white one.

I have been to Dr Evans this morning & he examined my chest & said you were right, my lungs are very delicate but he will write to you & tell you all about me; he drove me back in his dog cart. He thinks change of air & moving about from place to place will be better for me & to walk as little as I can. So on Saturday I take a return ticket for 10s/ & go to Sunbury & return on Monday afternoon. The next day I am going to Richmond to stay with Mrs Brown that's Ellen Darling's sister & then the following Saturday Ellen wants me to go with her to Schnapper Point & stay a week at her Mother's who has a farm down there.

Dr Evans advises me to go, for the air is so good for invalids he is not quite sure that the Sea-bathing is good for me for my fingers & toes die away & I am a long time before the blood returns to them but only one hand died today so I think it is passing away. I thought on my return from Schnapper Point it would be time for me to return & that you would come & fetch me. Do try darling you could have a bathe in the Sea & such a long talk to Smith about old times—it would do you a world of good & me too. I spend this evening with the Webbs last night I went to Mrs Harriman's.

I should have gone to Mr Steadman's had I received an invitation in time but I did not get it until this morning. I am going to see the Baby & Mrs Cuthbert today. Read the enclosed then give it to Anne Maria it will amuse her & tell Mrs Steadman I wrote an answer to correspond. I quite regretted not being there to inform her how the Bachelor party went off—I am very glad to hear the children are better. Mrs Hughes hopes she will have the pleasure of seeing my Husband before I leave. Her daughter married a gentleman who lived opposite to us at Leicester—

Tell Anne Maria I have not touched the Piano since she left. I get no chance.

You would hear such nice singing if you were to come down— do if it is at all possible. I received 1£ quite safely. Many thanks dear darling Husband. God bless & prosper you. I do not sleep much but very singular when I do I dream of you & home. I do not think I have had one dream in which you have not appeared. I do long to see your face & have a few kisses it seems wretched not to have any. Good bye darling love

Your loving Wife
Mary

Let me get a letter on Monday & tell me do you approve of my plans—

1/57

[45]

Webster St
Saturday 21 January 1860

My dear darling Mary,

Yours of Thursday reached me safely and I was so glad to hear that you were better, and that you were taking the medicine prescribed for you by Dr. Evans: Ah! you have changed your opinion of him have you, well his first impression is not so favorable as is the one formed after a time: I trust you will enjoy your riding; I am much surprised at Brooke Smith being on sick leave, again, so soon too after his voyage home. He has never answered my last letter, nor yours written when I was on the sofa last April. Perhaps he is offended with me for telling his father, I did not consider his illnesses very alarming, at least what I had seen of them: I am sure I would come down dear love to bring you back, but really I think it would be very unwise—It is true I have been busy for the last month, but I look forward with dread & apprehension to next winter: the healthy season when there is no sickness; & I have not yet saved any thing: I have paid Bogle & Thom Gray: & part of Ned's & sent you money, but I ought to have £50 in the Bank: However we will see, I will not definitely say 'no', neither can I promise 'yes': I am very glad you are running about, I quite approve of it & pray that it may restore you & give you flesh, & a color once more in your dear cheeks! I am going to dine at Cuthberts tomorrow, Sunday: It is very handsome of John to pay for your Lodgings, you must thank him very cordially for me from my heart, it certainly comes very 'apropos' & will enable you to get a new carpet & curtains for the bed when you come back: You might perhaps buy them cheaper in Melbourne—The size of the front room is 12 feet 6 by 12 feet, it would require 17 or 18 yards which would do it well, you could get the best tapestry for 4/6 £3.12. & it might be sent up by Reynolds & English[1]. The present carpet is very shabby and will require drugget all thro' to the door of the back room & across thus [small drawing] if we do not get a new carpet: I have delayed it until you come back but the carpet in the back room is entirely gone, the children have torn sad holes with their little feet—They are both better, Baby has had the same low fever that Harry had for some days—Yesterday Friday was our hottest day of the season, this day however exceeds it there being a hot wind:

And so you dream of me nightly my darling? I am beginning to *count the days* & to feel *your absence*. God bless you; this will be the longest separation we have ever had:

Anna Maria tells me Mrs Graham[2] has gone down, that will be agreable company;

Sad thing that losing the two children: Ah *I have only lost one child:* I am not so busy now, but most likely this weather will set us running about next week; I went to the theatre last night, I felt so dull, with Kingston Cuthbert; was not home till 1, brought home Dr. Wills & we smoked till 2, up at 7. Could eat no breakfast owing to the intense heat & dread going out in the sun!

You need not have sent me a list of your expenses. I am perfectly satisfied my dear wife that you would never be wasteful. Mary has been trying her hand at breaking just to keep in practice until you come back.

4 PM This has been a terrific day Ther 105° in our parlor. Harry & I bathed at 12 & after dinner I lay on the floor & so did the children: we bathed again at 4.

All enquire for you very kindly. Mrs Winch, Mrs. Haywood, Mrs Park & Mrs Searle called; the investigation into Searle's conduct has taken place result not made public

Saul [?] Foster married—Adieu my love.

Your Walter

1/54

1 Carriers in Collins Street.

2 The wife of George Graham, a Melbourne doctor and later member, along with Walter Richardson, of the Victorian Association of Progressive Spiritualists. The Grahams became close and longstanding friends of the Richardsons.

[46]

Heathville House
Tuesday {24 January 1860}

My dear darling Husband

I received your kind letter when I returned home last night. I am so glad you are well love. The weather here has been worse than Black

Thursday. I do not know what the Thermometer stood at on Saturday but Sunday was 130° in the Shade & 160° in the Sun. I was up at Sunbury but not able to move about on Monday when I came home—I was quite fatigued not able to sleep all night on account of one of my old attacks at the chest & stomach so I have been to Dr. Evans about it; he told me he had been too busy to write to you but would do so at the first opportunity. The Grahams came here last Saturday & took apartments here for a fortnight. So today an immense sale of the most exquisite things I ever saw took place in St Kilda at Mr Powell's who has made his fortune & returning to England. The street was lined with carriages for it is the fashion here for ladies to go to Auctions. I could have got some splendid bargains had I had the money to spend. I only bought 1 doz Spoons washed in Silver for 1£ & they ask three in the Shops so everyone thinks I made a good bargain. I tried for a Carpet for they were all Velvet pile but the worst one sold for over 6£s—so I let them alone. The G[rahams] spent over 16£'s *well* to *be them*.

I was too poorly & tired to go to Richmond today so am going tomorrow—I do hope my darling Walter will come for the change will do you a world of good. Smith comes to take me a ride on Thursday. I had a letter from Miss Cuthbert & she says you promised to go to dinner but they did not see you. So I suppose you were called out on Friday.

I go to spend the day with Mrs Evans & Saturday I am off for a week to Schnapper Point. Let me hear from you on Friday morning love & then I will answer it & put in my address on Saturday morning when I go to Ellen's to know it. I shall have to leave here by nine o'clock on Saturday morning & the post would not come in until 11 & then I should not get your dear letter so do write if it is only a line. The dinner bell has just rung so I must say Good bye for tonight. I will add a line presently—Brooke Smith's sisters have sent me a lovely workbasket fitted up with such nice things as a present & their Father has sent you a book. I have not seen it yet. It is getting quite dark so I must say Good bye to my own darling Walty.

God Bless & protect you. I have a sleeping draught to take so hope I will sleep & dream sweet dreams of you. I do so long to see your dear face again. I think it will be kissed all away. Good bye dearest with kisses many from

> Your loving Wife
> Mary
> do not forget to write

P.S. Wednesday morning—I am so ill not able to move scarcely. Sick 12 times already & it is not 12 o'clock yet—The sleeping draught had no effect. Graham will post this hasten & write to me darling—

Mary

1/58

[47]

{Heathville House}
{28 January 1860}

if it was possible you might come down by some Friday night mail & we can return on Monday morning.

I am sorry to hear about poor baby she never seems to be well, am glad Harry is such a good boy, give my love & a kiss to both. Trotty never mentions or seems to care about them she is very fat but perfectly well. I think the change has done her good.

I shall finish this in Town & then I will enclose address—Goodbye so far dear darling

The address is Mr Jelfs

Tanti [?] Hotel

Schnapper Point

that is where the letters are left & then I go there to enquire for them. If you write on Monday I will get it Wednesday or Thursday & then I will write you again. I feel very poorly & am behind time so Good bye darling husband. God bless you with all love & kisses from your loving wife

Mary R
excuse this pen won't write
Goodbye dearest

1/60

[48]

Westbourne Terrace
31 May {1860}

My dear dear Walter

I arrived safely per coach to Geelong where John met me it was very cold riding & so muddy until we got to Meredith, there had been no rain & dust was blowing.

Melbourne's very like Ballaraat constant drizzle. Mrs Patterson is very kind & I am enjoying myself. I stay here I think until Monday then I go to Turnham's for a few days. We went to the Ball & enjoyed it very much. You were invited as well. I wish you had been there it was very gay the crowd was very great but upon the whole I think our Ballarat Balls compare very favorably with this. There was such a very common vulgar appearance amongst the ladies present not thirty good looking women out of about a thousand. I was introduced to several gentlemen but not the Governor. We went in a carriage & pair & returned the same the building was well lighted & ornamented and everything passed off well. I saw Mrs Reid & Mr & Mrs Henderson the latter will be up tomorrow night. The Ministry have resigned, the Land bill not being passed (as it was) in the Upper House.[1] John seems to think they will be asked again. He does not seem to care very much. I have not seen Harry but am going to do so when I have posted this. I called on Mrs Wanliss[2] yesterday. She returns home next week, looking much better. She expected Mr Wanliss today. My blister is still very bad constantly running & the smell from it hardly bearable, nothing but matter & blood from it. I am obliged to carry a bottle of scent for fear others should smell it. I bathe it in cold water every morning but cannot get the lint off. I danced very little owing to it.

I hope darling you are well & happy & do not miss me very much —I take *you* to bed with me every night. I look at you the last thing at night & the first thing in the morning. John gave me a white head dress composed of pearls & frosted leaves. I hope to have a letter tomorrow & one on Monday morning before I go to Pentridge. I hope Trotty is a good girl give my love & a kiss to her. Is there anything I can get for you in Melbourne? because I will do it if you send in time. I am rather tired so shall say good bye & God bless you. With all love & kisses

Ever your loving wife
Mary

Send the enclosed to Miss Cuthbert, put it in an envelope.

1/51

1   The *Argus* of 31 May 1860 (pp. 4–5) reported the resignation of the Nicholson
    ministry thus: 'The Land Bill has come to grief . . . The opposition of the Lords has
    gone even deeper than anyone expected. The amendment of Mr Bennett shows them
    to be averse even to the very framework of the Bill—the disposal of some country
    lands at a uniform price. The leasing clause—the proposed mode of deferred
    payments—was attacked in its threshold, and by a majority of 17 to 10 the
    Council has decided against subdividing the allotments for the purpose of leasing.'

2   Eliza Wanliss, née Henderson. Eliza and Thomas Drummond Wanliss (1830–1923)
    were friends of the Richardsons. Thomas Wanliss was a mining investor and
    newspaper proprieter who owned the *Ballarat Star* from December 1856 until
    about 1870.

[49]

Webster St
Saturday {2 June 1860}

My own Mary,

I expected a letter from you on Friday and was much disappointed
however I suppose that you were better engaged: I am delighted that
you are enjoying yourself and that Mrs. P[atterson] is kind. You say I
was invited to the Ball *I never received the invitation* as you know! I have
made arrangements to have our names put down in the book at Government House so that we may get an invitation next year & go if we
choose. You had better apply a bread poultice to the blister at bed time,
that will remove all irritation, it must be very distressing for you—
Trotty is very good. Julia takes her out often—King has given Julia a
stereoscope & Joe a lovely Brooch of Ball[ara]t Gold.

Nothing doing—I was occupied all Thursday with Mrs. Gray, was
sent for 6 AM. baby not born till 7 P.M.—

It is fearfully cold today; Ther. while I write 3.30, 48° with rain
clouds coming up over Warrenheip—No particular news—All well.
Johnson was here last night & tried to operate on Harry but failed
owing to his laughing so—had better success with Mary *put her to sleep,*
a natural sleep only, after half an hour. We are going to try again this
evening & I have asked Irwin to come up.[1]

I hope you will stay away all next week & derive some benefit from
it. Never mind us, we feel of course very lonely, but if it does you good

as it may, that will counterbalance it. Brooke spent Tuesday night with me. He saw Julia—Wednesday night I was alone all evening reading, Thursday night I went to a lecture by one of 'Green's' friends, & last night I have told you of. I lunched one day up at the Cuthberts. Saw Bunce today. Bitter against Creswick wretches, for I can call them by no other name, *ignorant deluded* beings: headed by Nicholson of whom he speaks in bad terms: No sickness still—

I have discharged Harry he leaves next week.
If matters don't mend I will go to Snowy River.
You had better remain where you are—

Good bye dearest love,
Your own husband
Walter

1/72

[1] Experiments with hypnotism.

[50]

Pentridge Stockade
5 June 1860

My darling Walter

Many thanks for your kind letter which I have only just received. I thought you had forgotten me but your sending it to St. Kilda made it a day later as I left there on Friday for here & shall remain at Pentridge till next Wednesday. After that address my letters to John at the Post office & he will forward them to me for Mrs Marsh wants me to stay a few days with her & then I return to Mrs Patterson's until I come home. I feel much stronger & am very well, blister healing at last but have a gathered[1] finger. John wishes Harry to return & live with us if you have no objection dear. I said yes for I thought the money would come in useful because he will pay for both now.

Harry has quite left school & will stay at Pentridge until I return. He looks shockingly ill & John wants to have your advice about him, his head is one mass of ringworms. Uncle has got the Doctor here to come & see him he has had a bad cough for the last six weeks but that is a little better. I am glad Trotty's quite well & also yourself. I hope you do not feel very lonely. I had a good laugh at your sending Mary to sleep. What did Brooke think of Julia? Why was he not at the Ball? Did he bring the Music?

I think John will perhaps pay my expenses up to Ballaraat. I try to save though things are now very cheap in Melbourne. Baker the Book-seller[2] is going to sell off is there any book or Medical book I could get for you if so send me word.

I had an unpleasant dream about you on Sunday night & woke up sobbing. I have been quite uneasy about you darling until I got your letter. Aunt & Uncle are both delighted to see me. We take a good walk every day. I hope you will write soon. Shall I go to the Mesmerist in Collins street or not? Aunt would go with me.

Give my love to Julia, Mrs H—, Anne Maria & Trotty & they all join me here in love to yourself & with kisses many dear dear Walter

> Ever your loving Wife
> Mary
> God Bless you too dark to write more—

1/70

1   Affected with a 'gathering' or festering sore.
2   W. Baker at 71 Swanston Street, Melbourne.

[51]

Tuesday {5 June 1860}

My dear dear Mary

I did think I would have had a letter today in answer to mine written on Saturday. Dear me you are very chary of your letters: Lucinda came down from Castlemaine yesterday & is off again tomorrow her machoir[1] was broken.

We are all well: I have had to give her £3.0.0 & she wants a cheque for £5.0.0 as soon as you return—No practice—No money: do not think of asking me to come down for I could not do it.

I have a dull time of it and sleepless nights, from excessive cold & mental anxiety: Will be glad to see your dear face again!

I am going to drive Lu. out this afternoon:

Expect Smith tonight.

No news at all—

Mrs. H. back, looking very delicate; had no word from you; did not see you except at the ball:

Weather very, very, cold:

Letter from Ned this morning wh' I will keep for you. Nicholson is sure to go in again & John as well tho' perhaps not as P[ost] Master General.

Trotty suffers from the cold very much.

Your affect Walter:

Luc. sends kind love & regrets much not seeing you. WR.

1/73

1   False teeth; see *The Fortunes of Richard Mahony*, p. 711: 'Aunt Zara called her teeth her *mashwar*. Why did she, and why did they click?'

[52]

Friday {8 June 1860}

My own dear Mary

I only received yours of Tuesday *this morning*. I thought it very negligent of you to keep me 10 days with only one letter from you, feared you were ill, did not know what to think indeed!

I have been very lonely indeed and longing for you every day. Got no sleep the first week:

I have been away since 10 at a labor in the bush: & have now been sent for to go to the Asylum as Dr. Alison is ill again.

I was so glad to get your letter I wrote one yesterday to Uncle about you, then one to yourself. Neither of wh' I sent—I have nothing worth telling you: Weather cold:

Many enquiring when you are coming we did hope you would have been up today Friday but I suppose now we shall not see [you] until next week—Well perhaps it is all for the best as you are evidently enjoying yourself, made much of.

L. off on Wednesday morning.

Trotty well: Mr. & Mrs. Williamson called & Mrs McQueen.

Brooke promised to see you today & drive you out he will be disappointed again he was at S. Kilda but you ran away one day before your time.

Sorry to hear of Harry's illness, want of proper treatment doubtless. Does he wish to come back?—

You can easily telegraph up if you are coming suddenly: I will drive down to Corduroy to meet you let your box go on altho' I don't know about Harry I think I might manage it to Buninyong. Excuse haste my love as it is to catch the Post and believe me my dear dear Mary. Your own loving

Walty.

1/105

[53]

New Prison, Pentridge
9 June 1860

My ever dear Walter

I received your second letter on Thursday it was kind of you to write to me before you could get mine for if I do not get them posted before 1 o'clock they do not leave Pentridge till next day—You did surprise me about Lucinda being down. I am sorry I was not at home to make her comfortable. I hope that you are keeping well. I want to come home very much & am only stopping because I feel so well & perhaps if I come home quite strong it might do me good in the *sense we both wish*.

You did not say whether I should go to the Clairvoyant. I should like to do so if I could afford it. I have little news to tell you for all's so very quiet here. We went into Town on Wednesday but I did not see John he was so busy. We hurried home because it came on to rain & since then we have not been able to go outside it is so wet. I leave here on Wednesday morning & go to Mrs Marsh for a few days & the week after I return to my own dear Walter & how my heart throbs while I write it. I want to stay until <u>something</u> is over but I have lost count of when it ought to be. Can you send me word what day it was last month, as soon as that is over I shall start. I will not ask you to come for me dear as you wish besides I shall have Harry with me & I think I shall go to Geelong by the Afternoon train & sleep at Skarratt's so as to get a good seat in the Coach that leaves at 10 A.M. then if I do that I shall not put anyone about at St. Kilda by having to start from there early in the morning. My blister is well & my finger getting better.

I have a bad headache. Harry's very noisy. I hope Trotty's a good girl & quite well. I hope I shall get a letter from you today. I am to see John at 12 o'clock on Wednesday so if there's to be a letter for me that day let it be addressed to John for I do not get my letters here till afternoon. I hope to see you looking well when I return. Till then God bless & prosper you is the prayer of your ever loving wife

Mary
Many kisses—

dear Walter I have just received another dear letter so I have opened this to tell you to send me down one of your visiting cards to leave at Toorak as all have to go & leave their cards. I go on Monday week as that is the day Mrs Timmens stays at home to receive callers.

Next Sunday I am going with John to Mrs. Francis's. I have not time for more darling as John takes this in Town tonight so as to ensure your getting it on Tuesday, he is very very kind. God bless you dearest

1/69

[54]

Webster St
Tuesday 12 June 1860

My darling Mary,
Your letters are '*like Angels visits, few & far between!*' 3 in 14 days are not many!

The one I received this morning is dated June 9. Saturday. We are *pretty* well only very solitary, & having been very idle the last fortnight, I feel it more.

Nose bled twice yesterday once in the middle of the street on horseback when I was out in the dark: Weather very cold & damp

I am glad you are enjoying yourself. I expect Brooke up tonight which will amuse me a little—No news.

Took tea *once* at Mrs. Henderson's.

Dr. Stewart has gone down to get married to J. H. Taylor's sister: Holmes the lawyer is married: Dixie kindly asked me to go & dine with him yesterday but as I was in riding costume I declined—

I am so delighted you appear to be better & enjoying yourself so much, there is nothing like variety of scene & society. I made L. as comfortable as we could—

Tuesday May 15 *was the day* dear, so I suppose it is Monday this time & that you will be here on Saturday next: Go to the Clairvoyant if you wish certainly & ask her any questions you choose, you should however write down the answers. Kind love to Aunt & Uncle—I will meet you at the Coach instead of coming to Bun[inyon]g. I send you my card.

I do so long to kiss you once again do come on Saturday if you are at all able & if not why make it next week.

I hope you will like Mrs Francis & give me a good acc[oun]t of your doings when you come back.

I am writing to L today. I have paid her £7.0.0 since you were here—She got £5.0.0 of goods from Thom & Gray down to me—So that we are square all but £5.0.0—

Providence is wonderfully good & the money still comes in to keep house going: You have never *asked me for any!* I understood from John's letter that he would make it all right. It was a farce to say I got an invitation to the Ball for I never did!

I am suffering very much from cold feet & cold altogether. I am never warm—

Good bye God bless you

I see the mail is in

Your loving husband Walter.

1/55

[55]

My darling Mary

I received letters last night from my mother & sister & your sister Lizzie. Nobody dead: I am so glad to hear you have at last fixed on a day to return, I have been so miserable—no sleep from cold. I got last a better night as in addition to the bed clothes on the bed I put on Ned's rug & four blankets & having found a night cap only awoke about $\frac{1}{2}$ doz times which was decidedly better.

I have no end of a headache today & suffer much from the cold still:—

You will see or have seen Brooke by this: he does not expect to come here any more if he does next week send me latest intelligence.

Mr Bond & Mrs. Farley have been ill, both recovering. Dr. Stewart sent me cards this morning.

Very bad news of *The Times* it is reported to have lost Mr Henderson £3000 & to be for sale. Julia as romping as ever. I enclose you £1.0.0 in case you run short. Am going to send £5.0.0 to your mother for Sam wh' ought to have been done last month, but which may perhaps be in time. Very fair but cold & frosty: You say my dear you answered all my letters but you let many days pass without giving me my first one.

Smith says Madam Carol was a Mrs. Caroline Dexter the inventor of Bloomerism[1] & is a decided humbug—I send you two newspapers in one and have little else to say. Trott is well but she should have pinafores to cover her arms & neck or she will most likely be carried off by croup or influenza this winter as she cannot be kept out of the kitchen & the door is always open:

I keep Lizzie's to us for the pleasure of your reading *it here*.

Good bye darling. God bless you & restore you safe to the arms of your fond husband

Walter—

I hope you keep my letters safely from the eyes of the public—

1/101

[1] While not strictly the 'inventor' of the new Bloomer costume for women, Caroline Harper Dexter (1819–84) lectured on Bloomerism in London and the provinces in 1851. After emigrating from England to Australia in 1854, Dexter opened a 'Mesmeric Institution' at 114 Collins Street in Melbourne in 1859, which she maintained until 1864. She specialised in women's medical problems and employed a combination of clairvoyance, mesmerism and homoeopathy. Dexter is likely to be the Mesmerist whom Mary proposed visiting in her letter of 5 June 1860.

[56]

Tuesday afternoon {1861}

My dearest P:

Yours reached me this morning—Hope Leopold has not Scarlatina or Diphtheria—but that you are all well—& enjoying the change: I am doing very well—I dined with Mrs. Saddler on Sunday & at Hudsons[1] last evening. Met the Emblings[2], rubber and some good fun. He sang & accomp[anied] himself *Maid of Indal in German* Bridegroom &c

I saw no conceit or very little. *Certainly no bumptiousness.*

Mrs E very plain—

I was out all the h[ou]rs last night & have now a bad case of Placenta Praevia in—

Invitation to party at Morrisons for Tuesday April 2d—

You must sign the enclosed & get it witnessed—

Newingtons had a run on them yesterday sold at £4.0.0 then back to 3.10.0.

Dons up to £5.0.0.

I send today's *Star* with this—No other news—

Kind regards to the Kabats.[3]

Your affect H.

W.

1/95

1   Presumably the physician Robert Fawell Hudson (1834–98). Married Elizabeth, née Bath. Chairman of Ballarat Gas Co. and Ballarat Banking Co.

2   Presumably a reference to Thomas Embling (1814–93), a medical practitioner who later became a parliamentarian. Married Jane Chinnock. Their son, William Henry Embling (1840–1912), also became a physician and surgeon.

3   Leopold Kabat (1829–84) was a Polish soldier who arrived in Melbourne on 15 May 1852. Member of the Victoria Police Force 1878–84. Married Emily Murchison in 1856.

[57]

Bull Street
23 May 1861

My darling Walter

I write today so as to get John to post this in Town tomorrow morning. You will see I have arrived safely after the long journey & feeling very tired. John met us at the Station & was very glad to see me also Jeannie. I like her very much there house far surpasses ours in furniture it is most elegant. You would be very pleased with everything. My boxes have not yet arrived it is very vexing. I cannot go out until I do get them. Trotty behaved very well though she is suffering very much today. *No rest* day or night for coughing her face & eyes all inflamed quite a fright.

I forgot dearest to tell you that the day before I left Mrs Porter called & told me to ask you to send a Nurse, a temperance one you promised her, also send back the books I had from Davis & pay 1/–. Travelling in the Coach was a party who knew you when at Smith's at Mary's Cray & her name was Golding. You attended her Mamma. She knew you directly she saw you at the coach—She is married to Mrs Turnball's brother & lives far back in a paddock opposite the Turf Hotel.

I had to put this by last night so have got up early this (Friday) morning to finish it. Such a night I do not wish to pass again. I have not had one hour's sleep since I left you. Trotty sleeps with me & all night long she was either crying or coughing. I struck a light & such an object as her face was, like a spotted pink dress. Well I thought it very funny but said nothing. Wrapt her up & made her perspire & at daylight I looked at her again & my suspicions were confirmed. She has either Measles or Scarlet fever. John & Jeannie are not up yet so they don't know—a pretty state of things. She either caught them in the Coach where there was a sick boy or else in Skarrat's Hotel. He told me as we were driving to the Railway that all his children had been ill with Measles though we did not see them. I suppose John will send for a Dr. It has quite put me about.

No boxes have arrived & here I am & cannot get out.

Jeannie has only been in the Colony 7 months has no relations whatever earned her own livelihood & is not ashamed of it. Says she is thirty years old. A great deal to say for herself & will make John an excellent wife. Very very different to Poor Susan. She is anxious to return with me to see Ballaraat but John does not like that but she will come before three months are over. You must come down, a beautiful room for us both. I showed her your likeness & she thinks you very good looking & would so like to know you. John says the trip would do you all the good in the world.

By the bye send down the prescription for Trotty. Cough mixture. We were to have gone to the Turnhams to spend tomorrow but we shall not be able to go on account of Harry. I cannot tell you anything about Melbourne as I have not been out. I feel very tired already & hope you will be down in about a fortnight for me. I shall not stay [for] the Governor's ball I think. How do you & Sam get on? I hope Bridget attends to your wants & cooked the Sucking pig to your liking. I hope to get a dear *long long* letter from you on Monday & I will write again on Tuesday. Give my love to Sam & accept many kisses with all my loves to yourself. God Bless & prosper you darling is the prayer of

Your loving Wife
Mary

1/67

[58]

Saturday 2.30 p.m. {25 May 1861}

My dear Mary

You have certainly not had a very nice time so far—I should advise a *separate* bed *for you* as sleeping with a feverish child is not good for you. I am glad you got down safely and hope you will enjoy yourself next week. You have escaped our miserable weather—wet & cold—It is certainly very trying. I shall not be able to write much now for I have to go again a long round and my hand is so cold I can hardly hold the pen.

I was called out last night & not in bed till one—*Night mare* both nights—first so tired that I could not catch my horse who walked away from me, & 2d a large bone got into her foot & lamed her.

You will understand these were my dreams—I have a case of broken jaw & I have to go every day 2 miles off—Queen's birthday wet spoiled everything.

I send you *Times* of Friday.

Sam well—Bridget doing well.

Volunteer Ball a great success—I enclose acc[oun]t from Wanliss which I will pay today—As to Trotty you will find a good article in the book I send to our new sister. I could not find your letter to Sarah. Kelly has just been & we put in a vine at each end of the house & a few other plants & that has warmed me a little—I will write you a longer letter next time say on Monday evening and with kind & fond kisses to yourself & regards to Jack & Jean I am Yours

ever W.L.R.

1/157

[59]

Bull Street South E
27 May 1861

My dear Walter

Yours I received this morning with the book to Jeannie which she is much obliged for. Your letter was very short but I hope dearest you will let me have a long one on Wednesday morning. Trotty is a little better—I think the rash seems to be going in today & she is not so feverish. Her cot came on Saturday so I put her in but it makes very little difference as I have to keep getting out of bed to her. I am *nurse* & doctor both. Coughing constantly.

I do hope dearest you will make up your mind to fetch me home as soon as you can. Harold was here yesterday he looks very well. Suffers so much from cold—he says if it would not trouble you too much he would like to have his rug it is under one of the beds marked EHB if you can write a day or two before you come I am to write to him & he will come on purpose to see you. Jeannie is very anxious to return to Ballaraat with me & send Trotty to Pentridge but I want her to let me come first & get the house in order & them to take Harry back. She does not believe in never going away & intends to begin as she likes. Very different to Poor Sue. John not like the same man quite a pleasure to be in the house, he says he does hope you will come & Jeannie too so I said I knew you would. You will be so delighted with St Kilda if fine. Jeannie & I are going to town tomorrow.

I wish you would send me word the exact width of the Drawing room window from wood to wood. I saw such a beautiful Gilt Cornice for 25 shillings it measures 6 feet 4 inches they look better than poles & must fit just round the top wood mark. I shall also get a set of new dish covers for two pounds. I find my hat & cloak will not cost me quite so much as I thought for I shall have money enough to buy those if you don't object; the cornice is very handsome. We have not been out anywhere nor anyone here. All frightened at the Measles so Jeannie & I walk about. Seen nothing of Turnhams. The little book says diarrhoea often sets in when the measles disappear. Send me word what to do in case such a thing occurs; she won't eat anything. I give her Aniseed Tea to drink. I am glad to hear that Sam is well. You must tell me what you do all the evening & how you amuse yourselves.

Shall you bring the Buggy down? Mind you write good long letters dear. I forgive you the last one. I hope you will sleep better. I can sympathise with you for I am as bad myself. I will give John the Bill when he comes home there was such a row about the things the charge was 35 shillings & when they came here they wanted 5 shillings for fetching the things from our House. John would not pay & there was a regular scuffle. I do not know how it will end. I think I have told you all I can. My head aches so I shall leave off—God Bless you darling with love & lots of kisses ever yours

Mary

do let me have a dear letter on—*Wednesday*—

1/65

[60]

Tuesday {28 May 1861}

My dearest Mary

I know my last was very short because I wished to post it on Saturday, and therefore I was prevented from writing more owing to my having to go out. There is no fear of Trotty if she does not take cold. I would recommend a good large Mustard plaster between both Shoulders if Cough continues. You say you want me to come but do not say when, if matters go on as you describe your visit is made a punishment instead of a pleasure and sleepless nights will soon injure your health again & do away with any good that might arise from your trip—I think of going down on the 11th June so as to be present at the installation of the Grand Master. I have been asked to represent the Ball[ara]t Lodge: so if that is not too soon, the ceremony takes place on the 12th. I could stay until Saturday 15th that would make your stay under a month:

I do not think the gilt cornice would look nearly so well as poles: the width from wood to wood below is about 5 feet 6. but the cornice could easily be altered, up above it is about 6 feet 6 inches I should think. I have no news to tell you on Saturday eve[nin]g Sam went to theatre and I staid at home.

Sunday I went to Church. Monday played chess 3 games—Tuesday Boyle spent eve[nin]g with us—Tonight I am going to Hospital Committee Meeting.

Have been & am fearfully busy the days are too short and I will either have to leave at 9 or stay out till 6 & 7—

Mrs Henderson gives a party tonight the Smiths & O'Haras, Sam & I have been asked. I told her I would not be able to go until late but I would be in time *for supper*. I thought of her treatment of you:

I cover myself up at night with your dress & I have managed very well, the last two nights—Weather fine yesterday & today but much dirt & sludge. Do you get the *Star* daily let me know. Bridget is behaving very well—I have not seen or heard of any of your friends—& so have nothing to tell you of them.

Kind remembrances to all.

You will see by the *Star* if you get it that Vowles has tendered for £1600 for Cuthbert's house & has been accepted—

I have literally nothing more to add & so Farewell if I thought you burned my letters I would write much longer & fuller ones—

Your affect
Walter

I have had a terrific cough & cold in consequence of getting wet twice daily for 4 days—

I see rain coming in again tonight or tomorrow.

1/75

[61]

Saturday morning {1 June 1861}

My dearest Mary

I am still very busy, occupied every night until after dark, I cannot give you any particulars about my coming down yet for of course something may occur to prevent it even at the last moment: so do not be too sanguine my dear—

Of course we are *very happy* & *not at all dull*: there was a fire this morning ½ past 5. Star Hotel & Binney & Broadbents both destroyed—

Weather intensely cold—but anything rather than wet:

No news whatever of any body.

Sam went to Hendersons & I popped in at 10.30 & had one Polka then just as we were sitting down to Supper I was called away & did not go back again: Dr. Bunce is going thro' the insolvent court again![1] I will not keep the Foresters[2] longer than next Xmas & perhaps may not be re-elected this month or next month I am not sure which—No accouche-ments this week only two last week altho' 24 down.

Gray[3] got in to the Hospital as Dispenser. Shepperd very nearly succeeded Gray 11 to 10.

2.30 I have just come in, quite knocked up & have to go all over the Town again & up to Little Bendigo—I have determined to resign the Foresters they are a low mean set—And my attention is too good for them, besides which I feel I am killing myself. I get no sleep now after 5 every morning, & the worry & wear & tear is terrific.

I have nothing more to add. Good bye.

God bless you
Your own husband
Walter

The sucking pig came this morning. I shall not get home tonight before 7—

1/102

[1]   Bunce was also insolvent in 1856.
[2]   The Ancient Order of Foresters, one of the many friendly societies established to provide medical services, sick pay, funeral and other benefits to members and their families. The lodges, or clubs as Walter sometimes calls them, would usually each elect a doctor as an officer, to provide medical services to members in exchange for an annual fee.
[3]   Possibly Andrew Sexton Gray (1828–1907), medical practitioner who founded the Victorian Eye and Ear Hospital in 1863.

[62]

Bull Street
3 June 1861

My dear Walter
    I am sorry to see by your letter that you are so put about, resign the Foresters if you cannot give satisfaction besides your health is more important than any lodges at least to me altho' you are so cool in your

two last you have never sent me even your love or a kiss it seems very hard but I suppose I am not missed very much. No matter what my faults are I thought you would have had kind feelings towards me. Your letter has destroyed what little enjoyment I might have had today in Town & coming after my dreaming all night that you had your arms round me was very chilling. I must put it down to your being so busy but those two are the first really cool letters I have had from you. Jeannie is going into Town today for a new servant, hers leaves tomorrow—will not stop, too much work, it must be on account of the children I expect but so far she has had nothing extra to do for I have washed & dressed Trotty & done my own room & she has never done a single thing for me since here I've been. On Saturday we went to Pentridge they were glad to see us but more delighted to hear that you were coming down. Very anxious for us to stay there but John would not hear of it. I promised for one night.

Yesterday we went to church & a walk on the Beach afterwards. I saw Harris one day in Town but he did not see me. I shall not stay for the Governor's Ball. I hope if possible dear you will come for me. I feel dull. I hope you enjoyed the sucking pig & that Bridget cooked it to your liking.

I think John intends taking us to the Theatre one night this week.

It was very vexing about the supper at Henderson's but your usual luck. I am not very much surprised at Bunce he is a man who will never do much good. I hope you will write me a little warmer dear next time [m]y back aches today & head & perhaps I felt it more. John's honeymoon is not over yet. Give my love to Sam & God Bless you darling love & kisses

Ever Yours Mary

1/64

[63]

{4 June 1861}

My own dear Poll

You never meant half you wrote to me. You must make some allowance. I have never been so worried in my life.

I enclose you a list of my patients that I have seen today—On Saturday night was called out to *Mrs Allen* home by 12. Called out again to *Mrs Pearmain* at 2 Sunday morning, home by 4—Sunday night called out at 11 to *Mrs Rogers*, home by 3, as I got to my home found some person waiting to take me to *another,* home by 4, as I got home found *Mr. Rogers* back again, had to tear away there, home by 11. Last night called out to sick child & called up to prescribe—

I was riding up Creswick road last night after dark & a dog flew out after the horse she shied stumbled & came down a *fearful smash*, I got clear providentially *without much injury* but she is done for—I have felt shaken all day & hands hurt: I had to walk all morning & hire a horse afternoon 10/- I fear this will stop my trip to you dear—as it is at least £10 or £15 out of my pocket—

I must say you do write punctually altho' your letters are short & contain little news.

You must excuse the shortness of mine for I am always fitter for bed than anything else.

I will give up the Foresters & then I will have a little peace—

I am glad you saw the Turnhams I should like to see them & to come down—

Sam is very well. I asked him to write you—The Potters called & Mrs Wayne & Mrs Walker and the Adairs—I am sorry to hear you feel dull my darling the reason I have not said any more about ourselves is that we do not wish to make you duller or to hurry back until you have enjoyed yourself well:

Wednesday morning. Called out again 8 PM last night not home till 4.30 this morning & have got six new places to go to all wanting me first—

Another confinement on hand = 7 since Saturday night:

I will try & write a little more at lunch time. I am going to try & walk this morning & go to a sale of horses at 12–2. PM. went. Could not buy—An awful Catastrophe has occurred to me. Puerperal inflammation of the worst kind has attacked 2 of my confinements & I must be off at once.[1] Very likely I will be down tomorrow or next day. Good bye love till then Your own Walter

1/74

[1] Puerperal fever (childbed fever)—a highly contagious infection of the reproductive organs after childbirth.

[64]

Webster St
Thursday 30 January 1862

My dear Mary

In accordance with your wish I commence a letter to you this evening, to be in time for tomorrow's post—I have been just as busy as usual, out all day today, from 10 to $\frac{1}{2}$ past 1 & from $\frac{1}{2}$ [past] 2 to 6. Regatta tomorrow, I have some remote idea of going, but of course will be prevented by some mewling & puking babies; I hope you got down safely and that Lucinda did not laugh too much of a guffaw.

I hope she is better, & that you too my own are better also—No pains or aches but that the change of air & scene is enjoyed by you—

Did you breakfast on the road?

Did Ned meet you I suppose he did—

Fine weather since you left: I slept so well the first night: never waking: last night nearly as well, called up at $\frac{1}{2}$ past 5—

Bank holiday. I think Sam is going to the regatta: I could not lend him the mare; for I have work in plenty for both: I send your newspaper with this: Mrs. Haywood has another son—Stewart was sent for to Creswick, to Lewer's son, and so Bunce attended her for him!

I got your letter this morning & hasten after lunch to finish this: *O'Connor has been in for an hour* 1 to 2. Glad you got down pleasantly—take care & rest.

I see the *Great Britain* is off. The *Latona* is not advertised for any day so it may possibly be March.

I have no news—very cross—Sarah can't write the names of the people coming & confuses me very much: I believe I have lost two private patients today.

Sam pretty well—Kind remembrances to Uncle, Aunt & Ned—explain that I have no time to write to Ned. I shall expect a long letter about Tuesday.

Ever Your affectionate
Walter.

1/79

[65]

My own dear wife

I am so grieved to hear about you, I declare your letter this morning filled my eyes with tears. It appears you are suffering a great deal for Lucinda's sake and she ought to be very much obliged to you—I wish you had never gone—I do not see my dearest any chance of my going to you just yet, wait patiently. On Saturday I started at 10 & went over Ball[ara]t West & Hospital, home by one found of course several waiting, & a confinement; started to Golden Point, found I should not be wanted just yet & so went round by Specimen Hill, Eureka, Little Bendigo, Soldiers Hill, back to Golden Point, home by 9—dined, off again at 10 to another, home by 3. *Slept well.* Sunday just as busy & another confinement this morning. Could not sleep last night owing to sore throat—dreamed I was choking—Called out at 2 home by 6. Got no sleep, sent down for Chloroform—dosed from 8 to 9, up to a *dozen people* & out again in a broiling day till 1.30. Rain threatening: Confinement 1st do 2d do 3d of this month & another likely to come off this evening. Bunce could not do $\frac{1}{2}$ my practice so I do not see *my own*, how I am to leave just now. Suppose you take Lodgings *at Williamstown* Sandridge or S. Kilda, away from bugs. Ned would see to it & I will send money down & try to come down at end of month—Let me ask Dr. Tracy to call & see you: I hear Mrs. W. is coming back soon—There will be but little use in my coming down if you put off going to Dr Tracy till then because his treatment will require a week or two & I could not stay.

I am so glad of Uncle's rise—Capital! Remember me kindly to them both & thank them for their love of you.

Sarah is very good indeed—so sorry to hear of your illness.

Hudson knocked up: Elliott sun stroke—Rumor says that Mrs. Dr. H living on the Main Road who went home you remember some years ago, before marriage *had a child at home*, & that H has found it out since & has kicked up a jolly row. Scott told me & vouched for the truth of it.

Sam went to the Picnic came home brown as berry—*No rise*:

Remember me to Ned & Lucinda.

You have not said a word about John or family.

Ever your fond husband
Walter

1/76

[66]

1 to 2 Wednesday {5 February 1862}

Received yours my own love this morning. I had been anxiously expecting it & was overjoyed to find you better at last; the change will be of benefit, do not talk of hurrying back just yet, there's a dear, I will try & come end of next week, or the beginning the week after, but I have *so many bad cases* that *cannot* be left, that I am unable to fix an earlier day: 'Absence makes the heart grow fonder'. You know *it is true love* that dictates this advice, and not selfishness, for I feel your absence every night, and want of rest makes me ill—
After an awful week, a cool breeze has set in & a cloudy day without rain—Still busy & likely to be, have ordered a new pair of wheels and when they are ready & on, so that I can lend Bunce the buggy, I may think of coming but I am *certain* that I cannot see Lucinda off, I am sure I regret it heartily, but I have *a queer lot to deal with*, & am but a poor man & can only hope to get on for your sake—L. ought to be content with *your presence* & the sacrifices we have made for her!

I send £1. in this & will send another in the next, so give her 30/– for your mother for the *Ill{ustrated} News*—I am surprised at Ned! Poor chap. I will buy a chain from the Warehouse it will be a good chance. One with a *bar*—they asked me £7. here & £9.0.0. Sarah is very good! Sam has his salary raised to £150.0.0 & is *Ledger Keeper*: He is in good spirits about it. No news:—

I think I shall sleep in drawing room tonight or try to sleep.

Swamp going dry no rain—

Kind love to all: I send a newspaper with this. I will expect another letter *Saturday at latest*.

I was too busy to go to Church last Sunday: Went to bed Monday at 8. & last night at 10. served them out; they kept coming to the

Surgery & Sarah managed them. Her hieroglyphics on the slate are *very amusing* but very *difficult to make out*. She misses your instructions & is going back!

Do not disappoint me of a letter on Saturday dearest & tell me how John & family are & if you have been boating since: the *Latona* was advertised for 4th. I do not believe she will sail punctually on the 8th. I may perchance be in time to see L. off yet!

Mrs. Ocock[1] called I think that is the only one; Watson is back, Bunce has got the Asylum.

The people won't have him, so I intend giving up the Foresters as soon as I have paid Cuthbert. Ochiltree is in town.

Nothing else of interest *but that I love you* and will be so glad to fold you to the heart of your dearest on earth

Walter

There is some talk of you being *sub poenad* in a case likely to come off soon vis that girl formerly of Mrs Smith Melbourne Road who is commencing an action against her for defamation of character £200 damages! I said that whoever subpoenaed you would get the worst of it —I shall swear you are too ill to appear in a Court of Justice.

1/81

---

[1] Presumably the wife of Richard Ocock, a Ballarat solicitor. In 1859 he was a member of the Ballarat Horticultural Society while Walter Richardson was vice-president. He was also a foundation member, along with Richardson, of the Victoria Lodge of Freemasons.

[67]

1 to 3 Friday {7 February 1862}

Dear dear Polly

Your last cheered me up, & was the best & longest you have written me: I have heard nothing more about the law case it is to come off on the 11th so I should have heard had there been any truth in it.

You are far from well yet my dear; *bath daily in cold water* drink plenty of beer & try & rise early: going to bed before 11.

I have not much to say but I wish you not to have to wait one Sunday for a letter & so answer yours today—I received the newspaper.

I was called out at 7 this morning to go to a labor, found I could not manage & sent the case to Bunce. He comes in to see me at 8. I get up at 8.30 see half doz people swallow cup of tea & sent for at 9 to another labor—get *there too late!*

Bunce has had a charge professed against him by the Governor McGee of *coarse & rude behaviour* & an investigation will take place before the Sheriff.

Weather cool today, & not nearly so busy this afternoon!

Mrs Bell and Mrs Newman called.

Go on board my love & enjoy a little sea sickness & a fresh breeze, it must do you good. I met Mrs Ochiltree she is thinking of going down to Queenscliffe she says—

If weather keeps cool & no sickness, you may see me *next week* but don't be too glad or too delighted & wait quietly if I don't come until the week after.

The house is very lonely especially midday—Sarah is very good all except the messages, those certainly she cannot manage.

Nothing of interest except that I love you *still as ever* and that I want *20 kisses right off,* & the remainder of the hundred as soon as possible. If I don't squeeze you when I catch you! But try my pet & get stronger or you *won't bear my love*, and will be *too weak to* <u>*return it*</u>. For goodness sake *burn this letter,* or keep it out of sight.

I must now conclude my own dear love it is very hard to have to wait until Tuesday morning to hear from you but I suppose there is nothing for it but patience—

Your loving husband
Walter

Kind love to Aunt, Uncle, Lucy & Neddy not forgetting Willy & Harrie.

Saturday What can I do to make up for not sending this yesterday to my dear one? Why write another to be sure—Well dear I wrote it and stamped it & having to go out with Whitcombe walked, intending to post it myself. You know my head for everything *except my patients*— More cholera today!

I feel anything but right—bad cold, from yarning last night at front door when wind from S[outh] was blowing in—Was John kind? They did not ask you to stay there?

Very cold today fine—at breakfast—How I do long for you to come back & make breakfast for me & pour out my tea—it does not taste half as good now.

Does L behave more pleasantly to you now? What a happy thing for her when she is alone in the wide ocean. I fear the Captain's wife & she will not agree very well—

You will get this on Monday don't serve me as I did you but be sure & let me have one on Tuesday morning, and then I will write & tell you what day you may expect me—Meantime good bye dearest on earth —it is very cold at nights now & I used the opossum rug & my gig rug last night—

You will come to meet me at the station won't you? Good bye again

Your own Walter. ✳

1/77

[68]

Saturday 9 {August} 1862

My own dear Polly

I have been almost delirious all day with this blessed 'Tic'.

I went out at 11 & felt it first coming on, hurried round home by 12.30 & never had a moment's intermission from pain till about 6 when it abated a little. I took Chloroform for an hour & woke up ten times worse—20 drops of Chlorodyne!

Fortunately no one at all came since morning—It has been a nasty dusty day I believe, but now the wind is round to the S[outh]—Kabat looked in for half an hour & had a chat: says he saw you looking very well: glad to hear it, hope you sleep better—I see nobody everything is very dull & you will feel the house very lonely when you come back after Sam & Alick.

I see the 'True Briton' is postponed till the 15th inst: Kabat asked me to dine there tomorrow & so did Bunce but really I declined first because I dread another day such as this & 2d because there may possibly be a lot of people about this place after me—

Sunday morning.

I was called out last night 10.PM to the Plank Road Mrs Dunstan: home by 2, pretty good night, but can feel my enemy coming on again —A nice cool day—I am writing to Alick by the same post. I am not certain whether to address it to the agent or to the ship Sandridge pier. I think I will do the latter.

Sunday night—I have not suffered so severely today but still have had it, but managed to sleep thro' the worst of it from 3 to 5.

I have been to Church tonight. Mr P preached a capital sermon. Good night dear ✳

Monday morning. I send you £1. in this & will enclose the other next time. Another fine day, very little sickness. My face is paining me a little it is *not* toothache but genuine '*Tic dolereaux*'. I believe there will be some good sport today at the Copenhagen and I am going up to try to keep me from my usual sufferings every afternoon—

William is doing pretty well. I have allowed him to get up on crutches—My new boy is a very good boy so far—

Kabat has asked me to go over tonight. I do not know whether I shall be able or no—English mail I am glad to see just in: What a pity John was not at home or that you could not have gone to the 'lawn party'. Kind love to Jeannie. I hope Harry is behaving himself better.

Your affect husband
Walter

You will observe how much longer my letters are than yours so that if I do not write again till the end of the week it will [give] you the opportunity [of] writing *a long* one in reply. You never said a word about the opera—

4 P.M

I have been up to the Sports—great fun but I was obliged to leave my old enemy in full force: the tortures of the damned—a large fire somewhere about the Melbourne Road.

1/78

[69]

My dearly loved Walter

You see I have arrived safely at St Kilda. Ned & Jeannie met us. Alick left me at the Station. I fancy he was a little afraid of the Captain; he began to tell me in the Railway a little of his affairs, he said he had no idea he had spent all the money he had done, he had quite mismanaged his affairs. I told him if he had told you you would have helped him but he said he did not like for it was his own fault.

I felt quite sorry at parting with him he looked so lonely & unhappy. We enjoyed the trip, had the Carriage to ourselves all the way did not do any reading, talking all the time. When we got to Melbourne it was raining very heavily so we came straight home, found all well. Trotty very thin. Harry quite yellow neither improved in looks & according to all accounts very naughty. Harry shocking taking *improper* liberties with Trotty. Jeannie will not have him in the house after John comes home. My heart feels sad to think what is to become of them. Thank God we have none to be such a trouble. The baby is such a fat fair little thing. Very like Jeannie & will be very pretty, not very well on account of teething, got a dreadful cold on its chest, no trouble, put to bed wide awake & never cries it is a really good child. Ned is looking very poorly, though I have not seen much of him but shall see him today as we go into Town this afternoon. I have not seen anyone else at present.

I shall have more to tell you in my next. I hope darling you are quite well & do not miss me very much though I do you particularly in bed. I shall be glad when I get back. Jeannie just the same as ever talking all the time, full of the children. I shall go to Pentridge next week—I will write again on Thursday.

I send you today's *Argus* to amuse you. It is a lovely day. I hope Sarah takes good care of you. God bless you my own darling with all my love & kisses ever your own wifey

Mary

1/66

[70]

Wednesday {12 November 1862}

My own dear Polly

Your nice long letter gave me greater pleasure this morning than any that you have written before. I am so pleased that you are enjoying yourself among friends. I hope the change to Pentridge will do you further good—I had ease yesterday thanks be to God and altho' I feel it today it is not yet bad—

I have lost 3 pounds weight since you left for I weighed myself the same day.

I got a letter from Sandy this morning tho' not in answer to one I had sent him which I suppose he had not received. You did not say if you had got the £1.0.0 safely so I conclude it must have been abstracted from the letter but I will not write the Post Master General on the subject until I hear from you again—Last night was the coldest night I think I have felt for many years. I could not sleep for some hours—the night before I was so poorly, I went to Kabats & was better.

A nice party *Sherard Burton Robertson Pooley Mackay*—

Pooley & I won £6.0.0 each—Bob Cuthbert was almost the winner of the ladies' cup. Willy Welch first Robert 2d—What a low fellow that Skipper of the 'True Briton' must be. Remember me kindly to 'Joe' & Aunty, bring her back if you can & keep her till Xmas when 'Joe' can come up for her—go out for a walk every day—go & see the gardens again—I am going to operate on the Hair lip this afternoon.

Not much sickness, Sarah says she thinks the people are giving me a holiday—

I intended to have gone to hear Black last night but prevented—I am going out tonight to the L.O.L.[1]

5 PM. I have just come home & have to go to Specimen Hill & Main Road so must cut this short.

I send you a newspaper acc[oun]t of sports & fire poor Treon burnt out.

Ever your own dear
Walter

I shall be so glad to see you again—

1/107

[1]   Presumably the Loyal Orange Lodge.

[71]

Pentridge
Thursday night {13 November 1862}

My own darling Walter

I am sure you would feel disappointed at not receiving a letter from me in the morning but I did not get yours until 7 o'clock this evening.

I came here on Tuesday afternoon & Uncle then asked for three days leave & got Thursday, Friday & Saturday so he went into Town & hired a nice four seated buggy to take us about in so we set off this morning before the post came in & drove to St Kilda for Jeannie & baby took lunch there & then drove right along the beach to Brighton & got back here at 7 o'clock very tired. Tomorrow we start at nine in the morning for the Yan Yean & on Saturday for Heidelberg so you see I am having a fine time of it. I am dreadfully tired & am writing this instead of going to bed.

I have Jeannie & baby for bedfellows, how I wish it were you darling. You did not say in yours whether you had any English letters for me. I saw one from Mother to John. She is in great trouble again. Sarah was in the train at the time of that fearful collision on the Midland Railway had been in bed a fortnight & lost the situation she was to have gone to. No bones broken but a shock to the whole of the body & nerves will be a long time before well, expects to get compensation, always something happening.

Ned had a letter from Lucinda, had you one? Also from Lizzie. I am so glad to hear that you are better. You want me at home to fatten you. I know I did not make you thin. I wish you could get a change, ever so little would do you good—I think of coming back next Wednesday night. Could you not afford out of your winnings to come down by the 6 o'clock train in the morning & return with me by the seven train in the evening? You could have a bathe darling & it would only be a single fare for return ticket. Oh do come darling it would do you good & you would see the time so nicely. I hope you will send an answer. You could leave your patients for one day. I leave here on Monday afternoon so be sure & let me have a letter either Saturday or Monday telling me to meet you. I got the 1£ all right, thought I told you so. I wish you would come darling it seems ages since I have seen your dear smiling face. I long to kiss it again & again. I expect to see Alick tomorrow to say good bye as I believe they sail on Saturday.

I hope darling you will forgive me for writing so short a letter this time but I am so tired I can scarcely hold my pen. God Bless you dear dear Walty with love & kisses

Good night. Ever your own loving
Polly
Absence makes the heart grow fonder.

1/71

[72]

Friday morning {14 November 1862}

My dearest Polly

I have been a little more occupied since I last wrote. On Tuesday night I told you I was called up to Mrs Merry: on Wednesday evening I went down to Hamburgher & played whist till 12. Found in the evening that John had walked off, so put an advertisement in *Tribune* & got up yesterday morn[in]g early to groom my horse myself; at 8 got a message to go off at once to Mrs Blair, did not get home till 12.30 found several boys waiting & engaged one: last evening John walks up to the front door to know if I would give him the money I owed him: I told him he had left me without notice & I would not.

I am delighted he is gone; the new boy last night got up *in his sleep* & *walked about* the room kicking up a terrific rumpus talking & laughing. I called out as loud as I could before I could awake him. There is a most disagreable hot wind with clouds of dust blowing today. 'Murton' is building a fine new brewery *80 feet by 24* which will shelter our house very much—Bunce came in last night & played 'Ecarte' till 12.

I have just received yours and regret so much about your not sleeping, try & take a sponge bath before you go to bed & drink a glass of wine.

I am delighted you are enjoying the days.

I am sure I will be very happy to see Feldheim when he comes up & there is no doubt it would do Ned good, remember me kindly to the old fellow—I see Mount & Harrison's race is talked of in the *Herald* about end of month at Melbourne.[1]

When your letter arrived O'Connor was here, he came to ask me to put my name to a bill for £50.0.0.

Walter Richardson in his thirties

Mary Richardson in her twenties

I declined most decidedly. Mrs Heine is keeping very good. H. took her out in buggy yesterday & walked out in eve[nin]g.

My face is very bad again: agony all day—

Assisted Bunce at an operation—Knocked up—fairly beaten: so you must excuse this short letter.

I will write you a longer one on Sunday.

Love to Jeannie

Your ever loving husband
Walter

12✳

1/106

1 The *Argus* of 17 November 1862, p. 4, reported that the 'third and concluding match for the pedestrian championship of the colony, between the well-known amateurs Mr. H.C. Harrison and Mr. L.L. Mount' would be taking place on the Melbourne Cricket Ground.

[73]

15 November 1862

My own dear Walter

This is only a scrap to say I got the second 1£ all right, also English letters. Many thanks for your sending them. I am looking forward to Wednesday to see your dear face once more. I hope you will be able to come for me it would do you so much good. I am very tired we have just come in from a long drive to Heidelberg & when we have had tea to drive back to Pentridge.

I shall not tell you now where we have been to but leave it until I can talk to you & describe the scenery. I am so glad to hear you are better.

I have not seen Alick & I hear they are going today. I should like to have seen him once more. That was a sad accident Sarah met with.

I visit the agent (with Mr Marsh on Tuesday) for W. P. White & Co[1]—So shall be able to tell you some news. There is so much talk going on around. I hardly know whether I am on my head or my heels —Send the enclosed to Miss Cuthbert as it saves fourpence. I have not seen Mrs Haywood; twice I started & it came on so wet—be sure & not write to me after Monday morning at Pentridge.

Will you also ask Mrs Kabat the name of the New Waltzes I was to bring for Miss Cuthbert I have quite forgotten.

No news of John yet. I wish I was home again. I feel lonely now. Give my love to all friends & excuse more as I wait an answer from you. I shall only have to write once more.

Tell Sarah to have the Carpet up, & now Good bye my own dearie & with all love & kisses ever

Your loving wife
Polly
I am longing *for some kisses*

1/68

¹   A shipping company.

[74]

My dear Polly,

I am very much disappointed at your not coming up today: There may be a great deal of difficulty about Alick's bill of exchange: & it may not be payable except to himself *personally.* You had better not delay any longer *but come at once.* I should prefer you coming by this evening's train—

But I will excuse you if you will go *now* with John either to Tracy or Dougan Bird¹—this afternoon—bring up the prescription or get it made up & begin taking the remedies at once—I am sorry that Alick has made so bad a commencement by getting into debt—I had made all arrangements for your coming this afternoon & think I had better not make any more as I do not know when to expect you now—

I have nothing to do & if you were at home could take you out nicely & enjoy ourselves. When I want to do so I suppose I shall be busy again & prevented—

Your affect Hubby
W

Thurs morning

1/82

¹ Dr Richard Tracy (1826–74) was founder of the Melbourne Lying-in Hospital, a lecturer in obstetrics at the University of Melbourne and President of the Medical Society of Victoria. Dr Samuel Dougan Bird (1832–1904) established a practice in Melbourne in 1862 and was appointed honorary physician to the Alfred Hospital and the Benevolent Asylum. A lecturer at the University of Melbourne, and the author of several medical books.

[75]

Wednesday morning

My own dear P:

It was very good of you to write without waiting to receive my reply to your first letter. I was very glad indeed to hear you were well—There appears to be some awkwardness about the postal arrangements of the neighbourhood in which you are now:

I have been very busy since you left—I posted the last to you on Saturday morning. Well I had a busy day and dined with Hudson went back & spent evening.

Too busy on Sunday to go to Church dined with Cuthberts:

Monday night labor & called out to another case Tuesday out all day & 5 miles on the road past the Cuthberts. Rubber at my house from 8 to 11.30 bed by 12—called up to a case of very protracted labor at 3.30 on Plank Road where I now am & likely to be for some hours. It is very annoying because it will upset my day's work & cause me to neglect my patients: & as I promised to go to the country patient the first thing I see nothing for it but running home at 8: & breakfasting & finishing this to you—

Do not be in too great a bustle to return: you may not get away again this year. Mrs. C. & baby all well. She came down to dinner with us on Sunday & played a chant—

Just had a letter from Ned about the box he says he may send it up today: Bill's Carte de V. very good.¹

No home letters for you. Enclosed from Sam.

Never seen Leop. since you left. I am too busy. I see Felix loafing about.

Nobody has called.

Weather wet this morning.

I send *Star*—and now I will either have to close this or put it off till the afternoon. I think you wd not like the latter.

Your affect husband
W.

I will give you a longer one next time.

1/104

¹ Abbreviation for carte-de-visite—a small photographic portrait mounted on a $3\frac{1}{2}$
by $2\frac{1}{4}$ inch card.

[76]

Monday evening {6 March 1865}

My own dear Polly
    You need not be cross because you did not get a letter in the morning, as I was prevented from replying by return post. I am glad you arrived safely and that the journey was a pleasant one. I hope the whole trip may be as pleasant: You must not talk so soon of returning but make up your mind for the entire month of March—Leopold went down Tuesday afternoon. I dined at the Saddlers, we had a very pleasant dinner.
    I found it very cold last night & told Maria to put on some more blankets.
    Jim called me at 7 & we had a bath—I have been pretty busy today—and as I was at tea in walked Albert from Woods Point. The account of his life is like a romance—sleeping out in the open air for weeks. No covering from rain or snow, wading in rivers & swimming them night & morning. He says he is better off than he has ever been since he has left home—I am glad all are well—I will finish this in the morning.

    Tuesday morning.
    Another cold night: Had a bath this morning—the weather is pleasant, not too hot.
    No news of any interest.

All going on well in your absence. Enjoy yourself as much as you can—go to Abbotsford & Pentridge & the Murchisons and on board the *G. Britain* & try & come back *fat*.

Ask Turnham for my acc[oun]t. Remember me to them & to Jeannie. I think I will not write to Ned this time as I have nothing to say.

If any English letters come I will send them to you.

Hudson did not come back yesterday—I am much obliged to Ned & Jeannie for their invitation but must for the present decline altho' I may run down to Geelong to meet you & stay there *one* day & have a bathe —We might arrange it so as to meet on Saturday & stay till Monday.

Jim has just called to ask me up this evening for a rubber.

Good bye dear says

Your affect husband.
W.L.R.

1/103

[77]

{10 March 1865}

My dear dear Polly

I know you will like to hear from me altho' I have no news to interest you—I am exceedingly busy.

It is very strange that the letters are not delivered at Toorak—I am writing this on Friday evening & I will post it myself before 6 so that you should get it Saturday morning—I spent Tuesday at the Saddlers & met Mrs. Dawbin[1]—a wonderful woman plays & sings correctly & offered to ride any horse we could bring her—her rings are a sight.

Wednesday dined at the Mitchells a bachelor dinner & whist party. Thursday my chess club. Tonight O'Connor has asked me over but as I dread Miss Mooney & the musical box, I am doubtful whether I will go—

Hot morning. Shower of rain about 1. cool since—

Hudson not back yet.

I am sure the Saddlers can not go down. I enclose letter from Sam.

You did not say anything of the Turnhams or Leopold—or Ned! or the children—

Be sure & stay away the month—I have nothing else to say as I am very tired. Pooley I saw this morning, he was going off by this morning's train to say good bye to the Murchisons but was taken suddenly ill. Maria is very good, cleaning up, putting up clean curtains &c & takes messages very correctly—

And now dearest you must excuse this, but really I am not able to write any more—English mail as you know has not yet been heard of.

Kind love to all & believe me Your
affect Husband
W Lindesay Richardson

1/88

[1] Annie Baxter Dawbin (1816–1905) recorded in her journal, 7 March 1865, what appears to have been the same meeting: 'In the evening Dr Richardson, Mrs Sherrard & her sister, Miss Welsh; were at Mrs James': we had some music, and quantities of scandal'. See *The Journal of Annie Baxter Dawbin: July 1858–May 1868*, p. 520. The reference to Mrs James would seem to be to Mrs Emily James Saddler. As Lucy Frost has noted, Annie Baxter Dawbin and Walter Richardson also had a mutual friend in Alexander Brooke Smith.

[78]

Monday morning {13 March 1865}

My own dear Polly

Yours written on the 10th & posted on 11th came to me this morning most unexpectedly at breakfast. Of course you have received before this, one I wrote & posted on Friday evening—

I like your photographs very much—the one with the head on one side full face in the dress with the white border at the bottom is the best, and I should be very well [pleased] with this even if he gives us no better. I send them back but should like to have kept it.

I think I will go down to Schnapper Point for a fortnight—as I do not feel at all equal to my work.

I went to church last night—but was obliged to *leave before the sermon.*

On Friday even[in]g I went to O'Connor's.

Saturday to chess club.

Hudson arrived Saturday last train pressed me very much to go to dinner yesterday but as the Saddlers had given me an equally kind invite for same hour and as I did not feel good enough company I remained at home. There is every probability of rain today. Yesterday was one of Saxbys [?] prayers were offered up in church last night for rain & altogether ruin is impending from drought—Black Hill works are about to be stopped. One squatter at Echuca lost 5000 sheep—I am so delighted you are enjoying yourself, it quite makes up for my suffering. I hope you remember my advice about the bathing not to stay in it but just go in & then come out. I think by your feeling sleepy after it you stay in *too long* & if so you are better without it—

If you go giving away my likenesses there will be none left.

To one of your questions I say Yes: you know which it is—

Jim says he cannot manage to go down—I am sure I cannot, *it would be quite impossible for me to bathe* at present.

1. PM. I have just come in from my morning round, such a day *equal to Black Monday* only not so hot.

I am so pleased with your likeness. I should like *six of each* for my own self—but especially do I love thee in the *front picture* with that elegant dress.

Maria is behaving very well & making everything as comfortable as possible for me—she does better than any other for she never bothers me to know what I'll *have*.

I feel in a little better spirits today after seeing your dear face—still don't hurry home—you can do no good—I do get some sleep—

Send me up one of the other likenesses you get done—

Mrs Saddler & Jim kindly came down to see me last night about 8—very kind was it not?

You cannot see the Turkish Baths.

I dread going out this afternoon.

Say good bye to Flora for me.

I have seen none of the Cuthberts since you left or Nixon.[1]

Good bye dearest—God bless you says your affect Walter—

1/108

---

[1] William Nixon was a broker in mining shares who was sometimes used by Walter Richardson.

[79]

Wednesday {15 March 1865}

Your letter dated the 14th reached me my own dear Polly this morning, with one from Ned. I was much pleased to receive your dear picture again, and can now make you happy by saying that since my last *I am better* so you need not be in a hurry back but can stay and derive the full benefit of your trip. Monday was a second edition of black Monday without the fires, towards evening heavy rain set in & fell in torrents most of the night—

The Saddlers had arranged for a whist party but in consequence of the rain it did not come off: Yesterday Tuesday, I took tea at Hudson's, & found them very happy & pleased with the house, which is indeed very nice, I afterwards went to the Saddlers, & met Mr & Mrs Sturt, & Welsh & we had a rubber—they had asked me up to dinner to eat a goose, but I *quite forgot all* about it till 8 o'clock. Today was showery & very unfavourable for the review & the show.

I hope you are still enjoying yourself. Mrs. L. says she misses you very much—

You will have to do without me for I do not see how the house could be left without one of us: other reasons also prevent me from accepting *Ned's invitation.*

9 P.M. Jim has just popped in to borrow a pair of white kids fortunately I found a new pair—they are going to the Volunteer Ball both of them. The Wynns called & took them to the show & review.

16. I got a letter from Brighton this morning. There are none for you as yet. I presume you will get them by Ned. Henry, Caroline's husband, has been appointed Registrar to the Court of Probate Cork a very good billet & they have left Dublin—

It is a fine pleasant morning after the rain—Sickness has somewhat abated—

The ball was not very crowded last night—the old set were there. Sherard of course.

I suppose I may expect the Kabats up by the $\frac{1}{2}$ past 3 train on Friday. I will have dinner ready by 4. The second week of my bachelorship is nearly over—

I do not think of any more news to interest you. I will send you down £5.0.0 in my next week's letter. I send you the *Star* with the acc[oun]t of the doings yesterday.

It was very cold last night, I could not get to sleep for some hours
—Good bye dearest says Your lonely husband

W.L.R.

1/83

[80]

Monday {20 March 1865}

My own dear Polly

I was very disappointed at there being no letter on Saturday and
again this morning.

Yours of 18th reached me however this afternoon. You are always
going to write a long one next time but that next time never seems to
arrive—Yes, the Kabats came on Friday & Maria had a nice dinner

A few friends dropped in during evening & we amused ourselves.
Mrs S. keeping saying how strange it appears that there is no Mrs R;
they remained on Saturday & left Sunday morning. I was glad to see
them to relieve the fearful dulness & monotony of a silent house even
Dilly's screaming was some relief. Mrs. K wrote the enclosed & put it in
an envelope. I did not see why I should send an envelope—so I read it—

And so you really think you will be ready *to come to my arms* this
week—I shall have forgotten how to kiss having been so out of practice.

Forbes has left, but I may go down to Geelong on Saturday to meet
you—I do not intend to go to Melbourne.

Hudson never told me he had a letter from you. He certainly
offered to see my patients but there's sure to be some rows if I go away.

I am far from well yet in fact I have *been very very* poorly since you
left.

I thought last Sunday week that I should have to keep in bed and
altho' I would dearly love to have you back yet I do not want to spoil
your trip.

I miss your nice little dishes.

Yesterday Sunday I dined at the Saddlers very pleasantly tomorrow
evening I have a few bachelors for a rubber

I am not busy now

Ask Turnham how much I am indebted for the door plate and I
will send him a crossed cheque

No letters for you from home

Weather is pleasant—

We lunched at Pooleys on Saturday so well that we could eat no dinner—I suppose you enjoyed Ned's party altho' you do not say one word about it—

I was up at ½ past six this morning to Mrs W. M Brown. Got it over by 8 & went & took a bath.

I have been too ill to have any since you left—I have lost about 10 lbs weight—

Kind regards to Joe & Aunty & ask when they are coming up again—I suppose your next will be your last. I enclose a crossed cheque for £5. 1/– to be paid thro' Ned's account—

God bless you dearest & bring you safely back to your own dear & fond husband

Walter

1/91

[81]

Friday afternoon

My own dear Polly

Yours dated April 3d reached me last night at 12 o'clock—it had been brought down by the Coach & not posted—I had been out all day & taken away to a confinement at 5 o'clock. Kept there till 12, a case of twins—

I am glad to see you are enjoying yourself & that the thumb is better—You will have seen what sort of a place Portland is—it would take us 3 months to clear out of this—but I should [enjoy] the change & [especially the] Sea-side it would [set you] up too I am sure.

I dined at Hudsons [one] evening on the Turkey.

Went to see 'Arah na pogue' on Tuesday very much pleased.[1] I am going to Melbourne tomorrow morning Saturday, will be back on Monday—so that when you get this I will most likely be at home again. I am very busy & hardly know how to manage leaving.

Mrs. Saddler promised to write you yesterday. Of course I shall go to John's he wrote me a letter & asked me—Ned also wrote one of his epistles, about being determined to 'protect her' 'innocent creature' &c —The spoony—

You will have been away 3 weeks next Tuesday.

[Text missing] for some poor [devil]. You will be glad to hear that Newingtons were sold at 4.12.6 on Thursday: going down with the shaft well—about 40 feet on Saturday night—Jane is doing as well as she can: I see she has washed the things but stupid like she has put them up again.

You will not get this before Monday. Remember me kindly to the Kabats—Very cold here.

Mrs Cuth & Mrs. O. called today. Mrs. Stewart Dr. asked us to her house last Thursday.

Good bye Your loving
Hubby
WLR ✳

1/94

₁ *Arrah-na-Pogue; or, The Wicklow Wedding* by Dion Boucicault (1820–90) was first performed in 1864.

[82]

Ballarat
Friday evening

My darling Polly

I received yours this evening & I was sent for hurriedly out just as I met postman. I was not therefore able to write you by return. I am glad to hear that you arrived safely after your long & tedious journey—how singular that Mrs Kabat's letter was never got. What became of it? On the morn of your departure I was sent for to the Springs 6 miles at 7 o'clock back by 10 to breakfast: House full.

Mr Cummins called on you—told him I cd not afford anything.

Busy day, to Essex meeting, home by 11—Yesterday busy also. Paid a late visit to Cuthbert's & dined there—Whist—Nixon there. I am glad to say that Mrs. C. is doing as well as could be wished. The baby is admired more daily. Leopold is away. We will have no whist party this week. Mary is doing very well she is becoming more particular about the messages & the addresses.

I have sent you a *Star* every day. Letter today from Lucinda another from Alick nothing of interest in either so will keep them until you come. None from your Mother. I hope you slept well & that you are pretty well: make up your mind to enjoy yourself & try & come back with roses in your cheeks & with your lips red & ready for kissing. I cannot deny that I sleep well—never awaking.

No news of any interest except that Bunten *has been dismissed & suspended*, & has cut & left his wife & family. It seems he has been a *regular scamp*, & Elliott got him away from this so that nothing might occur here: Nurse Millar says the trip will do you a great deal of good 'and it will do you good too Doctor' she said—I was on the point of saying none of your impudence!

I am at home this evening—Mary gets me everything very nicely & I make myself eat.

I have not seen Hudson since you left.

Saturday morning
Very cold—
did not sleep owing to the cold. Must have more blankets—I have told Mary.

Good bye dear.
Your affect
& loving husband
W

Love to Mrs. Kabat & Flora. Kind regards to Mrs. M.

1/93

[83]

Ben Air House
Monday April

My own darling Walter

I thought I had better write this morning as it may be a week before you get another letter from me & I have had no letter as yet from you & cannot now get one before Thursday, so you need never say again what a time elapses before you get one from me for it will be 9 days before I get yours as today we start for the Station & there is only a post every two days.

I hope dear you are keeping well & do not miss me too much and that Mary is taking good care of you. I am enjoying myself very much. Everyone seems so kind & hospitable. Mrs McKenzie is such a nice person & although there are 4 children I never saw any so obedient & well behaved it is a pleasure to be with them. There is a Mrs Gibbons close here used to live on Ballaraat, he an Engineer you attended her once for Dr Holthouse on the Melbourne Road rather fond of *Pale Brandy*.

We had a drive in the carriage to Broadford 10 miles from here such a nice Macadamised Road & Magnificent Scenery all hills & valleys everything so picturesque. The trees are quite different from those about us & so thick. Close to the Garden here there is one tree with I should think an 100 Magpies on it quite covered. Yesterday we went to church a much handsomer building than any on Ballaraat but a very poor clergyman not 50 people in the building.

In the afternoon we had a long walk thro' the Police Paddock & to the Resovoir. We have no walks so pretty with us. When you write will you send some simple thing for Dilly, they think she has got worms. She starts in her sleep & her hand always at her nose. Mrs Kabat's brother is very like Mr Kossack but much taller & finer looking altogether so dark with bushy Black beard & Moustache. Not like any of the others.

The O'Haras left here long ago Dr Bingley has all the practice, something like Hudson. He has just built himself a large Brick & Stone House with Verandahs all round both Stories, one of the best houses here. The weather is very pleasant cold mornings & evenings but very nice during the day. How is Mrs Cuthbert getting on & baby? I hope the Nurse continues to give satisfaction. Give my love to them. Have you seen anything of Leopold? Mary must have the Spare Bed Room dusted when I come back because they will stay a day or two with us before going to Hamilton if they can. Has Felix gone yet? I shall be able to tell you how I like the Station in my next. I received two papers.

I was dreaming about you last night & felt very lonely when I awoke & found you were not beside me.

I have a bad cold in my head change of air make take it away.

I hope your cough has not come back take care of yourself darling you are all I have to love in this world & it would break my heart were anything to happen [to] you. I suppose I shall get home letters in your next. Send me word how much you weighed direct the letters as follows until I write again. Mrs Richardson care of J Murchison Esq—Kerisdale Broadford.

I can perhaps tell you in my next when we shall be likely to return. Mrs Kabat is waiting to hear from Leopold. Good bye darling with love & kisses as ever

> Your loving wife
> Polly

1/47

[84]

Friday evening

My own darling Polly

I have just come in & got your letter. I am sorry you thought my last so short but really I had nothing to interest you no news—and moreover I always found such a difficulty in getting the time unless by staying up at night—I wrote you the day before yesterday. Yesterday morning I got up at 7.30 breakfasted & started off $4\frac{1}{2}$ miles & busy all day till dark. This morning out at 6 to Mrs Loney who kept me till 12 —Hudson dines with me tonight—He went down to Brinds wedding —I asked H. Cuthbert but of course he couldn't come. She (Mrs. H.) looks so pretty that he could not leave her: the old gent threatened to bring her out today but fortunately it has been raining very heavily & so they are prevented. I told you I dined there on Sunday. I am delighted you admire the scenery & that it is so charming. I wish I were with you —Mary is doing very well. I hope she won't burn the dinner tho'. No sign of the box altho' Ned has passed it & wrote to me Wednesday.

I sleep pretty well. Of course you do not. You must not abuse Hudson about promises if it was any one's fault it was mine. I do not see the use of giving Flora's love if she accepts Mr. Pooley's lock of hair!! however we will have a talk about you all this evening.

No news. Letter from Watson he has been to Woods Point.

I will keep them all till you come—or I will send that.

No parties—I have never yet seen Leopold—I do not know where to find him.

Well I suppose Mrs. Kabat's letters are filled with details of auctions & removals & meetings of creditors—What does Flora say of it all? Is she looking as well as she did—You ask me for a prescription for the little boy. From your description I make out that the fits are caused by a *determination of blood to the head,* & that they are apoplectic. A good smart purge of *salts* wd be better than oil—preventing the overloading the stomach by heavy food as puddings. The treatment adopted was good. I enclose a prescription if there is heat of head, redness of eyes, pain in head or loss of power in any limbs for any one of these the medicine will be useful as directed—Heavy storm last night & today. Hope you will get rid of your cold & come back *quite well*—Weight day you left 10 st 7.

Remember me kindly to Mrs M, Mrs K & Flora. I hope Dilly is improved & does not cry 'uppy Mamma' quite so often. Sat[urda]y—Leopold, Felix & a stranger came last night & we had a lot of rubbers, they stayed till 12—Leopold says you are not coming home next week that he shall be at Smythes until Sat[urda]y & then he's going down to Geelong—May 1st. He said why shd they hurry back let them enjoy themselves.

Very, bitterly cold this morning. Rain.

Winter in fact

No box yet. S. has not come up. I hope you are still enjoying yourself and that it is doing you good—Ned wrote to say that Aunty had been very ill—Two doctors, about the illness he did not say a word—No news—

And now my dear wife—May God give you his blessing & may you come back safe & well to the arms of your own dear husband when I shall make up for the absence of kisses during the past fortnight by taking you on my knee all the evening—I suppose you will come back by the 11 PM train. As ever Your own.

W

Sam has just turned up by this morning's 10 o'clock train. He says he has nothing to say, looks very smart.

1/87

[85]

Friday

My dear Polly

I got your note yesterday & was glad to find you had reached Streatham safely. I have not seen Mackay yet but Pooley told me last evening that he had reached Carngham & spent the night at Russell's coming on here yesterday Thursday.

I hope you will enjoy your trip. I enclose you letters from Flora, John.

Ned's is here there is nothing in it—

The day necessary for me to go to Melbourne has been altered to the 24th April so that you will have plenty of time to enjoy yourself.

Sickness thank God has slacked off.

It rained nicely last evening & this morning showery & heavy rain.

I applied for your Newington Scrip. I cannot get it without the receipt paper you got from Wynn—They are down to *1.17.6.* Nixon bought some at that price—No more news—Kind regards to Mr. & Mrs H.

and remain Your aff. H.
W.

1/92

[86]

Ballarat
Thursday morning 22 February 1866

My dear Polly

I received your letter *only this morning*. It was posted in Ball[ara]t *yesterday afternoon*—so the postman says—Who was entrusted with it?

Of course I was much shocked to receive Ned's telegram about ½ *past 10* and feel deeply for John. Your letter this morning fills me again with grief—What an unfortunate thing.[1]

I hope Tracy will see you every day.

I had intended to have gone down to the funeral but as it took place *yesterday* of course it was *out of the question.*

Leopold left.

All are well.

I enclose crossed cheque for £5.0.0. Ned will cash it for you—do not hurry back—What about taking the baby?

Ask Ned to write me about your hand. Kind remembrances to all.

Your Walter

1/110

[1] Refers to the death of John Bailey's second wife, Jeannie.

PART 3

Return to England

1867–1869

ON 3 JANUARY 1867, Walter and Mary Richardson left Melbourne on board the *Red Jacket*, arriving in London on 7 April. Before resuming practice, Walter went on a tour around England, Ireland and Scotland, visiting old friends and relatives and also learning about current developments in treating such then common diseases as fever, tuberculosis and lunacy. In the first letter here, however, he notes that in his old university city, Edinburgh, he does not 'see much advancement in physick'. Although it is summer, he feels the cold badly and decides not to 'stay out the fortnight'.

During these months Mary was staying at Leicester with her mother, Elizabeth Bailey, now in the final stages of dropsy, from which she was to die on 8 July 1869. Walter's initial decision to set up practice in Eccles, near Manchester, towards the end of 1867 may have been influenced by a wish to stay close to Mrs Bailey. His cousin William Duke Richardson and his wife Carrie also lived in Eccles. Walter registered for English practice on 26 November 1867. Soon, however, it was apparent that Eccles was not suitable. As Mary's letter (no. 90) shows, inquiries were made for practices in Devon and

Brixton, but Walter eventually settled on one at Rawcliffe, near Selby in Yorkshire.

In an anticipation of their later moves to Chiltern and Queens-cliff, Walter's early letters from Rawcliffe are full of promise and praise of the new locality as well as details of the new house. Mary, meanwhile, was left with the task of packing up their previous house, selling off or packing up the furniture, with plenty of advice from Walter about how best to do this.

By late 1868 they were on the move again. The gold mining shares which Walter had been buying since the early 1860s were now returning excellent dividends; he could afford to give up work and live on his investments and they decided to return to Australia to do so in a better climate. Once again Walter's letters are full of plans and packing. Towards the end of October he left Rawcliffe to join Mary in Plymouth where she was staying with her sister Lizzie and family. His letters of this period, especially number 106, are some of his most playful and most revealing of his continued strong sexual passion for Mary. Subsequently he revisited Eccles, when an earlier coolness with William and Carrie was seemingly forgotten, and then went to Dublin to stay with his cousin John Richardson. After spending Christmas in Leicester, Mary and Walter sailed from Liverpool in the *British Prince* on 3 March 1869, arriving in Melbourne on 26 May.

[87]

{Edinburgh}
Friday evening {1867}

My dear Marie

Your nice long letter with enclosures from Mother and Grace was very welcome. I am obliged to them for thinking of me. I hope your mother keeps well—

Edinburgh is too cold a place for me and it will not be advisable for me to stay out the fortnight, the wind is always East or North—You will have the pleasure of seeing me then on Monday or Tuesday.

The North British is the line and the train leaves about 9 AM & gets to Leicester 7.30 or so—

Give my love to all. I suppose you wrote to Bayne.[1] What an extraordinary letter about the lady!

I hope your budget of Australian letters amused you—They want us back you see: Leopold must have been pretty well 'cocked' when he wrote that—

I like the people here very well, *but the climate*! I cannot get what I want in lodgings. *No milk* or dried fish—and as I do not see much advancement in physick, I hardly think I need run any risk but may at once go South, for it seems there is no summer going to be here at all.

With loves again—I may write again but as you would not get it before Monday night why you may see me same time, *or Tuesday* if I do not write again.

Yours faithfully
Walter

1/158

---

[1] Bayne Cheyne, second husband of Walter's mother, Lucinda.

[88]

Monday morning {1867}

My dear Wifey

I thought I should have had a letter from you this morning but perhaps you did not get mine early on Saturday. I start from this tomorrow morning Tuesday by the train that leaves this on the North British Line at 9.45 AM and gets in to Leicester at 7.45 PM.

We had a warm day on Sunday but the East wind is at it again today—I enclose you another letter from Bayne. Have you written? You see the distress you have unwittingly created—I think by that he is fond of you—

Of course I shall look out for your dear face at the station and shall see you a long way off—Have a little nice supper ready, of something you know I like, with a cup of coffee—Kind love to your Ma and Gracy I hope you enjoyed your visit to 'The Gorse'—Good bye and God bless you.

Your faithful and true
W

1/159

[89]

Saturday 6 p.m.{1867}

My dear dear M.

I am afraid you have been overdoing it—You should keep in bed and apply hot fomentations around the seat of pain—Don't hurry back if you are not better on Monday, of course it is dull but come back well —Mr & Mrs Bent called on Thursday *nice people*, He is something like General Yorke.

Yesterday I was out walking & met the clergyman Mr Sayers & wife, I lifted my hat & he spoke & we walked some distance together. He is an Irishman and of a better class than we have been accustomed to meet abroad—They said they hoped to have the pleasure of seeing you when you return. We shall have lots of visitors next week I am sure— will get the carpet down on Monday in case. Carrie's sister I told you has arrived they expect Mrs Fisher this evening—William returned Friday evening[1]—The oak chest & chest of drawers arrived this morning. *All* the *drawers except one open*, but apparently not meddled with. Anne is behaving very well indeed she cooks capitally and is getting everything cleaned up.

Do keep quiet Sunday and rest yourself. Your mother ought to be able to nurse you.

Bradshaw[2] I enclose 71.23. & 12.0. are the shortest 3 hours & 48 minutes—The nights & days are *very cold*—we shall feel this winter very much.

I had a newspaper from H. H. in America today[3]—Give my kind love to Mother ✳ to Grace & lots to somebody else—You know dear my letters are never burnt so must be careful—If you are not better send for Dr. Barclay tomorrow he knows me—I do not like the stump business in pairs [?], Yours and Grace's very much alike but especially Grace's!— I have no more news so what can I write—I am going to dine tomorrow Sunday at Swiss Cottage—

Lizzy cannot care about getting well; the medicine cannot be good, I am mending at last but it has only been by perseverance & *pushing the medicine*. I do not believe anything else will ever cure her—Camphor & pepper & spice the *Platypus* if they are moth eaten.

Good bye dearest. I hope to have better news on Monday morning —if I do not hear from you I will conclude you come by the twelve o'clock train from Leicester on Monday—& will meet you—If you have much luggage leave it at the station Manchester for the carrier & address it by carrier before leaving Leicester. I only paid 6/2 for the two & 2/– from Manchester by carrier—

God bless you till we meet & ever after.

Tell your Mother we will soon have a room ready for her—

If you borrow £15.0.0 you can repay it in the middle of November when my bill of exchange is cashed. Good bye Dearest says

Your faithful & true
W. ✳

Read the enclosed don't laugh when you read it be sure & save it for me. Let your Mother see it but on *no account anyone else.*

1/161

¹ William Duke Richardson, Walter's cousin; married to Carrie.
² *Bradshaw's Railway Guide*, a timetable of all railway trains running in Great Britain.
³ Henry Handel Richardson, another cousin of Walter's; source of his daughter's pen-name.

[90]

Wednesday evening {1868}

My dear old man

Yours safely to hand this morning. I was so glad you were all safe & so well pleased. Of course nothing can be done until you come back. Two letters came for you one from Devon saying he was in treaty with someone & the other from Mrs Dunne at Brixton; they have sold the practice to a young man so I suppose fate intends us for one of the two you are after. I have just had a letter from Mother enclosing one from John but I am to return it by tonight's post.

Captain Pope¹ had arrived safely John had a dinner party for him asked Ned, Turnham & Brooke Smith just half an hour before dinner the Captain sent word that he had a bad cold so John was vexed—John was at the Levèe Ball & all sorts of pleasures. No time to write to anyone but Mother, Ned sent his baby's likeness that I shall keep for you to see. I hope darling you will be home on Thursday I could not sleep without you. We have been in Manchester all day. We went to see a grand wedding at Eccles old Church such a grand affair. I am writing to Mother by this post. I hope you have had the same fine day as we have had, it was lovely. Mrs Sayers called but of course I was out also Carrie & William.

Come home soon darling I hope to have a letter from you in the morning. Good night

> God Bless you ever
> Your own,
> Marie

> in case my letter does not reach you
> Dr Richardson
> Eccles
> Nr Manchester

1/152

[1] Captain of the ship Walter and Mary had sailed to England on.

[91]

Rawcliffe
Sunday after Church {1868}

My dear M.

I arrived here safely yesterday about 3 PM. Harrie will have told you that he saw me safely & comfortably ensconced with a foot warmer—In consequence however of the guard putting me into a wrong carriage I had to change once before I came to Wakefield; then at Wakefield for ½ an hour & more, we got there 20 minutes to 1. & the train came up for us at ¼ past 1—We then started for Knottingley, reaching it a little before two—left it ¼ past—There is a *first class ladies' waiting room* both at Wakefield & Knottingley—Be sure & ask the porter for it as the stations are cold. Macauley met me at the station here & I had the traps brought on—After a chop we went out & saw two patients—He introduced me to four families—comfortable houses & well to do people; one family very pleased, the father clerk of the court (County) or some such thing said they were very pleased indeed to have a gentleman of my experience as they were getting a little anxious & feared they shd get some very young man—His sons are in one of the

Banks of Goole, nice gentlemanly young fellows—eldest about 20—
This morning went to Church—not bad. Parson an elderly man about
60 service well read, singing fair, 'Hymns antient & modern' used—
Capital Sermon—A lovely day, bright sky, more sun than I have seen
since we left Brighton.

I send you the measure of the parlor 10 feet by 19 feet 20 inches
without the projection of the fire place which is small—the Surgery is
12 by 14 about but if you send me word what you want I will measure them—Milk 2d a quart. fresh eggs 10 for a shilling—Coals 13/–
No. shops = Butchers three—a small Drapers, ditto Grocers—a little
P.O. I got your *Standard* this morning by ½ past 8—

I hope all are well. How is Mother's cold? & did you sleep? Harrie
got home all safe? & How is Gracey? Have you been up to Carrie? Did
you write to Mary Yorke? I have not coughed much. The air is so
delightful. We had a walk before Church & we are going out again now
so that I will not close this till we come back—Be sure and let me have
a long letter from all of you on Tuesday morning.

4 P.M. Just returned from a walk. Have seen three patients today
& been engaged for my first Accouchement—Have seen primroses &
wallflowers in flower & the birds have been singing in the groves at the
back of the house—

Am going to Church again this evening—
Good bye and God bless you.
Love to Mother, Grace & H—
Be sure & tell me of your visit to Fairfield.
Two large cupboards in my room.

Your faithful & true Walter

1/125

[92]

Rawcliffe Selby
Tuesday {1868}

My d. d. M.

Yesterday Monday was wet nearly all day. We called on several
more nice plain homely people, one a brewer with a pretty daughter;
another farmer who lives in a capital house—dining room I should
think 25 × 15. Drawing room like our Ball[ara]t one—His wife a nice

body. We talked about servants: they are paying £12.0.0 for a bad one. Thinks you may get a bad one for £10 *at Hull*, but advises us not to engage one in the village—I can see this will be a difficulty—

Was called up last night at 11 to see a child & called up this morning at 8 to Accouchement it will be on all day—

I saw the station master & he shewed me the rate of furniture from Manchester here direct 40/- per ton Insurance about a few shillings extra—luggage 28/4 per ton—he advises all the good things to be sent as furniture & insured, all the common things as kitchen utensils &c to be packed in cases or casks & sent as luggage—You had better write to Gibson & ask the charge for a man to come & pack all. I should think one man would do all in three days—I hardly would entrust Palmer altho' you might ask him—

The House is the worst part of it—the big room never will be dry for the house is on brick foundations & the damp creeps up—We must just hope to get another *if we stay* in a year or so—There is just a chance of the one I was in last night but there is no stable & the rent would be about £30.0.0—

The place that is the village looks worse than it really is, for I can see there are plenty of well to do people about—

My cough is quite gone I am so sorry to hear that you are dull you ought not to be so with Mother & Grace!—I do hope Mother's cough is better; put the feet & legs into hot water every night & mustard *to* the chest—Glad you liked Mrs. C.

You did not say how much the van held? but I think you might get the whole done under ten pounds—

I sleep on a nice feather bed wh' I shall try & buy—Where did you put the tape measure I have not found it yet? There is a capital cupboard in the kitchen, a pantry about 8 feet square with a gauze over the window like a safe—

In fact excepting the damp walls of the big room I consider it a more convenient house than yours. When you tell me where the tape measure is I will measure every room—Any sort of felt stuff will do for my surgery & the bedrooms—there are no bugs nor mice—Glad to hear Carrie is better, it was a lovely day for her—

I do not know how long the house will take to do but I will see the agent some day this week—

Am I happy & comfortable? pretty well—I eat well, 2 fresh laid eggs every morning ditto for tea—plenty of ham, bacon & Yorkshire pudding—

I hope dear Grace will make you sleep—You will quite miss her.

Do you think you can do with the quiet of a village life?—I believe there is as good an opening as at Cray except that there are not any swells of noblemen—Be sure & say before I pay the first installment altho' of course we can move in two years but then the expense will be great—

I weighed on Sunday without any great coat 10st. 12lbs. very good—Macauley is going in for getting me 11 st. 6. before you come— The Station Master—there is an opening for me *'against the world'*—that is his phrase. Dr. Robertson has a very pretty daughter, there are said to be several good pianists & we are likely to have a penny reading soon at which of course I shall go in—[1]

Give your Mother my kind love how glad I am that you have got her with you—think seriously of taking Anne with us—I shall have to keep a man servant soon & that will relieve her of the boots & knives— I have just seen 6 nice sticks of celery & about a dozen small curly cabbages bought by Macauley from the *garden at the Hall* for *sixpence*. Is not that splendid? we can get early potatoes & green peas, asparagus, & every delicacy there—as soon as they are up—for a nominal charge—Of course Mother will read this—

They are no relations of the Leicester family—

I declare to you that the day is quite warm, the kitchen door is open & the birds are singing around the House—I will give you full particulars of the Sale & send you a list.

Don't fret about being without me—cheer up take walks & let me have some roses on your cheeks to kiss when you come—until then dear Polly Adieu from your loving & true W.

> 1/129, 1/138, 1/147

[1]   Penny readings were a popular form of Victorian entertainment; admission was a penny.

[93]

Rawcliffe Selby
Thursday morning {1868}

My v. d. Marie

I got my first confinement over at 11 PM on Tuesday night— All well Mrs. Macauley remained with her all the time—Yesterday

Wednesday I saw two or three patients & we went to Goole: It is about 5 miles off by rail—a small sea port or rather river port for it is on the Humber. There are several docks & I saw some fine steamers & small craft—There is a trade with Hull & the continent. Pop some 5 or 6000 —Tidy shops Ironmongers, Drapers, Chemists, Hotels—&c. We came home & spent the evening at a Mr. Hernshaw's where we played a rubber of whist, *of course for nothing*—Mrs. H. enquired kindly how you were & if you were very anxious to know what sort of a place Rawcliffe was? Did you play? Were you a good sailor?—She was a clergyman's daughter —the boys are going out hunting this morning, as the hounds meet about 8 miles off & they keep a lot of horses & two traps—What a pity you started off on Tuesday before getting my letter. It is the Lancashire & Yorkshire Railway in the same station as the Victoria. They forward it direct here for as I told you *40/ per ton for furniture* with a shilling or two for insurance & 28/4 for luggage! I think I wrote this on Tuesday— Then of course it must be packed at the house & forwarded to the Station, as they direct it—I am afraid you applied first at the wrong station—I am sure you must have had a troublesome job—48/– a ton is too much for luggage they are imposing on us. The Station Master here turned up his book and shewed me the charge printed—

You must not decide on a *fixed day* my dear nor *engage people or carriers yet*, for I cannot say about the house—I certainly cannot bring you into it as it is! For goodness sake don't forward them on the 12th of February, or any other day *until I decide.* I am delighted Mother is coming with you—The accounts are not glowing my dear—plain people and a dull place is all it is but our happiness must not depend on others—I know there will be pretty walks in Summer—and is ten times pleasanter than dirty Eccles.

There are other doctors attending in the village now from Goole, so it will be some time before I expect to do anything—I must get a horse soon—Lie in bed for your influenza—the weather is mild here, we have not had one cold day yet—

My Surgery has a fire place & is 12 feet by $11\frac{1}{2}$—

Blackbirds singing at the Grove at the back.

4.PM

We have been driving out all morning from 11 to 3—& have been down to see the Farmers—

A high west wind we came home & I ate a capital dinner not of course as good as if you were here—I cannot say when the Sale takes place—they talk of beginning to do the place tomorrow—I have a fire in my bedroom every night—& they do their best to make me comfortable—I think a year or two here will make us both fat—You need not address at Mrs. Macauleys.

> *Dr. Lindesay Richardson*
> *Rawcliffe*
> *Selby*
> is quite enough—

My kind love to Grace, you will be more lonely than ever when she goes—

If anybody is writing to Sarah—be sure & tell her to send on letters & papers here. If you are not writing I will do it—Your mother can write & you can put a stamp on—I got the *Standard*s this morning —I wrote to Dr. Cheyne & Mr Hill & have had no answer from either.

I got the tape measure, where is the sponge? The passage is 26 feet 8 inches long 37 inches wide with a recess for a table 6 feet 4 inches in & 8 feet 4 inches long.

> Adieu Your loving
> & true W.

1/130, 1/144

[94]

> *Rawcliffe*
> *Saturday {1868}*

My dear Mary

We had a severe storm all night from the West wh' rattled against the windows with rain all night—When I came down I found no letter and was very disapointed, However they arrived soon after. I am glad you think 'it cannot be a worse place than this'. I like it better every day.

About the sketch of the carpet this is it. [small sketch] There must have been some other sketch of the passage perhaps near it in my last, for the wall opposite the fire is quite straight & even as I have drawn it above. Mr. Lake the agent for the estate called yesterday—they do the room and passage next Monday & will have it finished in the week.

The time will soon pass and you will soon see me again & come to our humble tho' I hope happy little home—The rates are paid by the estate, so we shall [not] be bothered by that expense—Mrs. Macauley says there are good enough servants to be got in the village & she is looking one out for us or she was yesterday—I will not stop her, but will see what they can do—She says they can *all bake*—You can have two if you like by & bye—I must have a man after hearing this of course.

I am somewhat sorry you concluded with Anne without consulting me further as I only said '*I would think seriously of taking Anne with you*'—

If you have to slave & worry as you have done it will be a pity—I am glad you bought more forks from Simmonds we can easily send to them from this, get a list from him before you leave—Buy me a dozen box of paper collars No 16. as the last I bought in Deansgate and a pair of driving gloves, small one leather fingers—you know.

You have managed very cleverly about the carpet & taxes—

What did Anne mean by it?

From what Mrs M says I should think we could get a good active girl here for about £9. to 10.

So do not bring her if she does not want to come but a month will not hurt.

I am so delighted to hear Mother is better—*The two front bedroom* windows 41 inches long & 37 inches wide for the blinds—I hope Fleming will make these better than the last—

We are having a regular gale—It was as much as I could do to walk out this morning—Give my kind love to Mother & Grace—The clergyman called this morning. He is a quiet elderly man. Asked when you were coming. I will be able to say next week when the Sale is going to take place.

Have got nothing more to say except that I do hope you will get well & strong before you come.

I will be just as glad to see you as you can be to come for I miss your good dinners!—So good bye from your loving & true W.

1/123, 1/145

[95]

Rawcliffe
Monday {1868}

My dearest

For you know I have only one of that name, Your last does not tend to make me happy—If Grace says you are looking thin how sad it will look to me—I fear you did not get to Fairfield today as it has been blowing and snowing and raining here all night & day—However we must get some wintry weather and the sooner it comes the sooner it will be over—I do not sleep very well myself—

The workmen commenced this morning & will have done this week and I have been asking Macauley when the Sale is to take place. I can see my way to £200 at least this year, this ought to cheer you up— Miss Fector 19 Lowndes St Belgravia London W.

I will write to Jack—There are rollers for the blinds but I do not know if they are sold with the house, or if they go with the blinds— There is a small table in the lobby that I shall bid for—I should like you to be here at the time of the sale but we will see—

I am too busy to send a line to Bill.

Did I tell you the parson called on me on Saturday? I suppose you will call & say good bye to Mrs Brett. I was at Church twice yesterday—

The girls, that is Bessie & Grace, will see much more of the country & have a better chance of enchancing young men here than in Leicester don't say this to them however. We must have them both down next Midsummer. Bessie shall never go to Rutland St again unless she likes.

I think we shall be as happy here as anywhere and there will always be two spare bedrooms—We can write to Gibson for any furniture we want. Do try and get strong & bonny for my sake—You will miss dear Grace—I got the two Newspapers this morning—I shall be glad when I can name the day for you to come, you will arrive here at ¼ to 3. Won't it be jolly?

Anything will be better than that lonely spot in that damp dirty street, still we must be pleased we did not do worse. Had we taken a £60.0.0 house how much worse it would have been—

Beg Mother when she writes to Australia not to say anything of our plans, as I do not wish it to be known yet that we are not going back—as we might have to do so yet and it wd look very foolish—We may tell them at the end of the year, and it will be quite time enough then—The afternoon has cleared up and the wind has got round to the North W.

I have taken the *Evening Standard* & so get it every morning at breakfast, you know how fond I am of a newspaper in my hand with you opposite me making my coffee *too sweet*, reading you bits of the news. My room is a much warmer one than that at Eccles, no draught at all; and all it wants is you and Mother—They do not give me good dinners —I shall give Mrs M. the first installment tomorrow & shall then enquire the day of the Sale—

Be sure and call at the P.O. and *write down my address* as several Australian mails will be delivered there yet—I will write to the *Lancet, Constitution, & Edin. Med. Journal* and have my address altered in their books—How does Mother like the smoke?

Be sure & tell me all about Harrie & Fairfield & what classes he is in & what Mother thinks of Mrs C.

No letter from Dr. C or Mr Hill—Good bye dearest and with love to Mother and many to yourself—

I am as ever
Your own
Walter

Don't bring any more 6d paper but some better sort with cross lines and thin yellow or mauve.

1/127, 1/140

[96]

Rawcliffe
Wednesday {1868}

My dearest
I am sorry to hear that your cold continues, you will soon get better here, my room is as warm and cosy as any one I ever sat in, no draughts at all, altho' the wind has been high enough all the time. The House will strike you as being small & poky at first, but you will soon get used to it and I am sure we shall be very happy & comfortable; I feared you would not be able to go to Fairfield and am sorry that Mother has not seen the place and Mrs Craig, for it is all so different from that unprincipled man's place at Tottenham—The afternoon was fine here— Poor Grace was in low spirits was she?—She has had a long holiday at all events—I think the best way will be to pay Jones up £14.0.0 and have done with it—I will send you a P.O. order next week. You will want some for yourself if I make it £20.0.0 will that do? I am sorry William should behave so cooly to you—I expect nothing else from his wife. However never mind be sure & don't ask them to come here for I do not want them—If you say anything, *regret* that you <u>cannot</u> ask them as the bedrooms will not be furnished—I wish to have done with them for

ever. His radical principles do not suit me. I do not approve of the way he talks about the Queen, and their treatment of poor Mrs Fisher shews what they are to their friends—No, Let us drop the acquaintance. Don't go near them any more. I don't want them coming here & spying out the place. Do try & not give them the address. *It is near Selby* that is enough—

The House stood the gale very well—tiles and chimney pots fell in the village but none off this house—I think you will like the paper I have selected—

I think Mother's pains in the bones are only the effect of cold—Have W. & C. been down to see her—What does she think of them?

I am glad you are beginning to take down & wash—our bedroom is a very snug one—it will require carpet of some sort, the size is $11\frac{1}{2}$ by 14 about—the small one 10 by 12 & the other irregular shape. Two have fire places.

The rollers of the blinds go with the House—

Twelve or thirteen stair rods—but those you have are ours—The eyes of Mrs Macauley screw in so that I think I would leave yours. The parlor is *on the right* hand side of the passage near the back window *I marked it.* My room door left hand.

Price a set of dish covers, so that if you have to buy them at Goole you may know the price—I have been obliged to *order a horse*, and have written to Jack to buy me saddle & bridle & whip at Leicester—I am already called out to the country 3 miles off yesterday & day before—& shall soon have as much as I care to do—

Why not come before the luggage? Bring some bedding for Anne & things for her food & we can stay at an Inn here—

I beg you will *not* stay at William's. I do not wish to be under any obligation to them now.

What is to prevent your employing *Mr Palmer* to pack the things, & *see them off* taking all responsibility off you; you must come *before* the things so as to let Anne get the rooms ready one by one. I can easily get rooms at one of the Inns here for a trifle, & it *will do me no harm*—This way you can come *before* the Sale & buy what you want. I should bring all the bedding with you as *luggage*—My cough is all right.

Lucinda's letter is amusing. She talks of *all heart,* what stuff! Do not write to her till you come here—Fancy rabbitts 9d each here! The keepers sell them at 1/– & Macauley says that the skins are ready bought by dealers at 3d each—We cannot get groceries here. No good tea or coffee every such thing dearer than in Leeds so the Macauleys get theirs from Leeds you must do the same & get a month's supply in every month. Bring some good tea & coffee with you to go on with—

There is a good opening here for an Ironmonger, Stationer & Grocer & Chemist all in one. A general store in fact. Of course those here in little bits of shops have made fortunes & are very independent. What a pity Tom is not in business—

Don't forget the Thermometer outside the Surgery window—I have asked Mrs. Macauley when the Sale is to be, she cannot say just yet.

A showery afternoon—I slept better last night did not wake till daylight—All are anxious to see you—The evenings are tedious—Make arrangements to come at the end of next week if possible but I will be able to say definitely by Saturday next. Kind love to Mother, lots of ✱ to yourself from Walter

1/128, 1/139

[97]

Rawcliffe
Sunday {1868}

My dearest

I am so sorry that you keep poorly—That nasty damp house cannot agree with you. *England itself* does not agree with you as you were far better in Australia. If you do not get strong & well here, it will distress me greatly—I fear you fidgett & worry too much—When will you be easy? What does Mother say to you—You ought to take a lesson from her—

Friday will do very nicely to send the things off—They will not be here before Monday I think, but I will make arrangements for them whenever they come—Macauley's sale takes place *in the yard.* I shall expect you then by the 11.15 train on Saturday but how are you going to do on Friday night for you did not say—There is a very nice Inn on the Eccles old Road 'The White Horse Inn'—You had better take two rooms there—*What is Mother's* objection to Inns? If you would follow my plans dear better, your health would be better! It is a nice clean place—I will send you £23 on Wednesday or Thursday. Pay Jones £14 & I will send *a notice* & form of receipt in my next—

Of course you will come first class. You can buy the dish covers if you like them.

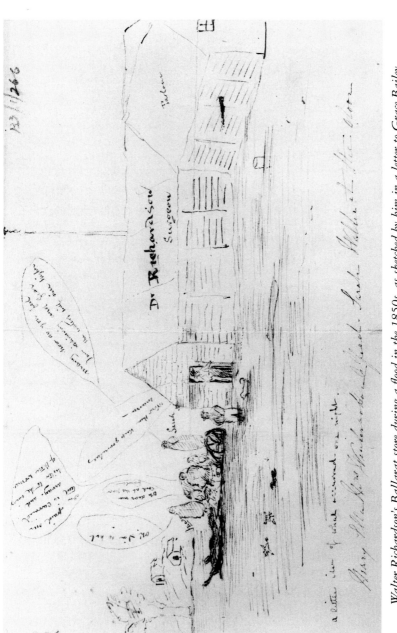

Walter Richardson's Ballarat store during a flood in the 1850s, as sketched by him in a letter to Grace Bailey

pre 1855
Ballaarat (Sunday)

My dearest,

I posted a letter to you yesterday, making the third since I left you. I trust they have all arrived safely, and that the contents pleased you.

I have some hesitation about writing this "Brown mother" as tho' I suppose I can depend on none of my letters going astray. We have a splendid moon after a sharp frost and I feel well & happy, how are you love? I am like yourself looking anxiously for letters from my mother & trust the mail will not keep us much longer in suspence — My mother is, or was when I last heard, at Brighton, where is yours? when did your father die? I lost mine when 9 months old, — where were you born? We have lots of enquiries to ask and answer each other, have we not? Of course I shall take more interest in you and yours than in any one else and all these little minutiae will possess vast importance when we come to hold dear converse, or to speak less à la Johnson, our cosy chat by our snug fireside — then I shall want to know what brought you out here, to tell you when I was living at home, ask you to narrate your adventures since you came here, & tell you some about Smith's family &c &c &c and so on.

I hope darling you will adopt my plan of jotting down a few minutes converse daily it forms a good sized letter each week, and as you are occupied pretty busily it will not be a tax either upon your time or your love — Moreover you write a charming letter both in regard to penmanship and composition but letter writing improves our style of diction which is much instead in life —

[left margin, vertical:] The vignette at the head of the chapter is a sketch of my place which I shall [...]

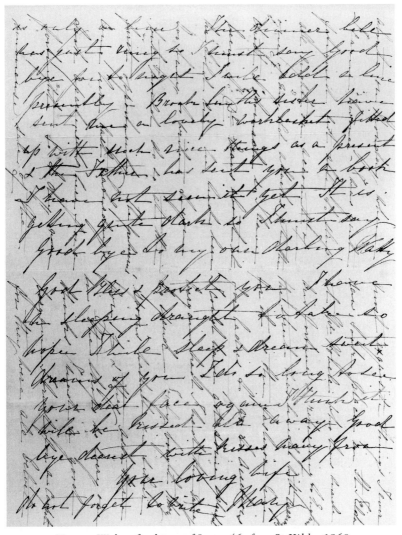

Mary to Walter, final page of Letter 46, from St Kilda, 1860

Mary Richardson in her late thirties

The Marseilles mail will be delivered in London Feb[ruar]y 13th. I suppose Mother's will come on here.

I had a letter from Mr. Hill this morning he says Bayne is pretty well—hopes we may like our new spot—Poor Caroline, Cork is too damp & relaxing for both H & her—We will be able to ask her over here when we get settled—I am sure you will get better here. This is a lovely bright bracing sunny day—

You must cheer up—you will see me before this day week if we are spared—The gas fitting bill you will find on the file & the cost of putting them in, I think together they came to near three pounds—

I think I would give over our old Hymn books—& should like one of the 'Hymns Ancient & Modern' with the Music & red edged leaves like Grace's—

I have booked *over* £9.0.0 in the two first weeks, without a horse— I think that ought to make you better you see I have a very comfortable & certain income & we can put by all our Australian Dividends & buy *Water Works shares* or Victorian *six per cent* Government Stock or *Three per cent* Consols—or leave in the Bank at $2\frac{1}{2}$ per cent—We will be just as well off as ever we were—

An old woman came yesterday

1/124

[98]

15 June 1868

My own darling

This is to say that I shall be home at a $\frac{1}{4}$ to 6 o'clock on Tuesday. The train leaves here at 2.10 & arrives at Wakefield at 4.50 I shall only have time to get out of one train & pop into the other I don't believe I shall have time to get a ticket but Mr Hill knows me so I must do the best I can. Mother is keeping all right; we are going out shopping this afternoon.

I don't believe you want me back but I am coming just to torment you—every day you say stay on. Mother won't hear of our not going to Devon says Lizzie will not be there another year & she would like us to go—

The weather fearfully hot, I hardly know what to do with myself. I am going to see for a hat or bonnet today. I hope your cold is quite gone. If I do miss the Train it will be 9.15 before I can arrive. Mother sends love & hoping soon to feel your arms round me I am your loving wife

Mary
lots of kisses

1/155

[99]

Rawcliffe
Tuesday {6 October 1868}

My dearest

I was glad to learn by yours of Sunday evening that you had arrived safely at Havelock Terrace—The Baby will die and the sooner it is relieved from its suffering the better—It is unfortunate that you have not decided about the ball—Surely you will go with Jack if it lives over Friday—it may linger some week or two. I am glad Edith is so pretty— Give her Uncle Walter's love & a kiss—I saw her donkey yesterday. Get a new dress if you feel you want it my dear. We can afford a fiver! I have just had old Bramley & his wife in they have *decided to take the house* if I would give it up by Saturday December 5th. I have agreed to do so—I shall borrow £100 from Mother so as not to let us run short & to take out plenty of nice things which are always better than what everybody else has—

Give my kind love to Jack & Lizzy. I am sorry for the poor baby— a drop or two of Chlorodyne would soothe it when moans are bad—I was over at Helliwells & had supper with them—did not get home till 11.30—Wale is doing very well—Cooks everything very nicely.

This is a wet day—I see by the *Argus* that Kabat is going to take charge at Beechworth for a time—J. H. Peebles has a son—I shall speak to Ellis tomorrow about making cases for the furniture.

The Bramleys seem inclined to buy—altho' I see they are mean screws—I hardly see how to run down to you: we must be packing up: if I leave this on the 1st Nov[embe]r & we are back Nov[embe]r 14—it will give us three whole weeks to get off—& I ought to go to Liverpool to see Ismay & Co—I don't believe I can do it, arrange about sale, see to the packing &c—Wherever I go now I hear regrets at my leaving—

I had a letter & *Argus* from Mother this morning—one from Lucinda with photograph which I shall not send but keep for you to see when you return—Mother writes in better spirits & is not worse—No line from Grace nice sister that—perhaps I will write to her again in a hurry don't she wish it—No letter from Mackay—Your faithful & true

W.

1/142, 1/137

[100]

Tuesday evening {6 October 1868}

My dear M.

I have just had Nunn in looking at the furniture & asking him as to the probable cost of making cases for it—He seemed completely bamboozled at it—says the legs will *not* come off the tables; the cheapest stuff he could get for the job would cost $1\frac{1}{2}$ the running foot will think it over & will try to let me know if it will cost under or over £10.0.0. I fear that we shall have to pack it all off to a Manchester Broker—if it cost £15.0.0 to pack I know it will cost £15.0.0 more for freight & insurance that is *30.0.0* we could surely get 22.0.0 for the lot & replace all in Melbourne for *£50.0.0* however we will see what he says next week.

Wednesday morning. Your letter dated 6th just come. Poor little sufferer eased from pain. Liz ought to be rejoiced that the moans have ceased. Truly unfortunate for you: I got your Sunday letter & wrote you Monday & Tuesday. Mother wished me to send *The Argus* to Harrie so will send you some via Southampton. No news of interest beyond what I told you. Agnes expecting another about end of August. Poor Ned or as she calls him P.B. His troubles are beginning.

You rather surprise me about *the style*. There can be no want of money then! I am glad to hear you walk, your mourning will come in handy now.

Did you see 'The Galatea' or has she left? I wrote again yesterday to Wigram—Yesterday Tuesday was a pouring day which was very hard on me—Today is fine so I must walk double—A letter from Harry—I paid my life money & Saddler—Wale is doing very well, is washing today. I am pretty sure Mrs. Fleeman had the small pox—She was at the Helliwells the other night & I saw her face is marked tho' slightly—the child I attended altho' the face was covered has not a sign—I am afraid I will not be able to run down to you but we will see. I do not see how we can spare the time if we have to be out by Dec[embe]r 5 Saturday—it would be better for me to do it afterwards when you are at Mother's—I would not be so hurried & would enjoy it more—I told you old Bramley had taken the House I saw Lake yesterday it is all right I give up the key to him I am 'shut' of it as they say in Leicester—

I told you also of the first div. of the N[ew] N[orth] Clunes £75.0.0 for August 1st & sent you Sam's letter. I will enclose him one & you must write him next week—He is a good fellow, tho' lucky—

The best thing for Lizzy's breasts is a piece of sticking plaster about 8 inches square *with a hole cut in the middle* warmed at the fire & put on each breast & left on—for two or three weeks, there will be no fear of abscess if this is done at once—

Lucinda has left the Limons, she could not put up with their anti-Christian conduct—does not intend coming home—She seems quite independent & in good spirits. I expect we will have some letters via Southampton—They are due in London on the 10th Saturday but will probably be delivered here on that day—If there are any I will forward them with a newspaper. I got your letter of October 6. that was Tuesday this morning Wednesday—so if the letters are posted early it is only one day's post from you—

Did you take copy of my Tree for Jack?

Your attached—
W.

1/143, 1/146

[101]

Sunday evening {11 October 1868}

My dear Poll—

I got yours of Friday this morning—I sent you an *Illustrated Australian Post* today. You will see Adolphus Sievwright[1] died of consumption. I enclose with this a letter from John. You will see he says he misses us and is glad to hear of our return. I had also one from Mackay with draft for £60.0.0—He is nearly sure to send another £60 this month October wh' I will get end of November—as he say the div. on N Clunes has been paid in to my acc[oun]t.

I am glad you are being taken care of so well by Lizz—It is impossible for me to leave before the last day of October—I walked to Snaith Church today; was much pleased—small congregation—Sermon for half an hour without any notes and very excellent—almost as good as Marchmont also Choral service—

Write to your mother—If I do come down it must positively be only for a week as it will take us all our time to pack and arrange about the Sale—I send money for Piano tomorrow and enquire cost of case—I dreamed about you last night our usual three weeks absence is nearly up—I hope you sleep well without anyone to trouble you night or morning. I suppose you begin to want me badly—No letters for you. Ned sent you that paper I posted today—Send John's letter on to Mother in your next to her. My correspondence is awful—Wale does very well, her great weakness is being out at night. I wish she'd do her courting in the kitchen!

I paid Mrs. Ibbetson for the Ham 1.3.0—Expenses of House meal &c so far 8.10½—No *Star Times* yet, *will post it when it comes.*

Have had Ellis to measure how much the casing will come to, he says he can do it in a fortnight.

Took Porter's children present of apples today.

Minnie H[elliwell] off to school—

With kind love to the Rifles

I am my dear Poll
Your affect cousin
—Walter—

1/126

[1] Died 27 July 1868. Sievwright was superintendent of the mail branch of the General Post Office in Melbourne. His father was Charles Wightman Sievwright, Assistant Protector of Aborigines at Geelong in the late 1830s.

[102]

{written on the back of letter from Ismay's dated 9 October 1868}

without the bother of being Surgeon at all, there is the difference however between £45 & £105. I know I can get no better offer than

Ismays. Ellis has promised to come in next week & give me some idea of what it will cost to case the lot. I have measured the table it is $5 \times 4 \times 2\frac{1}{2}$ cost of freight *2.5.0* without expense at Liverpool or case or insurance. The sofa $7 \times 2\frac{1}{2} \times 3 = 53$ feet—freight 2.12.6—my table 1.5.0 & so on.

It is difficult to decide. I had a letter from Grace this morning—Sarah is there—Mother is evidently getting worse—I am very glad you saw the Review; who is Dr Clind? They cannot decide to buy anything till you return. Mrs B—wishes to see you—I cannot leave this possibly before Nov[embe]r 1, even then I do not see how we are to pack up & get off by Dec[embe]r 5—

Wale is doing very nicely—cooks capitally—This is a fine day. Yesterday pouring wet all day—No newspapers or letters yet via Southampton. Kind remembrances & love to J & L—

It will be necessary for me to go to Liverpool to see the owners before we leave this—I can then arrange about the furniture &c—we can go to Leicester & London & wait there till we hear from them about sailing.

With fond love & hoping you will come back well, fit & rosy. I am as ever

Your attached W.

1/141

[103]

Tuesday morning {20 October 1868}

My dear Poll.

Yours of Sunday morning just received. You forgot me on Saturday so I shall see how you like it by not posting this till Wednesday. I shall most likely start from this on Friday week go on to Wakefield & from that to Birmingham that night, then on next morning. You say you are home sick, you cannot want to come back to this dull hole. No No! You want me to teaze you. We are jogging on quietly. No news. I am *not* going to have any open waistcoats, they don't agree with my chest, and I have already got a little cough and must grow my beard under my chin I believe! Medical men are never expected to dress in the height of fashion, and I have always had an aversion to three yards of shirt front being worn in the street. I have been obliged to put on one of the lambs wool undershirts from Scotland they are very cosy.

You did not send the key. I asked you how Mother was you said 'never heard since Tuesday'—but *how was she then?* We have frosty nights, and I fear she will feel the cold; I suppose by my having no word she is keeping better. Is Grace going to remain at home after Xmas?

I hope your likeness will be a pleasing one, you ought to have a smile on now, nobody to worry you. Be sure and save Holthouse's letter as I want to shew it to his brother when I go to London.

Wednesday. A dull wet day. 10 days after this reaches you I will follow it and give you fits. It is now 23 days since you left. I have got on pretty well so far but begin to feel precious dull. My case is better altho' not out of danger yet. One of Robinson's patients came last evening for me to attend his wife—they had not bespoken me—I declined to go—

I will attend to your dressing case. I think when in London I will get a better lock put on it—The piano case has arrived.

Love to Lizz. Tell Jack he must issue a new 'carte' when I arrive— that bill of fare won't shoot this child[1]—

How is Edith? I see that by leaving Birmingham 7 morning, we reach Plym[outh] 20 minutes past 5. You can tell me where they stop long enough for lunch or breakfast—Did you get your likeness taken? I suppose you will send Sam one, won't the others be jealous?

I must write to tell Mother to send *The Argus* on to Stoke, & not here.

Lake tells me Mrs Cregke comes here next week—I am glad we shall be away. Wale busy as usual washing, cleaning, scrubbing.

I did not sleep well last night at all—Did you?—What was the matter—you know, awoke several times—

I suppose you will meet me at Plymouth—Won't it be jolly— Your affect H.

W

1/134

---

[1] Here, as occasionally elsewhere, Walter uses minstrel show slang: whatever they have been eating will not suit him.

[104]

Thursday morning {22 October 1868}

My dear Poll:

Yours of 20th. Your Bradshaw is different from the old one I have. I can however make it nearly all out except the fares, and those we must leave to the clerks. I think I will start Friday morning 6.45. & get to Leicester about 2 as my getting there at 11 night & leaving so early would give me no time to see Mother & might upset her. I can then leave for Birmingham *you say 10 minutes to 7*. My old Bradshaw says 7. I suppose the latest is correct that is yours—

This is a charming day but the nights & mornings are getting cold. I am sorry the time passes slowly with you that is a bad sign—10 days today, one week only when you get this. I suppose the letters are delivered about 4 or 5 PM—I shall enjoy the run down & the swell of the sea once more before we embark on 'The Briny'—Not a word from Leicester so conclude all is not well.

My bad case is better and on the road to recovery—I shall be able to leave him:

Be sure & don't miss the Australian mail by *putting off*: Remember your letter must be posted on the 29th at the latest that is Thursday next. Wale says you have locked up your bonnett. Do you remember a double breasted silk vest I had, where is it? or did I dispose of it?

Shall I bring Lizz down a few pots of jam & keep the chickens for Mother—I see one of the hens is missing. There is only the Cock & one old hen now—I had better bring you apples, pears, artichokes, jam, & keep the fowls for Mother, as they are not looking well just now & they will get over their moulting by December 5.

Friday morning. I have just got yours of Wednesday with the Photos. I am very much pleased indeed—they are both very nice. *I shall have half* a dozen of *the reading & smiling beauty for myself*. The other is nice too but is a leetle bit too much of the 'Regal'—Wale likes it best. Which does Liz prefer? I will write to Mother. Your acc[oun]t is almost what I feared. The action of the heart was so fluttering as to alarm me several times when she was here, and the dropsy also a bad sign and one announcing the approach of the end. I trust she is prepared for the great change, I think she is for altho' not a demonstrative woman she read much and Grace gave her some nice books. Tell me of some clergyman I could ask to visit her. I will start on Friday this day week & spend the evening with her. I am greatly pleased she has in some measure settled her affairs. I think she ought to have *a young person entirely* to wait on her, for when once she goes to bed she will not get down stairs again, & Selina is unable for both & Grace seems to be unable to remain at home! We must be thankful we came home to see for the last time Poor old Dr. C., your Mother and our other relatives—

Wale says your black lace bonnett is locked up in the trunk in the box room—

See and get all your sewing done before I come to you. Yes, I do think these Photos the best you have ever had done & especially the reading one. You naughty thing it gives me quite the *thrill of the heart* when I look at you—The Helliwells came over last evening & took supper with me sitting for two hours—She says she feels quite lonely in your absence—I got the enclosed letter from Cork this morning with a likeness of Cheyne which I keep—I paid willingly the *extra twopence* on yours this morning—They have done the correct thing with Lindesay to send him away from wretched Ireland, to wealthy Manchester—This is a damp muggy day.

I hope to get another letter on Sunday at the latest—Remember I leave Friday morning—No letters after Wednesday from me here. *Oh! Yes I will post one on Thursday* as you will get it Friday afternoon.

Love to Lizzy & Jack—I trust they are fattening you up for the show for I mean to have a look *at your legs.*

The day has cleared up & got quite warm—

I can't say I admire the new envelopes much—Good bye old woman with much love & many kisses from Your

Affect cousin Wa R.

That gabby woman Mrs. H. is pestering me to go over there—I have refused half a dozen times.

1/134A

[105]

Rawcliffe
Sunday {25 October 1868}

My deary

We had a heavy gale last evening—I had to get Wale to shut the shutters, I thought at one time the windows would have been blown in —It abated before 11—I had a wretched bad night—Called out to a confinement (*the last*) this morning & did not get to Church. I have just seen the Helliwells they like the reading picture & Mrs. H has bespoken one—She presented me with the enclosed for you—Of course her head was a guy this afternoon—I think she is a little touched! She admires the white dress amazingly & there is no doubt you should never be taken in black again—Photographers are as a rule asses & don't know their business! I hope all are well & that you are enjoying yourself & working away. I shall soon start for you now. Don't be afraid I shall not be tired. I shall have some oysters at Leicester & a good breakfast before starting. You take a hot bath every morning that is a new dodge, however it is good for you I am sure & you look ever so much plumper in your Photo *but I must see* & judge for myself—I still take my cold bath & shall miss it fearfully on ship board. I must start for Liverpool as soon as we get back here so Lizz must not expect me to stay more than a week or at most 10 days. *Monday week after I arrive.*

Monday—I hear two pieces of news, one that Mrs Cregke returns on Thursday the other that Turner leaves Rawcliffe. My informant added *'there won't be many sorry for that'*. I am beginning to pack up—was rather disappointed this mor[nin]g no letter Sunday, no letter Monday—

Mrs. H. is without a servant again. H. has taken a lease of the Brewery for 7 years—a charming morning but turned very cold in the afternoon with showers.

You won't get many more letters nor write many more before I come to you now—

Tuesday I have just got yours of Sunday—a mere scrap. I suppose you got my other of Saturday, Monday morning when you didn't expect—

Get as many Photos as you like 1 doz Reading & 1 doz of the last that Jack likes—I don't believe you want me a bit, all Gammon! you won't have me will you? We'll have a row the first night—You'll want to put on my trousers! This is the last letter then but one—I'll attend about the jam—the apples &c.

This is a cloudless day. I wrote to Mother and told her when I shd arrive, & not to have anything but a *small tender beef steak* & a mealy potatoe. Of course Lancaster knows as I do that she is only likely to last a *very short* time—any week may be her last or she may live on with perfect rest & ease of mind for some months.

I do [hope] Grace has told Miss Wilson she must leave—She will be so sorry afterwards that she did not remain with her. She cannot say she has not been told. I think if she does not intend doing so you ought to engage a little girl to remain with her & to do nothing else as it is quite possible that a sudden seizure of syncope or fainting may come on & if no one is near she may fall & never rise again—this is a frequent termination of such cases—The bonnett in my hat box is a black Tuile one not lace—*it is one I never saw you wear not* the pretty one you had last winter with the Red Rose & long lace strings. Wale says that is put away in my box & I've not the key—However I will bring it.

The Cregkes come on Thursday—I'll write on Thursday—

Love to all—I suppose I'll get another tomorrow morn[in]g.

Shall I bring Edith a doll from Leicester?

Ever Your bullying & kissing Hubby

W.

1/135

[106]

Rawcliffe
Wednesday {28 October 1868}

My own old 'gal'

I know you don't want to see me at all & won't be glad to know I'm coming—I am tho' and when you get this will be at Leicester as I started Thursday morning instead of Friday—

Your letter will miss me serves you right you should have written sooner—

I have been packing up and getting all ready.

Hip! Hip!

Friday 5.20—at Plymouth instead of Saturday.

The fact is I couldn't go on dream dreaming all night—and want to punch you so bad and to give it you—

Won't I just—Tiddy iddy I do—You'll have much to put up with—Your affect friend

Sincerely yours &c
W.

1/133

[107]

Swiss Cottage, Eccles
Sunday {29 November 1868}

Dear M—

I arrived safely about 11 & after seeing W.D. at his office went to Fairfield & found Harrie all well & had an excellent character of him from Mr. C.—I took him out a walk & as he was fond of oranges gave him a treat—I told him of Mrs Helliwell's kind invitation—He is at the top of the first Geography class: there are several bigger boys than he is in the school.

I found W.D. & Carrie very well & glad to see me—I brought with me a little rabbitt skin dog which has given intense delight to little Lindesay—They were pleased with the rug—Mrs. Johnson & two other rather nice people spent the eve[nin]g with us & a splendid supper was served at 10—Some rich trifle knocked me up & I have not eaten any breakfast or dinner yet altho' roast goose was very tempting—

We had arranged to go to the Cathedral this morning but I was not able, however I have had a glass of beer & a bit of toast & am coming round—I hope to have a line from you tomorrow at Ismay's and to find that you go on as nicely as I did. Manchester was as usual, cold slippery & dirty! Eccles has improved—I hope Wale saw to all the luggage & that you have been resting yourself and are not obliged to resume nursing Grace. Give her my love and let me know if she enjoyed the chickens and Mother the tea—W.D. says we can buy in Liverpool just as well as here or in London—Both he and Carrie send love & a kiss from Lindesay —he toddles about & eats at Table *not spoiled a bit!* he is sent off when he cries! & so know[s] to be good is best.

Your next will be to Rathgar Road if you write Monday I will get it Wednesday or Thursday morn[in]g—Hoping you feel rested & slept better than I did, with much love & kisses I am my dear Mary Your fond & true W.L.R.—

1/160

[108]

23 Rathgar Road
Wednesday {2 December 1868}

My dearest Polly

I arrived safely in Dublin yesterday morning about 11 & came out here dined—Sophy was very glad to see me & I went into Dublin to meet John[1]—

We had a roughish passage & you would not have liked it at all— Miserable small bunks.

I got yours & *Argus* safely, they were here on my arrival—so you see letters do not take 3 days.

I also got yours & Mother's this morning. You will get this some time Thursday. Sophy wants to know if you would like the stocking white or grey—I should think you could get them as well in Leicester to tell you the truth I am as *near full* as possible—However I will bring you half a doz pair of the best I can get. [New North Clunes] are looking amazingly well—

I have not had time to read my *Argus* yet. I can see nothing of Langley's dismissal but I see the Revd Seddon & two other ministers have had to resign in consequence of impropriety[2]—Of course S. & J. are full of regrets because you are not with me. I am sure Mother does not improve. I hope you will get a nice dress & will not think *of the price*, get a 30/ one *not grey! Claret*, or half mauvy

You must forgive me not writing yesterday—send on letters to me when they arrive—

Fine mild weather here—Is Lancaster suiting Mother?

Sophy chose the reading one & John the straight one—

We are going to see Mrs. Os this morning & then I am going to buy a guinea's worth of groceries to send to an old step brother who is out of a billett & who is supported by his wife.—We must do some

good with the dividends entrusted to us—I sent off Lucinda's parcel—
Love to Grace.

Have not decided about going to Cork yet—Am glad to have a
line from Mother. I will write her next time—Get all you want don't
think of prices—There is *already* £325 safe for us when we land in Melbourne. Money laid out here in *good* things really good things will be
doubled when we get to Australia by their increased value—I intend to
buy a 20 guinea gold watch at Bennetts in London—Get three new pair
of boots at Selina's friend, also your underlinen let it be the best—See if
you can buy it ready made—I intend to make you a present of a writing
desk for your birthday so don't buy one. I think I shall buy one here or
in Liverpool. I am using one of Sophy's that I like not a little, one like
we saw but a good one—

I am quite well again & hope you will soon be rid of your cold—

I went to hear Bellew read[3]—It was acting, recitation, dramatic. I
counted 30 priests there—the most magnificent Hall I have *ever* been
in. You will be delighted with Liverpool—The Southampton letters will
be delivered Saturday or Sunday.

I will write again tomorrow—I have bought some photos of
Ireland 6d each—I could not find my kid gloves I bought 2 pair of
calves skin $8\frac{1}{4}$, 2/6 each in Sackville Street.—Write & let me know when
the cleaning takes place; tell Mother—That won't get the fever out of
the neighbourhood—fumigate with sulphur every day in the kitchen
until you feel the fumes up stairs—Good bye God bless you dearest—
Get out as soon as the weather gets fine & try & get well for your
Attached Husband

Walter

1/114

1   John Richardson, Walter's cousin and brother of Henry Richardson.

2   On 12 October 1968, the *Argus* reported that the Reverend D. Seddon of Christ
    Church, St Kilda had to 'relinquish his charge in consequence of an accusation
    which he was unable to refute, of having been guilty of a serious impropriety'. It
    also reported the resignations of the Reverend Joseph Beer, a Congregational
    minister, and the Baptist minister, Reverend James Taylor, as a result of sexual
    scandals. It did also report, from the *Police Gazette*, the dismissal of First-Class
    Superintendent Thomas Edmund Langley.

3   John Chippendall Montesquieu Bellew (1823–74)—an author, preacher and public
    reader who was known as a powerful orator.

[109]

Thursday afternoon 3 December 1868

My dear Walter—

I have been in a regular fright thinking you had not arrived safe. I have only just received yours I really think if it had not come I should have Telegraph'd to Sophie. I sent to the Post Office & they told me if I posted before 7 at night you would get next morning so I made sure you were ill at Liverpool. I am a little more composed now but it quite upset me this morning when none came. I am very glad darling you are better & I hope you will keep so—Be sure & don't bring grey stockings they are my aversion besides they are for evening wear & must be white but never mind them I can get them here—You are very good to buy me a desk but don't burden yourself with it. I would not wish a prettier than Grace's—& hers cost a guinea Walnut inlaid—I could not carry a large one about—I have just found out I am writing on two sheets of paper. My usual trick—I am glad you are seeing all old friends remember me kindly to them—Langley's dismissal was in the gazette news—I suppose you will be telling me one of these fine days, when to come & meet you. My cold is a trifle better but my mouth all broken out, the cleaning is nearly finished. Grace talks of returning to Mansford on Tuesday. She is quite well. Mother a little better.

We went in to see Uncle yesterday he is as well as ever—Mother had a present sent her of a couple of Rabbits & a Pheasant which she is going to keep (if she can) until you come.

The weather is so wet that we can't go out. I went to Gray's about the Silver & ordered it for I was afraid if I waited longer they would be sold for the small forks had gone, so I have 6 *new* small ones & they are doing the Crests for 6d each that is reasonable—Mother has bought you such a pretty present of course I chose it, a handsome Fish Knife & Fork. Shall I have the Crest put on it? You are quite right to make a present of groceries gladden some hearts for Xmas—

I had a letter from Bessie & one from Sarah the former will be home next Tuesday fortnight—Send me word if you go to Cork—I am sure John & Sophy will make you very happy.

Be sure you see the Phoenix Park this time—I shall not buy my under linen until we go to London—I find it difficult to fill the paper for I have no news to interest you. I shall be very delighted to see you again. What day will it be? If you tell me in time I will have a letter at Ismay's for you.

I have numbered the sheets so I hope you will make it out. Love to your host & hostess

& now my own Good bye don't be so long in writing again God Bless & keep you is ever the prayer of your

>loving wife
>Marie
>lots of love & kisses from us all—

1/154, 1/162

[110]

23 Rathgar Road Dublin
Thursday {3 December 1868}

My dearest

I posted a letter to you last even[in]g which I hope reached you this morn[in]g. The air here is delightfully warm equal to Rawcliffe in Oct. Yesterday Sophy & I went to a morn[in]g lecture by a very eloquent man at one of the Churches: the place was full—Then we went to see Mrs Osborne & her daughter & right glad they were to see us. I have promised them our photos. Nelson has left Dalker & gone to Sligo to be among the brethren. We then went & ordered the little hamper of groceries I mentioned in my last & I came home & wrote a letter. Spent the even[in]g quietly at home with them. I found time to read *The Argus* & saw Langley's dismissal, rather a good thing for Kabat, I suppose he was sent to Beechworth to supercede Langley.

I have not decided yet what day I leave this or where I go, but think I will stay over Sunday, they are *most* kind! I hope you are better & have chosen a pretty and *good* material for your dress.

Tell Wale to go to Mr. Cox at the *Advertiser* office & ascertain *how* & on *what terms* she can get out to Australia Melbourne.

Friday—Yours of Thursday just came. An unnecessary fright my dearest.

Yesterday we went over the Phoenix Park & I then took leave of Sophy & applied at the Castle for an order to go over Mountjoy prison. I presented my order & was shewn by the *assistant superintendent* over the women's prison. I did not tell her who I was for some time. You remember she is Alick's mother, my brother's widow.[1] She has still the remains of beauty and a subdued sweet manner. I went to her little house & saw her daughter Lucinda & was of course much affected. They are R Catholics—I am going out with Sophy this morn[in]g to buy her a new dress—also your stock[ing]s & John & I purpose going this eve[nin]g to see Charles Mathews—in two of his celebrated characters.[2]

I am delighted you are better & only regret you are not with me altho' our roads are very sloppy & without strong boots or goloshes you would most probably get constant colds going about with me—And so Grace is really well & going back. I think at this moment of starting on Monday but do not write to Ismay's as I do not return via Liverpool but Holyhead getting home to you *perhaps* same night—Kind love to Grace & Mother glad the old gentleman is better. It rains here at night but the days have all been fair—get the crest on all you like. If I decide to go to Cork I will tell you before I start.

Tremendous number of carriages in Dublin & many pretty girls—The streets filthy, the prisons empty.—Mr. Disraeli has resigned & the poor Queen obliged to send for that turncoat Gladstone—The Roman Catholics now rule everything & no Protestant has any chance of any help or support from them—I hope you are getting on with your work—Any letters via Southampton—you may I think send them here to me if you get them so as to post them Saturday—I will then get them Sunday—Most likely I will write again tomorrow to you however as you are so fidgetty—John & Sophy desire their kind loves—They talk of moving to the seaside next Summer or Spring rather.

You need not post all the Australian newspapers. They will amuse me when I come to you.

I have been obliged to take off my linen shirt the climate is so mild & wear my light coat.

Good bye dearest; get well and tell me when you would like me to come so as not to incommode Mother with much love & kisses ever Your Attached

Husband Walter—

You did not tell me the color of your new dress!

1/115

---

[1] Henry Downing Richardson had died in 1849.

[2] The British actor, Charles James Mathews (1803–78); son of another well-known actor, Charles Mathews (1776–1835).

[111]

Saturday noon 5 December 1868

My own darling

I am so pleased to hear that I shall so soon see you. I do so long for you again but still I do not wish to hurry you for this place will be duller than ever after such goings about as you seem to be having.

Sophy is very kind I am sure. Today I have a bad headache only when I move, just as though small stones were rolling about but I think it is from lying awake so long in a morning. My cold is nearly gone & the sight of you will quite restore me. We really can't get out here except in pouring rain, all the week we have not had a fine day so you are fav'or'd.

The enclosed came from Lucinda yesterday—I could not post in time—I half hope you won't go to Cork. You can come whenever you like as I have the Top room all to myself & I'll guarantee to make room for you.

I have had no other letters so after this shall keep all until you come. Be sure & tell me when you leave Dublin. I shall like to come & meet you. I have bought 3 nice p[ai]rs of Boots from Selina's brother 1 at 7/6, 1—6/6, 1—5/9—very good indeed.

My new dress is the same as the one you used to admire so much on Lizzie only trimmed with Blue instead of Black—I am glad you are leaving a good name with your poor relatives.

I hope you will enjoy the Theatre he is a good 'Actor'.

My work is nearly done. Wale is still with me.

Grace won't go back until you come, her old plan putting off till the last, but she is company for me—so I don't mind. Be sure & remember *White stockings.*

I should love to have been with my darling but I think the rest here has done me good. If you would like to spend another week pray do—I will do without you.

We are going to make you some 'Brawn' on Tuesday. I don't forget what you like, Mother better, sends her love also Grace. God Bless & keep you my own darling all love & kisses

from your wife
—Mary—

Wrap up well it will be cold travelling
Goodbye
❋❋❋❋❋❋
You need not ask me when I would *like you to come.* You know quite
well you teaze.

1/153

[112]

23 Rathgar Road
Saturday 4 p.m. {5 December 1868}

My dearest

This is to let you know that I purpose starting for you on Monday
morn[in]g at $\frac{1}{4}$ past 6—from Dublin and shall, all being well, be with
you the same evening about 6 to $\frac{1}{2}$ past—

Do not post any letters on Sunday—

We have just returned from Dalker—yesterday we went to the
Irish Academy.[1]

John recommends me to say that a pressing invitation from Cork
may alter my plans but I do not think so—if I decide at all on going to
Cork I will telegraph Monday morning—I hope I will not put you
about

if so I can easily get a bed at Cooks—

The weather is wet & fearfully muddy—

I am writing in the dark.

Love to everybody—I expect a letter from you on Sunday morning.

Your affect Husband
Walter—

1/116

[1]   The Royal Irish Academy, established 1785.

PART 4

Prosperity and Parenthood

MELBOURNE 1869–1876

THESE SEVEN YEARS were the most prosperous period of the Richard-sons' lives. Walter was finally able to live as a private gentleman, sup-ported by the dividends from his mining shares. Mary at last carried a child to term not once but twice.

Letter 113 appears to relate to a brief visit by Walter to Ballarat soon after their return to Melbourne, catching up with old friends, all of whom seem to have been delighted to see him. In October 1869 Mary, now pregnant with the future Henry Handel Richardson, was holidaying at Ballarat with the Cuthberts at their mansion, Beaufort House. After much urging from her, Walter also went to Ballarat for a few days despite the severe illness of their housemaid, Sands.

Ethel Florence Lindesay Richardson was born prematurely at Blanche Terrace, 139 Victoria Parade, Fitzroy on 3 January 1870, after Mary had endured a long and difficult labour. When she and the baby were almost recovered, it was Walter's turn to fall ill. In June 1870 he travelled to Sydney by ship and spent a few days there seeing the sights—he comments in Letter 121, 'The more I see of Sydney, the more I like it'—and a few more at Parramatta with his nephew Alec and his wife Fanny.

On 6 October 1870, the Richardsons moved to a larger house, 'Springfield' in St Kilda, where their second daughter, Ada Lillian Lindesay, was born on 28 April 1871. By the time of her birth, Walter was heavily involved with Spiritualism, as the first president of the Melbourne Branch of the Victorian Association of Progressive Spiritualists. During the early 1870s, he frequently chaired or addressed public meetings in Melbourne, Geelong, Sandhurst and Ballarat— Letter 125 may relate to one of these visits, but few others survive from this period.

On 18 April 1873, the Richardson family sailed to England on the *Atrato*, arriving on 11 July. Again, only one letter survives, no. 126, written from 7 Victoria Gardens, London, the home of Mary's sister Sarah. Mary and the children were, however, staying somewhere else and the letter mainly concerns Walter and Mary's planned trip to the Continent in June 1874. This was undertaken by Mary and Walter alone, the children being left at Cork under the care of Walter's sister Caroline and her husband, Henry Richardson. While in Europe, however, Walter received disturbing news about his mining investments. He immediately returned to Australia via India, arriving back in Melbourne on 21 August 1874.

In what was to become the pattern of the rest of their lives together, Mary was left to pick up the pieces—in this case, mainly the children—and follow him from London. As one sees from her ship-board diary, now in the National Library, it was a long and tedious voyage for her and the girls on the sailing ship *Sobraon*, lasting from 17 September to 12 December 1874. She was often seasick, the children had various ailments and the ship was for most of the time either becalmed or battling storms. On 14 October, she wrote 'Shall we ever get to Melbourne? Oh how I miss W—it seems ages since I saw him', originally writing 'you' instead of 'him'. And a month later, on 16 November, 'All talking about getting to Melbourne in three week's; hope we shall for I long for some one again'.

After their return, the Richardsons lived in a furnished house in East Melbourne while their own new house was being built in Burwood Road, Hawthorn. They moved there about August 1875, but the new practice was not the success Walter had hoped. Again, only one letter survives from this period, seemingly from later in the year as Mary and the children are holidaying at Sorrento with their old friends the Grahams. It reveals Walter's continued financial worries, mainly because of the money still owing on the house. In June 1876, hearing that Dr C. W. Rohner, another leading Spiritualist, was to leave his practice at Chiltern in north-east Victoria, Walter travelled to Chiltern.

[113]

Ballarat
Friday evening at Hudsons {1869 ?}

Dear M—

I have been about all day seeing old friends all sorry that you are not with me—Nixons very warm. Wanliss ditto Saddlers, Hudson, ditto.

Wanliss has invited us for 3 weeks—I think matters [at] the Bank are pretty right. All shares are but I do not get my pass book till tomorrow morning—I am to go to Reid's office Saturday morning to get some information about Newingtons, so that I may be delayed leaving this till Monday as I have not got the mining maps for John—Nixons have asked us to stay there.

Old Cuthbert says he knows there is a room there waiting for us— Lots of news. Saddler's bills all right—Love to all.

Your affect H.
W.L.R

1/90

[114]

139 Victoria Parade
Friday {1 October 1869}

My dear M:

I was glad to hear that you arrived safely. I have no recollection of ever mentioning the fact to Hudson. He must have inferred it from some indirect remark about you I suppose—

I hope you slept better last night—I went to see Bandman last night[1]—met Ochiltree there & saw Montgomery in the dress circle using his handkerchief to his eyes![2] as the people did when we saw *East Lynn*—I saw Bandman in Liverpool & did not like him then nor do I indeed now much—The piece was well put on however & is worth seeing—They never could play it at Ball[ara]t for the dresses, scenery, & get up are too complex. Sands has been in bed all day Thursday & must stay there today—a threatening of Rheumatic fever, with inflammation of the heart.

N.N. Clunes have had another rise and were sold yesterday at £159: If you see Wanliss find out if the reefs are making again.

Give my kind regards to Mrs C: Henry, father, & all the boys—I got yours yesterday evening.

Have seen no one since you left. Emma has just been over with a note from Mary asking me to dine with them on Sunday—[3]

Weather fine not too warm.

Ever your attached
Husband W.

1/151

1   Daniel E Bandmann, a German actor who was performing the role of Narcisse at the Theatre Royal in the 3-act play of the same name, written especially for him by Tom Taylor (1817–80), a popular British playwright. Bandmann had several successful seasons in Australia between the 1860s and the 1880s. He first appeared in Melbourne on 18 September 1869.

2   Walter Montgomery (1827–61) was another leading English actor of this period who toured Australia from 1867 to 1869.

3   On 24 July 1869 John Bailey married for the third time, Mary Atkins; their Melbourne house was called Vaucluse. Emma was the daughter from John's first marriage, referred to in earlier letters as Trotty.

[115]

139 Victoria Terrace
Monday evening {4 October 1869}

My dearest M.

Received yours this evening and am very glad you are enjoying your visit—it is very unfortunate about the tongue. Write a note to Hudson or call & see Mrs H. & him. Mrs Saddler is of course proud of her daughter as someone else will be next year—Did Mrs Colvin know you were there: I suppose Mrs Macdermott is as vulgar as ever—try & walk a little it will do you good. You have a number of visitors. Sands is better today for the first time she has been very ill with a sharp attack of endo-carditis, inflam[mation] of the inside of the heart, in bed since Thursday morning.

I have dinner in middle of day to save Cook. I went to hear *Ernani*[1] again on Saturday Even[in]g. Yesterday Sunday dined at Vaucluse & tomorrow dine with the Kabats.

Weather mild today rather cool—I have no news so that I do not know how to fill the paper.

John, Mary & I took a long walk after dinner up past the convent & Mary was very much interested about the Nuns—The mail has again arrived before its time & I expect the letters will be delivered tomorrow morning. I will go to the Warehouse the first thing & slip any for you inside this—I suppose you will get them tomorrow afternoon.

My kind regards to all at Beaufort House from Your affect H.

W.L.R.

Thursday Oct 7 is appointed a day of special prayer for rain—All are getting very apprehensive—

I sold 2 [New North Clunes] one at £157 & one thro' Nixon at £158.10—as Wanliss talked so depreciatingly about 7 pennyweights & $\frac{1}{3}$ profits etc & this being the last 3.0.0 dividend—

Mrs Kabat sends her love & says she misses you very much—I was at the foot ball match on Sat[urday] & saw Captain Ross & 2 other officers of the 14th playing with their men, stripped & begrimed, & knocked down & shouting 'now 14th'—

1/150

---

[1] Giuseppe Verdi's 4-act opera.

[116]

Blanche Terrace
Thursday morning {7 October 1869}

My dearest Marie

I am sorry the tongue keeps so bad see Hudson as soon as he comes back and do try & eat some vegetables—a change of food from bread & meat is most necessary. I have not read the letters I sent you

I just glanced thro' them to see that all were well.

You should insist on going to Mrs. Wanliss as she is sure to feel hurt if you do not.

I went out to Pentridge yesterday. It rained hard for some hours, lunched with Joe. Sands is a little better just able to sit up for a few hours —It seems she has been a sufferer from Rheumatic fever at Home—I am afraid she will never be fit for hard work again. I dine at Kabats again tonight to meet some doctor from home. Friday even[in]g *at the Atkins*.

I cannot leave at present as Sands is so poorly—there will be no cleaning done no washing this week. Cook has to answer the door—I am not going to have any party in fact it would be impossible—Grace ought to have sent out *the Transfer for you to sign*—write & tell her to do this in your next or she should have found out & said what it was she wanted—the share is not losing money by being there—You had better tell Mrs Cuthbert that I regret I am not able to leave home & then you must make your arrangements about your other visits. I am sorry Mrs Nixon is poorly.

You had better write a scrap to John for his letters if you want to see them as it is no business of mine and he has not offered them to me and you know his disposition—

Ever your affect Husband W.

1/165

[117]

Victoria Parade
Saturday morning {9 October 1869}

My dear Marie

If *I knew my letters were destroyed I would write differently* but you *will* keep them & I dislike the idea of any other having the chance of reading them. You know my wishes and have known them for years. Sands is a little better, I am really grieved for the girl. Yet I am not without hope that she may be pretty well again, but doubt if she will ever be strong.

I am sorry your mouth continues so bad. *I write Hudson by this mail—*

Mrs Kabat sends her love. Mrs Murchison is still there.

We had heavy rain here & the weather is now pleasantly cool. Dr & Mrs Blair left cards yesterday

I think they are nice people from all I hear. Also the Spragues & Mrs Nield[1] called—I am afraid Grace will make a great mess of affairs —John tells me that in one of the letters they said that old Hester would give them no peace *until they had given him possession of the House*— Can it be possible they have been idiots enough to give up House & land!—

I have really nothing more to tell you.

With love & kisses
I am your attached
Husband W.

Mrs Kabat wants to know if we still write every day.

I am glad you are going to Mrs. Wanliss. I am afraid your ideas of the people wanting to see me is a myth—they did not shew me much kindness when I was among them—I hope you will remain & enjoy yourself—We spent a very pleasant evening at Williams Road and had plenty of laughing—I am not going to John's on Sunday but on Monday evening for practice with Mary.

1/166

[1] Likely to be Edgar Sprague (1835–93), stock and sharebroker, and his wife Amy, née Govett; Susannah Neild (1831–1918), wife of James Edward Neild (1824–1906), president of the Medical Society of Victoria and a noted theatre critic.

[118]

139 Victoria Parade
Tuesday evening {12 October 1869}

My dear Marie—

I am glad you are enjoying yourself, I may run down on Friday but it must only be for a day or two—Sands is still too ill—I fear it will be necessary to get another house maid as soon as you return.

If I leave on Friday, I must return the following Wednesday at furthest; there will be no cleaning done during your absence—She is only able to sit on a chair. I got Dougan Bird to see her last Saturday. I am glad your tongue is better, I wrote to Hudson about you but he has never answered my letter—We had fine rain all last night. I don't feel very well myself today—I can't get a decent cup of tea at home, it is so different to what I get out—It must be the 2/– trash. I have told cook to take 3/– in future.

I was over at Vaucluse last evening & got a very nice enjoyable one there—I shall go out & buy some at 3/6 & try that—

You say nothing about Sam & he has never written to me saying whether he went to see Day or not—I have got nothing to tell you. I see nobody & have no news. I must see how Sands is before I decide about leaving on Friday. Cook is such a deaf old stupid, I cannot trust her, she stands & talks to the people at the door & lets them talk to her.

I find that this will not catch the post this evening so I must post it in the morning—

I posted my last Saturday morning—

Wednesday
Rain all morning. I could not go to the general P.O.

Hope you keep better and am so glad you feel the movement.[1] I suppose Mrs. C., Mr. N., Mrs. O. are all delighted. I think I will leave Friday morning $\frac{1}{2}$ past 11 train. Weather is not favorable for the boat, we shall have floods on the Yarra.

I will write again tomorrow Thursday with love & kisses

Ever your Attached Husband
W.

1/149

[1] Of the baby—the future HHR.

[119]

Bank N S Wales
Thursday {14 October 1869}

My dear Walter
I was very glad to get your letter this morning & I shall be sure to be at the Train to meet you at $\frac{1}{2}$ past 3 o'clock. I do hope Sands will get better. I am afraid I shall have a difficulty in getting another to do as

well. I am going back to Mrs Wanliss tonight as she is giving a party on purpose for me but if you only stay such a short time we shall have to go to the Cuthberts on Saturday & the Saddlers on Monday as I have put off going there until you come for I thought you would enjoy that best. I am writing to Sam to meet you at the Station he has seen Dr Day & he says it's liver & indigestion. You had better make no promises about when you will be back for I think you will enjoy yourself & I am so pleased you are coming. Mrs Ochiltree has given me three new dresses & three petticoats for the little one when it comes, everybody seems delighted.

It has rained here for the last 4 days it seems to be pretty general. I want to catch the morning post so will be sure to be waiting your arrival tomorrow.

Good bye till then with love & kisses from your

own wife
Marie.

I shall wait here till the post comes in tonight.
It is very cold here so put on Flannel. I have a cotton suit if it gets warm.

1/45–6

[120]

Royal Hotel Sydney
Sunday {5 June 1870}

My dearest M.

You see we arrived safely. After you saw the last of us it was very cold and I felt the benefit of wraps. On going down the Yarra we came on 'The City of Hobart' Steamer ashore. She had been stuck for 2 hours: a Lady came off her in a boat as pass[enger] to Sydney. We passed out of the heads about 7 or 8 o'clock. Had a fine day Friday with fair wind. She is what I call a steady boat altho' the ladies *never* appeared after the *first* meal at table. We sighted land on Saturday mor[nin]g & kept it in view all day sailing along shore about 6 miles off. The scenery is very charming & we kept one big mountain named by Captn Cook 'The

Dromendary' in sight all day. We got into Sydney heads about mid-
night or a little later & soon brought up along the wharf—our table was
pretty fair and of course I ate like a hunter. We got up a rubber every
evening & the Cap[tain] turned out to be a jolly little fellow—My cabin
was very comfortable and altho' I dosed only the first night I slept well
afterwards with the window open of course—I had no one else with me
—I am at The Royal—I find no mail leaves today so you will not get this
before Thursday. I hope you & the darling of our hearts are both well—
    I am going to Church this morning and will close this in the after-
noon. The weather is delightful & I have had to leave off my flannels
already—

Monday morn[in]g. I went to Church yesterday morn[in]g & to the
Cathedral at 3½. A great many pretty girls in Sydney. The table here is
all that could be wished—This is a lovely morn[in]g & there seem to be
good shops—Address to Post Office as I shall go to 'The Oxford' Hotel
most likely before long. It is prettier situated than this & any change is
good—I will be very anxious to hear from you. I see the *Agamemnon*
arrived—You will be getting your home letters Tomorrow—We lunch
at 1—dine at 6. I have just made a fine breakfast—first two pork
sausages & potatoe, then Ham & eggs—I am now going out 9 AM. to
post this & will commence another letter as soon as I have seen Alec—
    I see the *City of Adelaide* made a fine voyage of under 48 hours,
45½ from heads to heads. Good bye dear from your own

    W.

1/173

[121]

Skarratts Hotel
Tuesday {7 June 1870}

My dear Mary
    I wrote yesterday & posted it to go by *City of Adelaide* by advice at
the G.P.O. I am going to send this overland. I see by this morning's
telegr[a]m that 'Power' is captured by Nicholson & Hare[1]—You will
also have your English letters wh' will cheer your tedium, altho' I

suppose you do not miss me much having Baby—Bless her I hope she is well. I enjoyed Monday amazingly. I went to Wooloomooloo bay by omnibus 3d. there I found two steamers just starting to go down the Harbor I got into one & we went down among the Islands to a place called 'Watsons bay' most lovely scenery, the bay wooded along its shores in most places to its edge—Villas dotting the shores here & there & the sun bright & warm. I then returned to my hotel for lunch at 1. Out again in the afternoon to the Botanic Gardens wh' you will enjoy amazingly. They are smaller but much more charming than those of Melb. There is more lawn and finer trees, the grass plots presenting such a relief to the eyes and the flowers most luxuriant—In them is a fine collection of birds &c. wh' is very creditable indeed—

The more I see of Sydney the more I like it—There seems to be more business doing than in Melb and the weather is set fair wh' is a great thing—*You will enjoy it*—It reminds me of Devonport & Plymouth —altho' much finer.

I have not seen Alec yet—The table here is all that can be desired —I hope you and dear Bab. are well & sleep a little better—How nice it will be when we are able to travel about—I am going to the P.O. & will not post this till evening—

Wednesday morning I went to the P.O. yesterday & found nothing not even an *Argus*. Perhaps I may have better luck next time—I went out to 'Botany Bay' yesterday a pretty drive of seven miles by omnibus; there I strolled about for an hour at 'The Sir Joseph Banks Hotel' a charming & truly rural spot. The landlady said she wd charge us two & servant £6.6.0 per week to include servants.

On returning strange to say I saw Alec crossing the street, & he saw me *on the top of the bus*—We had lunch together & I went out to Paramatta 14 miles from Sydney—where I am now this morning. I am much pleased with Fanny. She is plain but engaging and has *charming manners* and is evidently a dear good girl. You will like her much. We are going out this morning to see the orange groves for which this place is famous—

I was fearfully attacked by mosquitoes all night—the bedroom swarming with them—I am writing to the P[ost] Master Sydney this morning for any letters to be forwarded to me here—I *think I am better* —I will return by the boat at the beg[inning] of next week as I am uneasy at not hearing from you for so long—

We will take apartments at Paramatta also if you like—No change in the weather every day since I left has been fine with me—

Kiss baby for me
& believe me
Your Affect H.
W.L.R.

¹   Henry Power (1820–91), a bushranger, was captured by Superintendents Nicolson and Hare on 5 June 1870.

[122]

Paramatta
Wednesday afternoon {8 June 1870}

My dear M.

I don't think you can say I do not write often to you. I posted my second letter to you this morning *overland*, and I begin this the 3d: I told you how I arrived here last evening, and how pleased I was with Fanny. I got a carriage this morning and we drove out to an 'Orangery' about 3 miles out of Paramatta. There the scenery is magnificent and we saw the orange groves; trees 35 feet high, laden from top to bottom with oranges and lemons. The estate is situated very romantically in a glen, & belongs to one man, the trees grow best in sandy soil and they are planted in terraces along the sides of a steep ravine—[drawing of trees] Fanny had never been there before, & so she enjoyed it as well as I did. She is a very nice girl & improves on acquaintance. Alec is very much altered, so quiet & thin. Got quite steady & has lost all his absurd notions—I believe he will get on. He writes to, & hears from, Miss F. every mail¹— There has never been any family and so Mrs Saddler must have been misinformed. I shall make up a box of books and other things useful to young house keepers when I get home. They are commencing just as we did, & furnishing by degrees—living very properly *within* their means—

I have written this morning to the P.O. Sydney to forward my letters & papers here so if there are any I will get them tomorrow. This is Wednesday & I have had as yet no *Argus* altho' I called yesterday after the overland mail was in—However I saw Friday's *Argus* in Sydney on Monday—Paramatta is a considerable town, 4 churches: jail, lunatic asylum & the old Government House where the Governor used to live when Paramatta was *the Capital*, the town is 2 full miles long.

Mary Richardson with Ettie and Lil, taken in Cork, Ireland during 1874

The former Star Hotel, Chiltern, where Walter Richardson stayed on first arriving in 1876 (photograph by Barry Webby)

Lake View, where the Richardsons lived at Chiltern from 1876 to 1877
(photograph by Barry Webby)

The Athenaeum, Chiltern, frequented by Walter Richardson
(photograph by Barry Webby)

I do not think I will stay much longer away. You will not get this letter before Monday, if I post it tomorrow Thursday, as it seems the mail takes nearly a week between posting & delivery—I will find out tomorrow if '*The You Yangs*' sails on Tuesday & if so will start. This is awkward being so far from Sydney. So you had better not write any more after receipt of news when I sail. The climate is certainly much more enjoyable than Melb barring the confounded Mosquitoes—I think I had a better appetite on board the steamer than on shore—I saw an old Ball[ara]t man at 'Skarratts' named Warren who lived in Webster St. He is going to 'Figi' [*sic*]—He knows Frazer very well—Alec is engaged as travelling auditor of accounts on the railway and is from home all day and nine nights a month. Fanny thinks this very hard—how would you have liked it when we were 2 years married? Friday. We were in Sydney all yesterday and so I cd not finish this. I got Friday & Saturday's *Argus* & saw by your initials that all was well up to Saturday. *The 'You Yangs'* sails about Friday June 17, that is the boat I will return by: Holroyd has got me made an Honorary Member of *The Sydney Club*. We are going over to his place 'The Scrubs' to spend Sunday.

Tonight we are going out to tea & talk to a friend of Alec's. The weather is still most lovely I have not had one really winter's day since I left home—yesterday was the worst and that was only very dusty—Tomorrow Saturday I am going into Sydney by boat along the river to see if there is any letter from you—As I cannot get them here somehow.

This is the place to winter!

A letter from Miss F. arrived by the mail containing an agreable draft for 35.0.0. They are spending this on furniture so that by & bye they will have all they desire—they make his pay cover all expenses & *are perfectly free from debt*. She is evidently a capital manager—Today I am going over the jail & in the afternoon I take Fanny over the Asylum & tonight we are going out to a little whist at the Station Master's—

I did not see Mrs. Kabat's name in the list by mail to Sydney.

I do hope & trust that you and the dear baby are well & that the house has been safe at nights. I wrote by *City of Adelaide* & she put off sailing till Wednesday then I posted one here overland on Wednesday & now *this* goes overland. I think Thursday is the day *The You Yangs* leaves not Friday. If so I will get in by Sunday—I have got some photos of Sydney. God bless you & baby says Your affect H.

W.L.R.

1/171

[1]   Miss Fector—friend of Walter's mother.

[123]

Saturday {11 June 1870}

My dearest Marie

I cannot tell you how pleased I was to hear from you this morning, only for the first time. You have I hope got my three letters posted Monday, Wednesday and Friday—I am still at Alec's but intend starting for home next Thursday or Friday by the *You Yangs*—I will tell you in my next the exact day—Friday we all went to Sydney to buy furniture—Saturday I went alone by Steamer down the river 'Paramatta' and a most lovely sail it is—I returned the same way. The weather has been all that could be desired since I left Melbourne. Not a single wet day— We went out on Friday evening to a little musical party & a rubber. Did not get home till 12—I bought them a little clock for the dining room—

Sunday morning—I was glad to hear baby was keeping well & that you were not obliged to get out of bed so often.

I think I am better as I certainly am eating better, & the doors are always open the air is so mild. This will be the place for our next winter quarters. We can stay at a very nice quiet family hotel and I cut the enclosed out of a Sydney newspaper—

Monday morning—Still glorious weather—Yesterday we went to Holroyd's and spent the day there, he got us horses and we went over his orangery and rode & walked about for hours—Had a capital dinner with the door wide open all the time, so you may imagine the weather —& he sent his coachman & trap to drive us home.

I suppose Sam got safely to Sandhurst and that he has written to you—I am going in to Sydney this morn[in]g by the Steamer again and hope to get if not a second letter at least Wednesday's *Argus* initialled— I got Monday and Tuesday's all right—*I shall* be glad *to see you once more*—We did the voyage to this in 58 hours from wharf to wharf. If I arrive at the Melb wharf *during the night*, I shall wait quietly in my berth till daylight & then take a cab, this will be better than disturbing the house. It was my mistake about 72 shares, it was 52—Of course Saddler never called—I hope dear Etty gets her gruel regularly. You did not say how the goat was so I conclude she is not dead—I hope you have not written after today, Monday, if you have of course we can write & get the letter returned to Melb.

Good bye dear Marie, try & be quite well when I come back— Baby will soon now be 6 months old, & I expect to see a great change in her—I trust the bad weather will have passed away—I will write tomorrow Tuesday for *the last time* just to say when the boat starts on Thursday or Friday—With lots of kisses for yourself & the wee pet from

Your fond husband Walter.

1/170, 1/171

[124]

Paramatta N.S.W.
Tuesday {14 June 1870}

My dearest Marie

You would not get my first letter until yesterday, Monday, owing to the unfortunate weather 'the *City of Adelaide*' steamer encountered. I have written & posted three since, namely Wednesday, Friday & Monday—Four altogether this making 5—I post this to say I have only had as yet one from you written the Saturday after I left June 4—& 4 *Argus*—I only hope & trust all is well. I am still at Alec's: I leave tomorrow for Hotel in Sydney—*The You Yangs* is advertised to leave on Thursday but it will be Friday or Saturday before she sails. So do not expect me before Monday even[in]g.

Weather still delightful—English mail closes here tomorrow Wednesday—I am sure I am better, fatter, & stronger—doors open all day.

Weather positively warm—No fires required except in the mornings & at night & if I had not been anxious about you & the pet I should have done better even still. From the wretched postal arrangements I do not suppose you will get this before Monday morning—but it will let you know I am coming—Fanny sends her love & will like to see you very much.

We can spend a fortnight at Paramatta very pleasantly next Winter & a fortnight at Sydney—ditto at Manly Beach—I enclose advertisement that I omitted in my last. I am going to the Post *again*. I have got nothing since Saturday. Kiss the Baby and believe me

Your ever loving Husband
Walter.

I have posted by Steamer as I have just got your letter & the home ones & Thursday & Friday *Argus* all together. The Overland takes 7 *days*.

1/164

[125]

Sandhurst
8 am Monday

My dear Marie
Arrived in due course found all well.
Heavy rain Sunday morning wh' I suppose you had also.
Saw splendid cake from Ext. H. 90/– oz. top of the list once more. Div. 1/6—
Am going down the shaft today. Emily S. is staying with Polly— I enclose photo of Grace which is the best we have—
I hope M. from Va[u]cluse is with you and that the dear bairnies are all right—I think I will start on Wednesday midday, as I am going out to Eaglehawk Tuesday.
The weather is most delightful, and every one appears in good spirits.
Kiss the kids for Papa and take a few for yourself.

from your affect
Husband
W. Lindesay Richardson.

I will have to bring the photo it won't go into the envelope

WLR

1/167

[126]

7 Victoria Gardens
Monday evening {c. May 1874}

My dear 'Marie'

Sarah tells me that you will not get this until tomorrow afternoon. If I had known this I would have written this morning—On Saturday I went over the Surgical Home and then out to Hanwell.

Sunday with Sarah to the Catholic Apostolic Central Church Gordon Square morning & to Westminster Abbey Evening—We arrived there at $\frac{1}{4}$ past 6 (service commenced at 7) & found the old Abbey nearly full—I estimated the number about 1800.

Today I went to Cooks, Fleet St & then to see Harrie at Tottenham —He is pretty well & getting on nicely. No complaint against him—

I dined with Mr. White & his family—& came home very tired to write this—We were glad to hear that you had arrived safely.

What a blessing that the little Indian is behaving herself at last! Sarah will write some other time.

She is worried to death about that good for nothing hussy of hers —It is difficult to know what to decide upon as to our Paris trip—A month will cost us £40.0.0 but for that we will see Paris & Exhibition go right across France from Paris to Switzerland see Lake Lucerne & Lake of Geneva & return to Paris & home—

I suppose I had better come down to see you all, as you are not coming up to me; you may expect me there by the 3.40 train on Tuesday —I suppose I shall see your face this time and with love to all.

I am my dear wife
Your faithful & true
W.L.R. ✳

1/148

[127]

Hawthorn
Tuesday evening

My dear Mary

I have just received yours of Sunday—I was beginning to get uneasy—Am glad to hear all is well & that you had a nice passage.

Sunday was cold with us but only a few drops of rain—More today—

So glad they like the beach I suppose they will take a dip when the weather gets warmer.

Do encourage them—about an hour before dinner is the best time.

Delighted to hear Sydney is so nice—They must be happy—Kiss them for Papa—All is well here. Cook going out tomorrow—Was awoke at 5 Sunday by the blessed ducks & cock & this morning $\frac{1}{4}$ to 5 by the sparrows that are getting under the eaves. I have sent to Davidson to get the holes covered—as I don't like to put down poison on acc[oun]t of the neighbour's pigeons—

Some callers—Am in better spirits. Fancy another dividend of 9d —on Kneebones—£30 in the month—

I bought another 100 have got 500 now the next div. will be for Xmas—We expect good news from the Newingtons *every day* & when that happens I am happy! & safe, & if it occurs *before Sat.* week *I will come down.* I enclose 6 stamps—

I see O'Connor has had a success at the Magdala & the manager speaks most favorably of his powder.[1] His fortune is safe—

Remember me to Mrs G

Your loving husband
W.L.R.

Wednesday morn[in]g
Am afraid you won't get this till Saturday—Heavy gale all night. Awoke at daylight by the sparrows. Am going to put poison in the verandah.

Love to all
W.

1/163

---

[1] See Letter 189, note 2.

PART 5
Chiltern

1876–1877

IN THE FIRST FEW WEEKS after arriving in Chiltern on 14 June 1876, Walter wrote to Mary almost every day—twenty-nine letters—until the arrival of Mary and the children on 27 July. One of his main concerns was finding a suitable house for them. On 28 June he was finally able to tell Mary that he had seen a 'decent' one—the present Lake View, now owned by the National Trust of Australia. Although initially uncertain of his prospects in Chiltern, Walter was now most enthusiastic, apparently in the face of hesitation by Mary at the thought of their leaving Melbourne: 'We can enjoy ourselves very well here & you & the chicks can run to Melb in the summer. We can ask friends to come & stay & we will I am sure save money' (Letter 143).

So again Mary was left to arrange the packing—though with plenty of advice from Walter—as well as the Hawthorn house. Initially, Walter advised her to try to sell it—'See Ham[1] about our house & offer it for sale £1500 would satisfy me—it cost £1800' (Letter 144). Then, Letter 153, he determined that renting would be better: 'You will have to take £120 & the tenant pay the rates' (The Chiltern house was costing £80 per annum to rent). By 18 July he was delighted to hear that tenants had been found, telling Mary the next day, 'You have done splendidly to let the house & to dispose of the furniture so well'. She was, in addition, also trying to get money out of patients who had not paid their medical bills!

The remaining sixteen letters are from the following summer. Mary and the children had indeed gone south to escape the heat, staying with the Grahams in Melbourne and at Sorrento and with the Cuthberts at Queenscliff. Walter, meanwhile, was enduring not only the heat but the worries of a declining practice. Although he still saw friends and remained active in town affairs, he felt Mary's absence much more than he had done fifteen years earlier at Ballarat. Scribbled across the first page of Letter 165 is, 'It will kill me if I don't get out of this soon'. Letter 166 relates the first serious signs of the illness, then diagnosed as general paralysis of the insane, that was shortly to kill him: 'I was just up at Maude's posting a letter & I found myself unable to articulate—I could not say what I wanted, I am very uneasy about myself. I lay down. I said I thought it was a faint & said I had been out in the sun—I am afraid it is something worse.'

Walter's later letters attempt to reassure the obviously worried Mary and to urge her not to come home early. It was clear, however, that he must leave Chiltern before the next summer. Letter 164, to his daughters, anticipates Walter's next move: 'I wish we could live near the Sea. Perhaps Mamma may like Queenscliffe and we might move there'.

---

[1]   C. J. and T. Ham was a firm of Melbourne auctioneers.

[128]

Chiltern
Thursday {15 June 1876}

My dear wife
        I arrived here safely last night—without any other misadventure than leaving my hat box behind me in the saloon carriage wh' I did not discover until this morning—The place looks much better today, the morning is fine, & sky clear—Rohner and Lloyd met me at the Station. Rohner is a very handsome man and a gentleman. I shall have great dif-

ficulty in coming after him. I hope & trust Ettie is better as I got no telegram from you—I look anxiously for a line tomorrow morning—

I have got a nice room at the hotel & they say they will give me a private parlor if I require one 30/– a week—Thank God I had a good night & only awoke by the train ½ past 6. I heard a cough & I thought it was my darlings Ettie or Lilly—& awoke to find me alone. I have been over to Arrowsmith's house I find the *front* about 33 feet—did not see him—out—all say he is not going away—that would give 15 feet for each room & 3 feet for door but will be more particular some other time—

I enjoyed the sandwiches & sherry very much—& was not at all cold—Be sure if *you come* to buy the 1d Railway guide as it gives you all the names of the stations as you come along. You must break the journey at Seymour—it would be too long otherwise. If you post every morning I get it next morning. I will write again tomorrow. Don't send the letter to James Bonwick as we need not tell the people I am gone for good as I may not like it.

Give papa's dear love to my darlings—he will write tomorrow.

Tell Sarah how sorry I was not to see her & that I hope she will come & stay with you.

Your loving husband
Walter—

I have just heard that Mr Arrowsmith is *not* going away.

1/175

[129]

Chiltern
Friday {16 June 1876}

My dearest M

I have just had your telegram—Your post card received this morning made me very anxious. I am so glad to know there is no danger —the white patch must be follicular inflammation which I cured in London by Guaiacum lozenges—get 3d from Rawle & give her half a one three times daily if there are any white spots on receipt of this— Give the darlings Papa's best love & kisses.

Brooke Smith & Judge Hackett[1] have been here yesterday & today so we have been lively—They are off today—The Hotel is full, good table—Rohner being here still, I am not doing anything but getting known—one patient yesterday—Revd Mr Green, English Clergyman, called this morning, nice little man—3 children grown up—lost his wife.[2] Says he is likely to leave his Cottage & to move out a mile off—Cottage is of brick he thinks it is as good as Arrowsmith's, only no ground. Said he was very glad to see me coming—as there must be a good practice in the district. Brooke sends his love, says I am to tell you he is looking after me—he admits now there is a fine opening here altho' he thinks it would be almost better to run off to Corowa, a nicer place & he says only one doctor. However I think I will remain here for 6 weeks after Rohner has gone & see what results—

Be sure & drop me a line every morning before $\frac{1}{2}$ past nine or send letter in to Town if you have a chance before 5. So then I will get it always next afternoon about 2. Yesterday was a pleasant day & Brooke & I took long walk—today is cold but not out of the way, there are lots of flies about & blow flies,—I had my cold bath & 2 eggs for breakfast, meat lunch at one & tea dinner at 6. Turkey, Bacon: Roast beef, pudding, cheese. God bless you all dear M.

I hope M.B. was with you, of course the wet kept her from seeing me off, even if she had got my letter.

Your affect Husband
Walter

1/176

[1] Charles Prendergast Hackett (1819–89), born in Dublin, was police magistrate at Castlemaine in 1854, then with the Melbourne District Court in 1856, and a County Court judge 1868–82.

[2] The Reverend Samuel Dutton Green, father of Arthur Vincent Green, the curate at St Peter's Anglican Church, Eastern Hill, where Henry Handel Richardson would later attend services while a boarder at the Presbyterian Ladies' College.

[130]

Chiltern
12 noon Saturday {17 June 1876}

My dearest Mary
Your post card made me very uneasy, then your telegram gave me comfort & finally your letter describing your anxiety all night was

grievous—Not having had any telegram this morning I conclude that they are better. It is just possible tha[t] they may have had a mild attack & it will be necessary to be very careful about cold & to watch the water they pass. If it looks thick cloudy, smoky like porter you may be sure it has been scarlet fever & this cannot be known for some weeks—I am no further advanced about a house. Mr. Arrowsmith does not know & will not know if he is going until the 6th of July—Everyone says he will be retained here—The clergyman's cottage is brick about 20 by 18 with four rooms in that space. Rohner has no house at Hamilton so Mrs R. will stay here—he tells me his shed cost him £500. I was half determined to return to Mel. today disgusted, but Lloyd chemist says that Rohner is going over to Beechworth tomorrow & Monday, & Albury next week, so that there may be some patients for me.

It is very dull now Brooke is gone. It was very cold this morning but it is clearing up now at noon—

2 PM—Just got yours of Friday—Glad to find things are no worse. Mrs Graham is indeed a real friend how shall we repay her?—No chance of a house here I fear—two offering but very small cabins—I am glad Sara is with you I hope she will stay. If we could get a house she should not leave. Love to my darlings & same to yourself from

Your Affect
Husband
Walter

1/182

[131]

Chiltern
Monday morning {19 June 1876}

My dearest Mary

Since writing on Saturday I had two patients Saturday night, & one last night. 4 miles drive into the country for which I will charge £3.3.0. Rohner has not been a favourite with everybody, as these people told me that if I had not been here they would have gone to Rutherglen 8 miles from them—I am sure I shall have a good practice by & bye— & there seems to be money in the district & no clubs a great mercy. The worst thing is about a house. I hear now that Arrowsmith is likely to go—He told me himself that his staying depends entirely on his being re-appointed Shire engineer which will be decided July 6—The Post Master says he will *not* be appointed, that the Shire council will *not* have him. His is the only decent shed to be got. We can *just* live in it—as it is about the size of our wooden cottage in Webster St. I went to Church yesterday morning. The clergyman's cottage is brick but very small— He thinks he was fortunate to get that. We have two or three nice fellows staying at the Hotel & I shall be very lonely next week. We had Green Sam's bank inspector Saturday but he left suddenly this morning before I thought to ask if Sam had left Corowa. This is a lovely morning. There is Paterson an old clerk of the bench of Ball[ara]t East who is only relieving officer—A nice young fellow in the bank also relieving some one. The Station Master & commercial men in & out every day—some $\frac{1}{2}$ doz. coaches stop at the house.

Monday 3 PM. I get yours every day at 2. I am so glad they keep better—But one is never safe—You must examine the skin carefully & if you see any signs of peeling, of scurf you may expect Dropsy. I think I should give them a good warm bath _occasionally_ & if you see any scurf about them *oil* them all over after their bath at night—

I was very delighted to get their letters—Rohner leaves next Monday—

Nothing further. Love to Sarah & the darlings, will write to them tomorrow. Ask M.B. for the book I lent her father—Your affect Husband Walter

1/180

[132]

Star Hotel Chiltern
19{20} June 1876

My dearest Mary

I got yours of Sunday evening this morning Tuesday. I am glad to hear that the little ones are recovering, but very grieved you do not sleep. Try & take a cold sponging before going to bed & a stroll if ever so little in the afternoon. Do think a little of your own health it will be dreadful if the chicks lose you & your constitution must break down if you do not get rest. You must do the best you can with the house. I fear you will not get the rent you asked—It cost close upon £1800 & there is £400 due on it—I think we might get £1500 for it & invest £1000 at 7 per cent for the chicks.

An extra room put up in the shed would not cost more than £30 & with new shed £40 to £50. I am glad Sarah is with you. I have done nothing further about a house. I would much rather you did not come for two or three months as it is a horridly dull place. Mr. Green's house is a wretched brick cottage. I have not yet seen the one 1 mile away as Mr Lloyd thought it would be nonsense to go there.

I had very bad nights at first but better now. I do not know what I should have done without the opossum rug—The food is excellent but my bedroom is small & cold at night. I get my bath—I have suffered from bad diarrhoea Saturday & Sunday but am better this morning. I cannot acc[oun]t for it unless the water. It is tank water from the roof & excellent but a change often affects me—I shall go & see Sergeant Ellis this morning about the house—Give my love to Sarah: I am surprised at M. never being over. Mr. A. could not have got my letter at the Yorick.[1] You had better send for Davidson & ask him to give estimate of the alterations his address is Mr Davidson Contractor Boundary Road Richmond—

The darlings are improving wonderfully in their letter writing. Ettie has a sore mouth Lilly says; this is a sign of bad cold altho' the lips are often cracked & the gums bleeding & sore after S[carlet] Fe[ver].

The house in the country is too far away, quite a mile off. I walked half way to it since beginning this letter, but find it won't do—

As long as Rohner remains here of course the people will go to him—I have just examined a lunatic—I am glad I shall get your letters in the morning instead of afternoon—

Kiss the darlings for Papa

Your affect. Husband
—Walter—

1/183

[1] The Yorick Club was founded by Frederick Haddon in 1868 for the purpose of 'bringing together literary men and those connected with literature, art or science'.

[133]

Star Hotel Chiltern
21 June 1876

My dear Mary

I get your letters every morning now—Rohner is certainly going Monday—I have not been so cheerful because I have not been so well. I cannot make out what has upset me unless it is my cold hole of a bedroom & my regret that you should have to come to such a place. I have written to answer the advertisement of Kiesser as it appears in yesterday's *Argus*[1]—the *climate* will be *better* & the house *may* be decent & we should not be so out of the world as this—You would be near the Cuthberts—I have been thinking it would be very unpleasant for me to be all alone here—In the event of your illness or the chicks or my own. So I will not hurriedly decide about this, especially as at present there is no place to bring you to—

You can get another bottle of Sanmora if you see it does Lily good or an injection of salt & water or lard rubbed around every night.

You had better see Russell about the house—I am not sanguine that it will let. See what rent he advises & what reserve we should put upon it—[2]

I am glad Sara is with you still—I have just been over the cottage where Mr Green clergyman lives—It is brick—Iron roof—two front rooms about 12 × 12 & two back nearly the same, snug little kitchen Col[onial] oven & stable—It seems a warmer house than Arrowsmith's —& being in the Town would be more convenient.

I see a fresh patient every day altho' there is no scarlatina—

I hope you have had better nights—No news of Sam.

Give Papa's dear love to my darlings & I hope they are not teasing & worrying dear Mama—

The mornings here are intensely cold. Rohner says he has 100 confinements a year & I see several women in that way—They are giving him a supper at this hotel tomorrow even[in]g. The people still run after him in the streets—

Nothing more

Your affectionate Husband
Walter.

1/184

1   Kiesser, a physician, advertised a 'Good opening in country district' in Carngham, near Ballarat, *Argus*, 20 June 1876, p. 1.

2   Thomas Russell, estate agent, Burwood Road, Hawthorn.

[134]

Chiltern
Thursday {22 June 1876}

My dear Mary

This is certainly a lovely winter climate every day since I arrived has been fine—mostly clear blue sky, sunshine with cool bracing wind from South. I am glad the darlings are well & able to go out & that Maria is kind. She must be good if they like her better than Nurse—

The landlady tells me servants are very difficult to be got here. Dr. Rohner's only has one—there is only one at the bank opposite who gets 10/– week. She gives hers 15/– I suppose M: would not care to leave Melbourne—I am sorry to hear M.B. is ill & in bed—I may be able to say something definite next week after Rohner is gone—

Everyone tells me that Mr Green's house will be the best for me as it is in the town & Arrowsmith's is nearly ½ mile off—Green's kitchen is best—it is a brick house & must be warmer in winter.

I am certainly not well completely off my food & a headache on rising—I fear that my bedroom is damp—I have nothing further to say except my love to the dear ones & yourself & Sara.

Ever your affect
Husband
Walter

1/185

[135]

Chiltern
Friday evening {23 June 1876}

My dear Marie

I was prevented from posting this in time today by one or two people. I got yours of this morn[in]g & again this afternoon.

I would have remained at Hawthorn if I had thought there was a chance of my getting any clubs even. I confess I feel the extreme discomfort of my horrid bedroom so cold & damp always—It gave me Rheumatism—I am a little better today thank God.

My great grief & sorrow is that you & the dear ones have to give up the comforts of our fine house & put up with cottage life—I spent an evening with Mr Green they keep no servant because they have no bedroom! for her! I wrote to Kiesser because I thought their house might be habitable at least—but we will say no more about it—I wish I had not hurried up here before the place was properly vacant altho' Rohner has *now* discontinued going out.

It is not nice being here all alone from the profession but perhaps I may get used to it—The dear chicks' letters improve each day. Ettie's & Lilly's are both very very good—I have more than paid all my expenses Railway & hotel since I came already. I have put an advertisement in the local paper for a month.

Dr. Richardson
Temporary Residence
Star Hotel
Chiltern

I will hire a saddle horse or a buggy as I require them at first—

Call & get the likenesses from Hibling & send me one, also get mine at *Hiblings* or *Botterills enlarged* for the children; which you like, I should also like *another* of yours taken for enlargement.

If you should decide on coming nearly everything will have to be packed away & stored—I don't know when you will get this perhaps Saturday night. God bless you.

We have gone up the hill of life together & now it seems we have to go down—

Your loving husband
Walter

1/202

[136]

Chiltern
Saturday afternoon {24 June 1876}

My own dear Mary

I missed the post yesterday but sent 2 letters last night wh' ought to have reached you Saturday night. I wrote to Slatterie asking for particulars of specifications. I intend to apply & if I do not get it I must make the best of this for a time—I was called out this morn[in]g 2 to 4, 5 miles for wh' I have been paid £4. buggy will cost me about 15/–

I told you I had more than covered all expenses since here— Mr. Green is very ill today & I have been busy with other patients of Rohner who declines to see people now—

I am much better thank God & have had a good lunch of cold fowl.

Your letters cheer me up & fill me with hope—

I never felt the cold so intensely as I did in my drive this mor[nin]g. In spite of my wraps.

Give my love to the dears & Sara & Sam.

Poor George Walker of Sam's Bank died 22d—sorry M.B. is ill. Kind regards to the Grahams, thank them for all their kindness—

Good bye dearest

Your ever loving
Walter

1/204

[137]

Chiltern
Sunday {25 June 1876}

My dearest Mary

I am anxious not to let a post pass without a line. I told you I had been called out Saturday morning 2 to 4. I got buggy at the hotel stables—I had a busy day owing to the parson being *as he is still* dangerously ill. I was called out 5 PM. 5 miles in another direction so that there

is a good prospect here of £700 a year to £1000—when Rohner is off—
I see there are two doctors at Corowa & three banks but that is a rising
place & this is a falling place—people are leaving this every day—no
mining—

Still there must always be some, & the farming district is good—

I am not able to say anything more definite about the house &
hope to know soon if we may get Green's, meanwhile my dear you must
be patient for it is best that you and the darlings should not hurry away
from comforts. If I get Green's house I shall only take it for a term as I
have a scheme in view of taking an old oddfellows hall brick like a
chapel about 60 feet long & 20 front & converting it into a dwelling
house it would make 6 rooms. It is just away from the town ¼ mile
opposite the P.O. & Telegraph office & I hear it can be had cheap to buy,
or to rent.

I am happy to say I am much better again & can enjoy my food—
Of course altho' I wrote to Slat[terie] I do not expect to get the lodge—
and indeed after yesterday's sample of work I hardly think it would be
wise. *This* appears a certainty the other only a *chance*.

I will move about Green's house as soon as he is out of danger—
Give Papa's dear love to our darlings he does not forget them.

I should not be at all astonished if some other doctor came here.
What a sad thing about Sam's friend Sawell absconded with £6000
& poor George Walker dead—The clerk of the bank here is very
astonished—

The nights are cold Ice ¼ inch thick on all the tanks & the streets
& fields covered with white frost—the days are warm the sun hot I can
hardly bear my flannels. I hope you are sleeping better my darling.

Is Sara still with you?

I sent my life premium to the Melb office yesterday—

Be sure & let me have a photo: also get dear Ettie taken again &
have Lilly enlarged.

I am really obliged to bank some money taken as fees—

We ought to be in better spirits—take the savings bank book to
the bank after July 1st I will send you a cheque—

Let me know if you want money which you must do if no one has
paid—

If you can come you & the chicks can run down to Sorrento in
February—

I have not been to church today—I have two bad cases of inflam[mation] of the lungs one case of Rohner's neglected, not seen for
5 days:

It is a great thing that our letters are sent off by the early train that leaves this 6.30 AM Monday—

The people seem to take to me very kindly & all are very civil & want me to drink with them.

Your loving husband
Walter

1/192, 1/249–52

[138]

Chiltern
Monday {26 June 1876}

My dear Mary

I am so sorry about your fingers—you must poultice them & take a few drops of Tinct of Arnica say 5 in water three times daily leaving off the Iron meantime.

I am so glad M. is good & kind & that the darlings take to her. You would see by my last that I was better & getting more used to the place. I think dear I will decide on remaining here as there is a good practice to be done. You must be patient however about the house as nothing can be done immediately. You had better see Russell & let him get a tenant if he can at what rent he thinks fair. I hope M. went to you Sunday & that you sleep better. Lovely weather here such days—but the mornings cold—ice $\frac{1}{2}$ inch thick—I get your letters regularly. I got your last on Sunday by favor of the Post Master just after I had posted mine to you—The people are all very pleasant & civil. Some are very pleased to get rid of Rohner.

The parson is not safe yet it has been a most troublesome case of obstruction of the bowels. I have a child with a broken arm at the elbow —Two cases of Inf[lammation] of the lungs & cases from the country every day. Everyone tells me I shall do well. The Roman Catholic priest stayed at the hotel one evening & told his people they would be lucky if they kept me—It will be very dull & quiet but there are no lodges & a pop[ulatio]n in the shire of *2000.*

Rohner is not going until tomorrow, he told me yesterday he should never come back—I met two doctors yesterday from the neighbour-hood, Yackandandah. They were very pleasant, they came to drink a last bottle with Rohner—

2PM Monday

Just got your two letters & one from Slatterie wh' I will reply to tomorrow—I have decided to remain here!—If I had got the other offer a month ago I would have remained & not broken up my house but I think *this* is too good a chance to throw up—I will decide about Mr Green's house *as soon as I can* that is *as soon as he recovers,* he is still in a critical state & I hope you will arrange with Russell to let the house.

Much love to my darlings—I will write them tomorrow

Your own husband
—Walter—

1/177

[139]

Chiltern
Tuesday morng {27 June 1876}

My dear Mary

I don't know that I have anything fresh to say. I thought it more prudent to accept *this* certain opening with all its discomforts, than to take the uncertain chance of Hawthorn with two paltry lodges & the expenses of horse necessary—The bank manager Cameron came into the hotel last night & we had a chat. He was queer, had been taking nobblers —I hear he always does so—We spoke about Sam he said he could get Sam Manager to Beechworth if S. liked it—Capital quarters, the manager there not a fixture. He seems to be quite independent, has been here 17 years or 20—Says there is plenty of money about Chiltern. I saw about Sawell & Walker last Friday—very sad.

Mr Green is a bit better today. Rohner not gone yet—

The weather has changed & rain has come at last. I hope your fingers are better.

2 PM. Post in & no letter—I fear the fingers are worse. See Dr. Graham about them—Nothing new.

Much love Yours ever W.L.R.

I will not expect you in future to write so often if all is well every 2d day will do, same from me unless I have something particular to say—

1/178

[140]

Chiltern
Wednesday 28 {June 1876}

My dear Mary

I have just been over a decent house, 6 rooms, kitchen, stable, fowl house, pigstye & fine garden with fruit trees—it is the best house in Chiltern. The owner wants £80 per year & to be taken for 4 years—the verandah is not floored—it is not papered—built about 18 mo[nths]— high & dry. Water tank—earth closets—small range oven & boiler wash-house & boiler built in. In fact it is a comfortable place. Of course it is a venture as if I were to die before 4 years! but after all it is only like paying 100 or 200 for the practice.

He refuses to do anything is quite careless about letting—He is the leading draper here—Of course if our house at Hawthorn can be let or sold—we might decide on this—& be really very comfortable & the possibility makes me quite happy—I should be inclined to sell Haw-thorn if we could, as the expense of repairs is constant; see Russell at once—

I have also seen another, 4 rooms & 2 smaller rooms for servant & me. Kitchen Col[onial] oven, not near so nice garden, indeed only orchard—He wants £75 & 3 years will floor verandah.

I am inclined to the first as we could be comfortable & the chicks have fine nursery & a room for me with splendid garden & orchard. I would keep a man to garden or at least a boy, he says I can get one for 3 or 4/– a week with keep—I wish you were here to decide but the distance is too great & the journey too weary but you can see what to do with Russell.

The freight on luggage is £4.4.6 per ton weight. Keep your eyes about for some man to pack, if we take this house we can manage nearly all our furniture.

No fresh patients: the parson a little better gastric fever—
Any news of Sam?
Tell him about Beechworth—I saw Brooke Smith passing thro' he sent me word by coach & I went to the Train & had a chat—He intro-duced me to some lady of a squatter great swell in these parts. She said *w*e would [be] quite an acquisition—have just been engaged to a con-finement—Rohner gone at last today.

Love to darlings same to you from Your

Affect Husband
Walter.

Glad your fingers are better.

1/188

[141]

Star Hotel Chiltern
28 June 1876

My dear Mary

I have made an offer to Mr. Hancock to pay the first year's rent in advance provided he floor the verandah. Mr Lloyd thinks this most liberal on my part & that his demand about 4 years lease is excessive. Brooke Smith has just sent a telegram saying he has fallen from his horse & requesting me to go to Wangaratta to see him this evening— I do hope we may get the house: I told you I think it was brick with verandah all round—6 fair sized rooms good height—not papered, walls soiled, detached kitchen—& washhouse, bath shed with shower bath. Water tank—large garden, fruit kitchen & flower—We can be quite happy & comfortable if we get it. I will send you the dimensions of the rooms if I get a favorable answer which he has promised today.

I am afraid my darling that the journey would knock you up. It is dreadful 8 hours—Still I leave it to yourself—

I wish you would go & see Miss Armstrong about your state generally—I will write to her by this post.[1] It would give me great comfort—follow her advice. I am very anxious about you—She lives in Russell St near Dr Campbell's & next [to] the detective office—

don't forget about the photos

Was called out again last evening 5 miles—

Mr Green's case has gone on to Fever & Infl[ammation] of the liver—

I am glad M. is so kind to the darlings—

Fine day but foggy morning.

My appetite is good & I enjoy the good fare. Wild fowl, Turkeys, Fowls, Eggs & good butter—Cold bath every morning—

I have written to Miss Armstrong & have asked her to go & take a cup of tea with you & prescribe for you.

Kind love to Mary B. Hope she is better—

Much love to Ettie & Lilly. Papa will jump them & give them swings every day when they come to their new home,

Your affect Husband
Walter

1/186

¹ Miss Armstrong was a well-known Melbourne medium—part of the Richardsons' earlier spiritualist circle.

[142]

Chiltern
30 June {1876}

My dear Mary

I have not seen Mr. Hancock since & he has made no approval of my offer. I was out again last evening 5 miles, up all night with a confinement that is not off yet, & out this forenoon *10 miles* to see a patient of Dr. Peele's of Corowa that he has neglected—So that I cannot complain of want of success at starting—If Hancock accepts I will telegraph at once—Cameron the bank Manager wishes me to take McLeery's £75 per an[num] 3 years—4 decent rooms & 2 small ones with detached kitchen orchard—not anything so nice as Hancock's.

I think I shall be obliged to accept his conditions 4 years—but will wait until you say what you think or come up to see it—Thank God I am keeping well—

I hope Miss A. will go & see you.

Love to Sara & 100 kisses to each of the pets from

Your afft Husband
Walter

It was quite impossible to go & see Brooke as I had the confinement on hand & the journey 5 miles into country—

1/187

[143]

Chiltern
Sunday {2 July 1876}

My dear Mary

I was too busy to write Saturday, so I telegraphed to you—Mr.
Lloyd tells me that he has arranged with Hancock about the house &
that I may consider it as settled, that I am to have it for 2 years £80. per
an[num]. Rent of year paid in advance. I am sure you will be pleased
with it when you see *the choice I had*—I did not give you all the details—
It is brick. 6 rooms & kitchen & washhouse with built in boiler splendid
cellar where you can sit in the very hot days—stable 2 pig styes—fine
garden & orchard full of fruit trees. Of course the rooms are not as large
as ours—the house is high & dry. I am told there are not many mosquitoes—I certainly have seen none.

I hope you may succeed in letting our house—Ham is certainly
the best. I am afraid there will be a difficulty, perhaps Ham might get a
purchaser more readily than a tenant.

I am sorry about Jos. Graham the medicine is evidently losing its
effect[1] but I had a letter from Miss Armstrong & she promised me to see
you so like a good creature be entirely guided by her & tell me what she
says—

I did not say much about your coming here because the journey is
so terrific. The house is one story—No gas—no coals. The picture rods
ought I think to be left—I am so sorry you don't feel well but I shall be
much easier if I know Miss A. has charge of you.

This is a splendid winter climate—the change will I am confident
do you & the darlings much good & by & bye I shall have a trap of my
own. The Coach Co treat me very well I only pay 7/6 for a horse &
buggy each trip—This is owing to Brooke Smith speaking to them—

I never had my clothes off for two nights & I have had a 10 mile
journey for the last 4 days—I have been paid over £15 & have booked
over £30 since I arrived & Rohner has only been away this week—

We can enjoy ourselves very well here & you & the chicks can run
to Melb in the summer.

We can ask friends to come & stay & we will I am sure save money.

Should you really come bring a box or two—I can store them at
the hotel & my Thermometer & more books—

I am sure Graham will be glad to hear of my good luck—If I [had]
not popped in here quick as I did there would have been others &

indeed I am not sure there may not [be] another settling—Everyone is pleasant & civil & the place is no doubt healthy—Do not forget to tell Sam what Cameron said about Beechworth as it would be pleasant for you—Let Sam write to me about it if he cares for it & I will shew the letter to Cameron—Lots of love & kisses to my darlings.

There is a nice stable for the pony & lots of pear & apple trees, plenty of fruit & splendid grapes

oranges 1/6 per doz.

Your loving husband
—Walter—

1/190, 1/191

¹ Crossed out material here: 'I enclose a prescription for you, Rawle can I think make it up. It is for 12 powders—divide each one into two equal parts and take one part daily in sugar to taste'.

[144]

Chiltern
Monday {3 July 1876}

My dear Mary

I enclose open cheque for £5.0.0 which Mr Rawle or Smith will cash for you. I hope you are better & that Miss A. has seen you. Mrs Bresnan lives next house to the Terminus Hotel at the back—I also enclose Bonwicks—

I have closed with Hancock about the house—2 years rent in advance with the option of 2 years after wood [*sic*] at a valuation—These were the best terms I could make & it is like paying Rohner for the practice. I am going over the place again tomorrow & will pay him deposit of £10. on account.

I am sure the change will do all of you good—So far I have done very well. I hope it may continue—Kind love to Sara & lots of kisses for my darlings—I will get possession of the house in about 3 weeks.

See Ham about our house & offer it for sale £1500 would satisfy me—it cost £1800—

I will enclose cheque for building society tomorrow.

I hope M. will come with you for there are none to be had here—You may begin to pack up so as to have the things ready for

Waddingham. You had better see if Slatterie knows a decent man to pack the furniture in cases—as Effey cannot be had—

Your own Husband
Walter

1/181

[145]

Chiltern
Tuesday evening {4 July 1876}

My dear Marie
I paid Mr H. £10. on acc[oun]t of the house & went over it with him today—
1) The best room is 13 feet 3 inches by 14 feet.
The fireplace comes out of the 13 feet width & is 57 inches long by 23 inches—
2) The next best room is 14 feet 1 or 2 inches by 11 feet, 6 inches.
3) The next best a bedroom is 13 feet 3—by 12 feet 9 inches.
The other three are nearly the same or a little smaller.
The passage right thro' is 38 feet 6 inches long by 46 inches wide.
There are outside venetians which he has consented to let stand on condition that I took the following at my own prices—a book case in a corner of the sitting room painted deal glass doors £3.10. he declares this cost him this for labor alone—Two curtain poles 25/- fireguard 15/- Mangle £4.0.0—clothes horse 12/6—a capital one—Hencoop 5/- 2 pig troughs 10/- & about 40 fowls at 1/3 each amounting to some 14 pounds then there is a quantity of wood to be taken & measured at 15/- a cord some 20 or 30 pounds worth he says—
He was quite independent & I could not do better—
He is to floor the verandah.
I am afraid your wardrobe will not go into the best bedroom. I think I *would sell the large dining room bookcase*—I hope you will put the house for sale into Ham's hands reserve £1650—as if it remains empty it will not improve—& there is the £10. 5. per month going on.
I enclose cheque for amount which must be paid to Mr. Bradley at the office next door to the Athenaeum reading room Collins St— Thursday next before 3. PM.

I hope you got my cheque for £5. safely. I think I will write to those owing asking them to settle with you—You had better write to Mr Box or send Maria they live in Pakington St Kew—It will be a pity to lose £25.0.0—You had better sell or kill off your fowls as we shall have plenty here—I will send you the dimensions of the other bedrooms if you need them.

Don't forget the garden tools—1 spade 1 fork 1 rake—

I think you had better get the front garden done up by Ludlow.

I enclose 3 accounts—You can send them by post—

He will give possession in about 3 weeks but it will take you more time to arrange & get packed—I intend to have one bedroom white washed—Give the dear chicks my love their letters are splendid & they are improving each time.

Your loving husband
Walter

1/189

[146]

Chiltern
Wednesday eveng {5 July 1876}

My dear Mary

Mr H. has given orders to have the verandah floored—also he leaves the venetian blinds which are *outside* the principal windows which are French casements. I do not think *these* will require blinds, with curtains inside. There are no blinds up now—no rollers & as these are always a bother I think you might dispense with them *for the present* as the verandah is wide & protects the windows from all but the west or setting sun. I think there are two bedroom windows without venetians facing the south—but I will let you know this particularly tomorrow—

Mrs. Lloyd & Mrs Peel the landlady strongly urge you bringing your servant if she is at all good—you cannot get supplied here except with some slipshod dollop at 10/– a week who won't do the washing—I should recommend your bringing M. there is a nice detached kitchen brick—better than ours, a washhouse with built in boiler & chimney,—a splendid cellar—You will perceive that the rooms are small but there are six—

I hope you will let Ham get rid of the house or try to for it will *take some months*.

The furniture must all be packed in cases & my name painted on each case or well labelled—You can fill the drawers & have them packed & sent first. Also the carpets—I hope the weather will be fine or else it will be damaged—Get some one in to help you—I am glad you are better and sorry that my darling eldest has got a sore finger. I have had a rest today & I am not sorry for it—The people are all very pleased to hear that you are coming—Archdeacon Tucker of Wangaratta came today & made quite a fuss with me. I hope some more people have paid —I said the best room is 14 feet × 13.3—& the fireplace is 23 inches out by 57 inches wide projecting out on the 14 feet side of the room—

The 2d best is 14 feet 1 or 2 inches by $11\frac{1}{2}$ feet & the fireplace is on the 14 foot side—fireplace in every room but one—the two passage doors are about same width 46 inches so you can see if the piano can get in, I think so—I expect the move will cost £100—The station master thinks Permewan & Co will do it as they have Lorries & men who can go to Hawthorn & load at Spencer St. Your loving Husband

Walter

I don't think you can get the full length of me enlarged it was done at Manchester & is not so good as Botterells or Hiblings—Love to Sara, Mary & Mrs Graham. The house is on the outskirts of Chiltern about $\frac{1}{4}$ mile from the Town Hall & my hotel.

1/198

[147]

Chiltern
Thursday evening {6 July 1876}

My dear Marie

I am sorry to hear about dear Lilly—She must have *more* salt sprinkled over her food—Injections—greasing her at night; if these things do not do I will give her some Iron when you join me. The Season is splendid I am always hungry—I have been very slack the last two days —What a sad affair about Sam. Surely there must have been something very remiss when they allowed defalcations of £6000 to exist without discovery—I should think Styles & Millidge would catch it hot—

There are two french casement windows & one door on the front of the house—Three ditto on the east side—one window & one door west & two windows & one door south—I shall go over the house more particularly by & by & tell you all details—

The inhabitants are endeavouring to reorganize a mine only partly worked but which by bad management fell thro'—They are very sanguine of its paying well & it will employ some 150 men—My patients are all well—Every one says I have got the best house in the district & I shall advertise when we get into it—You had better kill off or sell your fowls as we shall have lots when you come—Surely the gas bill was not 16/– The butter here is very bad—Milk good—all things I have bought are same price as Melbourne—

I don't think you will get a tenant or anyone to give £1600 we shall I fear have it on our hands—I hope some more acc[oun]ts will come in for you—They describe the summer as something awful.

I hope you will induce Maria to come as there are no decent servants here—

I am engaged for 3 confinements.

Rohner's sale takes place on the 18th. I am told there will be great bargains—Can you tell me anything to buy?

They are going to bid for the house for the parson—

Lovely days—I get my bath every morning—I shall be glad to have you again as my nights are very broken, noises up to 12 & $\frac{1}{2}$ past & servants about at $\frac{1}{2}$ past 6—

Love to the dears—
& same to yourself
from your fond Husband
Walter

1/199

[148]

Chiltern
Friday evening {7 July 1876}

My darling Marie
I am so sorry to find by your Wednesday's letter that you were in very low spirits. The rooms are certainly smaller than ours but they are better than anyone's in this place, parsons or doctors. If you only knew

the choice I had or the holes I had offered to me at first you would not wonder at *my* being in bad spirits or at my wanting to try elsewhere & writing about Carngham.

All the windows have venetian blinds some outside some in—no rollers to any—I do not think you need blinds with venetians—the verandah is 6½ feet wide—*The best* sitting room has 2 windows with good curtain poles up—& fireplace & venetians.

The 2d best sitting room has one window & venetians & one glass door ½ window leading out to the yard—

Bedroom No. 1 has one window—is 13 feet 3, by 10 ft 9. Fireplace & venetians—

Bedroom No. 2 has window with venetians, fireplace & is 12 ft by 13 ft—

Bedroom No. 3 has inside venet[ian]s is 10 ft 8 by—10.9.

Bedroom No. 4 has no fireplace, window with inside venetians & is 10 ft. 8 by 11.3. I am sure I hardly know what to advise about the furniture. We can get most of the things in. You must dispose of the large bookcase & drawing room glass *certainly,* the wardrobe might stand in one of the bedrooms perhaps in the nursery or spare bedroom—for No 1. would do for us, No 2. for the children, No 4 for servants & No 3. for the wardrobe—I should have to see my patients either in the drawing or dining room whichever was disengaged. Many would go to Lloyds & send for me there—

It is no use fretting over sacrificing the things—they are not worth more than they will bring & Steinfield will do the fairest—

There are no furniture shops here—the cornices would be out of place in a cottage or if they come the poles will do for some other rooms —It was a choice with me to take the few things or have the venetian blinds taken down—

I am afraid you won't get the house off—Times are so bad in Melbourne. It is very unfortunate that we had to break up our home but it was folly to build the house & now I am punished for it—

I am certain there is a practice here that will keep us from want & our wants are not [many]

[text missing]

thus [sketch] fireplace does not project

I think this will do for the two lower rooms but it does seem a pity to get good carpets for such a den—Mine will only be dirtied by the boots.

Front windows for poles $43\frac{1}{2}$ inches from extreme wood to wood.
Back one 54 inches for pole—
windows down stairs
two front & one back
2 front blinds—32 inches wide
                    49—long
Back window— 52— ″
                    41— ″ wide
Carpet of big room [sketch]
fire place comes out 30 inches
& the cut out of carpet is 60 inches

My room is 12 feet by $11\frac{1}{2}$
A cut out for fender & hearthrug of 43 inches long & 18 to
20 inches.

[text missing]

walls. I hope Sara will have a pleasant voyage. The ship she is going
in is a very fine one altho' very old. Am sorry I did not get yours soon
enough to send prescription for podop. pills—
   I fear if your coming depends on your *letting* the house that I will
have to live alone a long time—However I don't grumble I am earning
money & keep well—
   Kiss the darlings for Papa & accept love from

Your loving husband
Walter

1/193, 1/200

[149]

{7 July 1876}

My darling Pets
   Bring Maria with you—I am glad you like her and that she is good
to you—The railway is near our new house and the summer house is
splendid—

Have you written to Annie Cuthbert[1] you did not say what old Nurse said in her letter.

Your affect Papa.

1/222

---

[1]   The Cuthberts' daughter.

[150]

Chiltern
Saturday evening {8 July 1876}

My dearest Marie—

I have been rather busy again today & had not time to go up to the house to see if the large bookcase would fit into the parlor. The wardrobe as I said can stand in the spare bedroom & I should think it would take to pieces. I sent you particulars of windows in my last—There is plenty of room in the garden & *a summer house*—fine large yard behind. I should think there is about twice as much land as we have at Hawthorn—The verandah will be a splendid place for them as it extends around the front & one side of the house. The station master now advises to pack all the furniture possible *without* cases. 98/6 a ton—Tables & chairs packed with Straw he says will come *very well.* We *cannot* engage trucks but the department will fill as many trucks as our furniture will require for Chiltern & it will never be disturbed—Piano will require case—

Dear Mrs. Cuthbert perhaps she will ask you some other time! Give my last love to Sara—You will be lonely indeed—

I hope you are better. I am very hearty & feel the benefit of this splendid winter climate.

I like your photo tho' *not* as well as Botterells—

The station master is leaving & a married man with family coming —I have not heard of Brooke—

Give lots of love & kisses to papa's darlings. The summer house is large enough for tea parties & we will have birthday parties there with a table—I have got my eye *on a swing* that I think will be for sale—They can have their own gardens—

I have nothing more to say. Good bye.

God bless you says
Your affect Husband
—Walter—

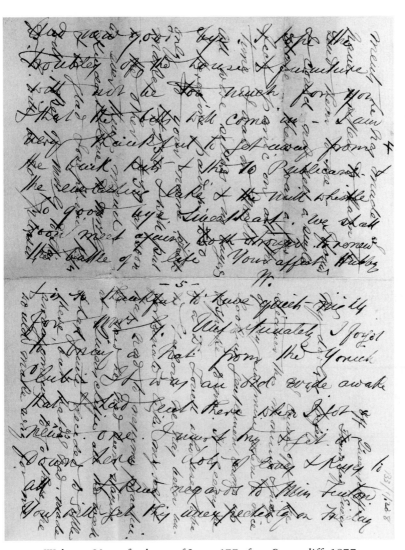

Walter to Mary, final page of Letter 177, from Queenscliff, 1877

Dr Williams's house at Queenscliff, now 26 Mercer Street,
where the Richardsons lived from 1877 to 1878
(courtesy Queenscliff Historical Society)

Sunday Even[in]g

I am afraid Russell & Ham will run up long bills for advertising. I don't think anything would do so well as a *notice board* 'To let'. Don't let the chicks eat any *colored lollies* I see by today's *Argus* that an analysis gives lead & other poisons in them—

1/203

[151]

Chiltern
Tuesday evening {11 July 1876}

My dear Marie

This is a sketch of the 2d best sitting room [sketch]

Mr. Hancock says he will be out about this day fortnight—I should take the house out of Ham's hands if he does not find a purchaser in 10 days—There are no buyers for things here—I am sorry to say many people are leaving—as they have failed to reorganize a great mine that they were sanguine of doing when I came here—I still think it would be wise to sell the *pier glass* & the *sideboard* & the drawing room *Chiffonier* & the large *book case*—There is an old dresser in the kitchen that I don't suppose he will take but it is not so good as ours & you had better leave yours if the people take the house & we can get an additional one put up—there are tables but of course he will take them—There is no room to store furniture in the cellar—I hope you will *not* think of storing things in Melbourne—

The repairs to the house will be a constant worry & any agent will expend what he likes without our control, being absent. Best to get rid of things. It is unfortunate that times are so dull in Melbourne but it cannot be helped—

I hope you had a pleasant day to see Sara off.

Magnificent weather here.

Strange about poor Mrs. Bright. She has her troubles. We are not the only ones—

It is very annoying the people do not pay you—It is very rude of the Boxes after my sending in my acc[oun]t twice—

Mr Uttier

Mrs Shaw

Mr Jordan

Mr. Box

W. Bonwick

Mrs Rutherford

Mrs Bresnan

If you do not write you will have to leave them—I hope you are better. I conclude you are as you say nothing of yourself.

With much love

Your loving husband

—Walter—

1/194

[152]

Star Hotel Chiltern
14 July 187{6}

My dear Marie

 I fear I did make the powders rather strong but I hope they brought away the worms, you did not say—They ought to have been given before breakfast *not* overnight. You did not say how you were yourself—Agnes wrote a kind sensible letter. She has had experience about moving—our house is not 700 yards from the railway station & I can get a man & a dray to load & get them over—The drawing room is 13 feet 4—by 14 feet 1. with the fireplace [sketch] in the 13 feet length. Two french casement doors or windows & one entrance door.

 I find I can get a man to whitewash & make the carpets he is a mattrass maker—& very handy

 he will hang the glasses & pictures—

 I suppose they will leave the dirty little dresser in the kitchen but the tables are good & will be taken away as I declined them at 30/–

 If Miss A did not go into house I would not give much for her medicine—however you may try.

 She only uses simples—

 I will look after the lamps at Rohner's sale 18th of this month & any cheap things I will pick up—

 I have not been so busy this week—It comes in rushes—

 I received the enclosed from the parson—The new station master is married man one little boy nice play fellow for our [*sic*]—about 2 years old & she is a very nice ladylike little woman has engaged me to attend her—

The bank manager's wife is pretty & stylish & her sister also.

I am rather uneasy about the house not letting—It will have to be shut up & the keys left with Russell—I hope the windows won't be broken—the gates must be fastened securely the front one with a chain —I hope Davidson has been. If not let me know & I will write him letter.

I am writing to Ellis about the scandalous work—our Ball[ara]t house never came down about our ears altho' we lived in it for 4 years after being built—

Much love to the chicks & yourself & The Grahams.

from your affect
husband
Walter

Will write again Sunday night.

1/196

[153]

Star Hotel Chiltern
Sunday {16 July} 187{6}

My dear Marie

I write according to promise altho' I have nothing to say—Have been rather idle the last few days—Have mislaid your last letter & so forget what you said—Shall postpone writing this until I get yours tomorrow morning—

I want you to call at the tobacconist corner of Collins & Swanston St, by the pillar box & ask for a meershaum pipe I left there to be mended before I came away—It will be a shilling or two.

Monday morning

Just received yours of Friday night—So glad the dear ones are well. You say nothing of yourself.

I have been better ever since—

You must not forget the filters—

I do not know what to do about Box—They have behaved scandalously & I have no redress but summoning them which I cannot do as I am away—Could you not give Russell the accounts to collect—he would send his boy—I write to Davidson by this post—

There will be no packing at the station if we have enough—the things will be put into one or two waggons for Chiltern by themselves—

I am afraid the house will not be let—Take it out of Ham's hands—put up a board & leave it entirely with Russell—ask him his terms for the agency—You will have to take £120 & the tenant pay the rates—There will be three or four nice families for you—Cameron the Bank—Martins clerk of the court—the parson's, the station master's—

I went to the Scots Church yesterday morning good attendance of well dressed people—

With much love

Your affect Husband
Walter

Take the pass book to the Savings bank & get it made up & let me know amount.

My dear Ettie and Lilly
Your letters are better each time—I know one little girl and one little boy to come to a party in the Summer house. We will not wait for the birthday but will have it as soon as we get settled—We will have plenty of fowls & eggs here—and I think you will be happier.

Your affect Papa

1/179

[154]

Chiltern
Tuesday evening {18 July 1876}

My dear Marie
I was so glad to get your telegram that the H[ouse] was let. Hancock has promised to turn out early next week so as to let the white washing be done on Monday. I have told him I will not *want the curtain poles*

the cases can lie in the goods sheds if we are not ready for them by Wednesday or if they come earlier.

Wednesday morn[in]g.

Just got yours—you have done well. You may send the things up as early as you like; the station master says they may come on the day after or they may *be a week*. So send them off as soon as you can. Get a load off on *Saturday if possible*. Carpets & some beds—The dray man who is constantly receiving & carting all sorts of things says they come much better loose & unpacked & if he was sending a piano he says he would send it *unpacked*. I enclose cheque for £5.0.0.

Rohner's sale came off & the things realised well. A good crowd of farmers in from the country the worst things sold best. I only bought one lamp—I have written to M. Bayles; her father has a book of mine—You had better accept Mrs Graham's invitation & stay there until Saturday or till I telegraph you things are a bit in [order].

If you can forward some things on Saturday I will most likely get them Wednesday & can begin. If you put them off till Tuesday or Wednesday we shan't have them that week—You can stay at the Hotel with the chicks—but if I could put up the servant a bed she could come up first & help me.

You may bring all you can for I see things sell well here. Love to the dear ones we shall soon meet now—I count the days

Your loving Husband.
Walter

1/197

[155]

Chiltern
Wednesday {19 July 1876}

My dear Mary

You have done splendidly to let the house & to dispose of the furniture so well—All I say is send up some as fast as you can without waiting for the whole—If I could have 2 or 3 beds & some carpeting early in the week—as the delay on the road may be great—I will have all the chimneys swept & the place ready by Wednesday or Thursday I hope but you had better stay at the Grahams & send M[ary] on 2d class to help me—as soon as you leave the house. You must indeed be tired with no one to help you amid all your excitement—I told you that the goods would be safe & could stand for 2 or 3 days in the goods shed if we had not the rooms ready—I do not know what to do about Box. Can you not get Russell to try?—All have paid except Box—Jordon—Uttier—Mrs Shaw —Mrs Bresnan

I shall be so glad to have you for my rest is sadly broken here— noises to $\frac{1}{2}$ past 12 & begin again 6.30 or at daylight, small damp bedroom—

I have not been quite so busy since—There appears to have been an unusual rush of sickness at first.

What shall we do about the oil cloth for the passage? I will price it tomorrow.

There are two large drapers & 2 small. Rohner's cottage—with 2 acres of land sold for £195—

We have never lived in such a hovel—Don't trouble about writing again until you send off something. I will send another cheque Saturday.

I suppose Ham's terms are 5 per cent—He had better receive rent & pay same into my credit at City Bank quarterly—forwarding me bank slip deposit receipt.

I hope there are no children & that they will take care of the house —explain the venetian blinds—Of course I would take the additions at end of lease & allow for them if done by Davidson.

Your affect Husband
Walter

1/201

[156]

Star Hotel Chiltern
Sunday {23 July} 187{6}

Dear Marie
I am sorry you sold your wardrobe for I am sure you will miss it— There is no oil cloth to be had here suitable therefore order piece 38 feet long by 45 inches wide—Could it be sent to Permewans & Hunt to be forwarded with the rest addressed to me—I send blank cheque for it & another £10 for you.

Hancock gives me possession on Monday & I have got man to whitewash & sweep all the chimneys—You must tell me dear positively the day you mean to arrive. There is only one room in the hotel that you & the chicks can occupy only one double bed—Don't you think it would be better to stay at Graham's until Friday afternoon? You will find the Saloon carriage most comfortable—there is a good hotel at Seymour 'Gills Hotel' if you like to break the journey & come on Saturday morning you will do it more comfortably. 8 hours is long & you do not get in here until 10.15.

Telegraph to me when you start. If you write Tuesday night I will get it Thursday morning—Mrs Cuthbert's visit must have tried you sadly amid all your packing; still she is a good friend & we will have a room for her here—

How I long to see you all once more—

I shall have 3 men to unpack the things as soon as ever they arrive —I hope the weather will keep fine.

Love to the darlings & yourself from
Your loving husband

1/195

[157]

Chiltern
Tuesday evening {25 July 1876}

My dear Marie

I expect another letter but not getting it I will have the room ready Thursday night & will meet you—with a man to take your packages into the house which is close by & what you need for the night to the hotel—There will be a comfortable bed & parlour for you & the chicks & I will have tea ready at $\frac{1}{2}$ past 10—

I hope you thought of the wine & the thermometer outside my window—

You will not forget to get a 1d timetable at the station Spencer St as it will show you all the stations along the line—Tea & Coffee at Seymour & Benalla—Ladies rooms at both places, stoppages 15 minutes at each.

You must indeed have had a trying time. Surely you got a man to pack—Telegraph to me about the luggage & yourself Thursday from Spencer St before you start—

Give my kindest regards to Dr. & Mrs G: & thanks for all their kindness—You will want wraps & possum rug for the nights here are bitterly & intensely cold—Wrap the chicks up well—They can sleep in the saloon carriage.

'The Springs' is the station before Chiltern—about ½ an hour—I have got a man in today sweeping chimneys & whitewashing 3 rooms— another one cleaning out the out houses & tomorrow to scrub out the house—I will keep the luggage untouched until you arrive—I will get them into the yard

Good bye
& God bless you
Your affect husband
Walter

1/206

[158]

Chiltern
Sunday {28 January 1877}

Dear Marie

As I expect a letter from you by tomorrow's midday post I begin this today so as to be able to post it tomorrow, Monday afternoon. Friday & Saturday were delightfully *cool* with South wind—Ida stayed with me till Saturday & went home by afternoon train—She is a dear good girl —I saw that she was so lonely sitting reading by herself when I was out that I thought she would be better among her sisters. She took the chickens, plums, honey & three books I gave her for herself, Gertrude & Jeannie—I had a telegram from Sam asking for the prescription I gave Leila last Xmas at Hawthorn so I suppose she is worse & dangerously ill.

Mrs. Porch was taken ill early this morning & I went 10. AM baby born about 3, nice easy time all well, & *all* much pleased. They are really nice people what a fool Rohner must have been to have alienated them. They said if I had not been here they would have sent to Wangaratta— I wish to God there were more people like them—Mary has done very well so far—

Monday morning. Just got yours. Am so glad you got there safely & well. We have had no change here yet. There is a strong North wind today with clouds but it will all blow away—I got the papers, does Dr. G. want them back? Am sorry about poor Mary. Do not feel very well myself today.

Not a soul coming near the house—Give my kind love to Mrs Graham & thank her for being so thoughtful as to write me the letter which I got Saturday morning; also thank Dr. G. for the papers.

Give Papa's fond love to Ada & Florence & I hope they are good & obedient—I hope to have another letter before you leave for Sorrento.

3 PM We have had a tremendous Storm of wind from all quarters with great heat but no rain.

Your affect Husband
W.L.R.

1/205

[159]

Chiltern
Wednesday {31 January 1877}

Dear Marie

I got your two letters and am glad you are all enjoying yourselves & that the weather is cool & pleasant. Of course I have nothing to write about so you must not expect many letters—There are no patients & I am doing nothing & the practice has gone. It is not a very pleasant look out for the future, so I advise you to value your money as it is likely to be scarce—Sam wrote asking me to telegraph again about the baby—I wrote.

Hancock's eldest son died of Diphtheria at Brighton a few days since & I hear that he has brought all the children back to Chiltern. Mary is doing very well indeed. She does everything as I like it. She had a friend in on Monday all day, helping her with the wash—it was a very heavy one for she was at it again on Tuesday.

The weather this week has been trying Ther 90 to 100. I am glad you are out of it—

Kind love to the Grahams & 100 kisses to the *little ones*—I hope they are good.

They are going to alter the trains next month. They are to start an hour earlier from each end & to do the journey in one hour less—

One patient in yesterday & two today.

[219]

3 PM. Just got yours of Tuesday with dear Ettie's, so good—We have had a terrific dust storm this afternoon—The town could not be seen from our house but only a drop or two of rain.

I think you will enjoy Queenscliffe better than Ball[ara]t & it will save the fares—

Glad you are getting bargains. I am better today but very little sleep—I hope you sleep well.

Your attached husband
W.L.R.

I will return the papers.

1/209

[160]

Chiltern
Friday evening {2 February 1877}

My dear Marie

I am so glad you are all enjoying yourselves, how fortunate to have a wealthy friend in Mrs Graham.

I hope none of the rest of you have been attacked, I have been so myself but I put it down to a plum pie as they were not ripe but acid. Sam has not written again about Leila so I fear she is worse. You are quite right to pick up bargains as you cannot get any here. I got a letter from Arthur Green today. A married man named Rhodda is appointed as clergyman. The new parsonage is nearly finished & the fencing of the church is really begun.

Mary is still doing excellently. She has cleaned out every room since you left, & my dinners are excellent—

No news of any kind at all. The Revd Ewing[1] lectures here on this day week & I have offered him a bed again—No rain & all are now getting anxious as the Barrambogie[2] supply is to be turned off except at certain times. Thank dear Lilly for her pretty letter I hope she is better & that dear Ettie will come back with a rosy cheek. The weather is bearable & still no sickness & no patients. Are you going to have a look at the house? if you do & see Mr Tully you might ask him if he is willing in the event of a purchaser coming forward to give up his tenancy before the full term or not—Of course I have no idea that Russell would find one, but he might—I told him to offer the house at £1700. Kind regards to all & love to the darlings with same from your attached

W.

Wain has sent in milk bill 8/3. I suppose it is correct.

1/214

[1] The Reverend R. K. Ewing of Beechworth. Walter chaired his lecture on the poets Moore and Campbell.

[2] A creek in Chiltern; name used by Henry Handel Richardson for Chiltern in *The Fortunes of Richard Mahony*.

[161]

Saturday {3 February 1877}

Dr. Marie

I received the enclosed this morning. Poor Jack has like ourselves been unfortunate. His Russian bonds have gone down fearfully. He evidently enjoys our letters. I will write again this mail. The weather is getting pleasanter & such cold nights. Lespinasse Martin has retired on his pension—The people are petioning to get up a new bank—I think they will succeed as the farmers declare New S Wales is not liberal enough to them. The Bishop's visit is postponed until after the 28th, evidently done by the Archdeacon because you are not here.[1] A few more patients since—I had to go to the Springs & to Gooramadda & was engaged today for a confinement—Things are however awfully dull.

Mary is still all that could be desired. Everything she cooks is excellent & she is always scrubbing & cleaning. Thank Dr. G. for his papers I enjoy them. Love to all, kisses to my darlings same to yourself from your attached Husband

W.

1/216

[1] Bishop Moorhouse visited Chiltern on 3 May 1877 to consecrate the church.

[162]

Chiltern
Wednesday evening {7 February 1877}

Dear Marie

I suppose you will be comfortably settled by the sea when this reaches you.

I think the weather here this week is the most trying we have yet had, there is no wind and the heat is so continuous, so persistently dry, there are great outcries about water & the Barnawartha people are getting alarmed & declare it will have to be carted: there is still 10 feet in our tank—

I have no news to write about. I saw Arthur Green passing homeward on Monday: he knew nothing about his family—Am glad you & chicks are well, how sad about poor Josephine—Thank Mrs Graham very much for the book.

I have heard nothing from Sam—I am surprised at his not writing—

Mary is still doing well. I think she is the best servant we have had. She is certainly the most tidy: & every meal is well served her pastry & puddings are excellent.

The Revd. Ewing lectures on Friday Evening—

There is still no sickness—

Kind regards to Dr. & Mrs G & love to the chicks.

Your affect Husband
W.

1/213

[163]

Chiltern
Monday {12 February 1877}

My dearest Marie

I was glad to get yours of Thursday on which day I also wrote to you. We have it awfully hot here also & so continuous a month of it & no change & no rain. The country is being ruined & all will suffer, hundreds of cattle are driven thro' Chiltern to go to the Murray—Yet no sickness—

Ewing came on Friday with 3 ladies. We had the Star Theatre nearly full & only got £8.15 total—I took the chair—I made them come home as the ladies seemed much afraid of driving back in the dark. Mary got hot coffee & eggs & they turned in about $\frac{1}{2}$ past 12; off next morning by $\frac{1}{2}$ past 5—

Mary is all that could be wished & I think she is the best servant we have ever had. She is doing the washing better. Lloyd took tea with me last evening Sunday—I do not like your lined paper. Go to Purtons. I am sure he will serve you better. I detest common paper & envelopes. You can see all kinds there & get them cheaper than any other shop it is nearly opposite McEwen's Ironmongery—

The tank is getting low & dirty—We shall have no rain worth speaking of until probably April. I am glad the darlings are happy & thriving & without lessons—Sam has never written a line. Have you heard if Leila is dead!—

I see that Wanliss family has had scarlet fever at Loutit Bay.

Hyndman was acquitted. I suppose you get the *Argus*.

I send an *Age* with this—

I sleep in the Nursery as I can have the window open all night—I am sorry to say there is still no sickness or patients. I go in for tea—three times a day—I find that is best. Business throughout Chiltern is frightfully bad & every one admits the place is done & will never recover.

No sign of Mr. Rhodda.

A tremendous storm appears to have been raging all round us but we have not had a drop—Kind love to all & the darlings from

Your attached Husband
W.L.R.

1/215

[164]

My dear little loves

Papa has not been well or he would have answered your nice letters sooner.

I am so glad you are happy and like the Sea. I wish we could live near the Sea. Perhaps Mamma may like Queenscliffe and we might move there—Mary is very good.

The bees are still hard at work and the chickens are all getting big—I sleep in the Nursery and last week three ladies slept in one room and a gentleman slept in yours, and they went away in the morning while I was asleep.

Your fond Papa
with much love.

1/221

[165]

Chiltern
Wednesday {14 February 1877}

My dearest M.

Yours of Saturday received Tuesday. The heat has reached Sorrento at last. It has been roasting here but as far as I can perceive our ther-mometers have not been so high as Melb. We had an hour or two rain Monday night but not enough to do more than lay the dust. I hear Mr Rhodda is curate from St. Jude's Melb & is to be here Saturday next alone. He is married & has family—The Bishop visits Beechworth *April* 28 & so will be here about that time. You need not do anything if you do not feel disposed for I am sure we will not & cannot remain here, the practice is gone, & is now a farce—there is *no money*, & *no sickness*!

Time hangs very heavily & it is very trying—I never could have believed things could have so collapsed from £70 a month to almost nothing—There is a good deal of sickness in Beechworth & Wangaratta I hear & the traffic superintendent whom I spoke to since you went, died a few days ago of Dysentery there—We have a few mosquitoes about—the peaches are getting soft, plenty of grapes 4d lb: they tell me there will be no butter soon—M. is saving & buttering a nice lot of eggs for you: She is really the best girl we have had. So careful & clean, always scrubbing—I let her go out as often as she likes—Green's buggy & harness sold for £16.

I feel very poorly again and hope it won't be long before you come back. I am very anxious & uneasy about you & the dear ones & am wretched *about the future*—I don't think I shall ever be an old man for I feel myself getting more feeble every year, and the worry & anxieties of life make me very anxious to go.

Thursday. We had a fine drop of rain last evening & the weather is pleasanter this morning—I am writing to Brooke Smith to see if the place he talked about is still open—It was a bad day's work that ever I came here—I should have gone back to our house & waited with the offer of the clubs.

I am really very distressed at the idea of your having to move again & to undergo the packing but there is nothing else for it apparently for this is done.

Love to all & my darlings.

Your affect Husband
W.L.R.

It will kill me if I don't get out of this soon. I would go away at once only I can't leave Mary.

Have just got yours of the 13th. I wrote & posted letter Monday. Am so pleased you are all well.

Not a soul ever comes near the house—It is very heart breaking.

I am too low spirited to write to the darlings & the continued heat is upsetting me—

A man called Mein who was Bath man & McLeerie's clerk is appointed clerk of court.

Martin remains as pay master—

I will not decide on another place until you have seen it.

I will attend to Dr. Graham's order about the wine. I think it is the best. Slocum has no more.

The carriage on 4 dozen will be 8/– I think but will enquire—1 doz case costs 4/– & 2 doz cases cost only 4/– I think the bottled will be best as giving least trouble.

1/212, 1/261

[166]

Chiltern
Saturday {17 February 1877}

My dear Marie

I was very poorly when I wrote last, am a little better today. We had some fine showers of rain Thursday night with such a storm of hail, rain & thunder that I never saw equalled.

I have really had six patients this week but this is very dull—The clergyman 'Rhodda' is not coming after all. What a lucky get off for him if he only knew it.

We have had no butter for days.

We have pleasanter weather & the woman has called today.

I was just up at Maude's posting a letter & I found myself unable to articulate—I could not say what I wanted, I am very uneasy about myself. I lay down. I said I thought it was a faint & said I had been out in the sun—I am afraid it is something worse. I have been so distressed about the practice I fear it has upset me—I am going in to lie down & must let M. post this letter—

Love to my dear loves

I will write or telegraph Monday morning early.

Yours
WLR

1/210

[167]

Chiltern
Tuesday {20 February 1877}

My dearest Marie

I don't want to say much about my attack on Saturday. I will tell you all about it when I see you.

I suppose it must have been mental depression & the intense & protracted heat—It seems settled that Rhodda is *not* to come and it seems pretty certain that there *is* to be a new bank.

The new mine expects to be on gold next Monday. The weather is still hot tho' of course not so bad as last month or the beginning of this. I am glad Leila got better; Sam might have written—I shall think twice before I expend 2/8 on a telegram for him again. I got your letter of Friday glad to hear you are all well—no news from this—very few patients indeed—

Scots bazaar opened today—

Two persons owing me accounts have become insolvent since I came here.

Wednesday Got yours of Saturday this morning & your papers.

Still very hot here—
Mary cleaning up every day.
Practice completely gone—
I bought a case of apples for 5/– for you & put them in the cellar
but I see the case is not full—
Lloyd had not got one person in his shop the whole of last Sunday
—Thomas the Wesleyan Minister has left gone to Rutherglen.
Am sorry you do not sleep better. I could not sleep for long after
you left. I always woke at or before daylight. I do a little better now I
take some wine during the day & at night. I hope Dr. G. got his wine
or if not he will I ordered it.
Kind love to Mrs G and lots of kisses to the pets happy darlings—
The drought & heat still continue—the mutton is very lean. We
have a fowl twice a week as I am sick of tough steak.
Good bye dearest, I suppose you will be off to Queenscliffe next
week—I don't feel strong enough to travel just at present.

Your affect Husband
W.L.R.

1/211

[168]

Chiltern
Thursday {22 February 1877}

My dearest Marie
Do not hurry back I am much better now. The trip to Queenscliffe
will benefit you. I would not have written on Saturday only I was afraid
I was going to be ill *all alone*. Stay on until the weather improves for it
is still unbearable. I am so sorry about you being ill yourself. My going
first would be bad but *your* leaving the darlings would be much worse,
let us pray you may be spared. I have got one or two patients. It is my
writing that has upset you. I should have kept my complaints to myself.
It was all my anxiety about you & the darlings. You did not say what
side the pain is in. I suppose it is the left—the old pain the heart always
brought on by worry & care *about others*: poor dear: I hope this will reach
you before leaving Sorrento. I am so sorry I wrote as I did. You will be
easier now dear won't you, & try & get strong for my sake & for the
darling's sake, think what they would do without you. I shall expect

you back the week after next. I think by that time you will have enjoyed Queenscliffe. We will make up our minds until that time & altho' I am afraid the hot weather will not have gone it must be going—

Thank dear Mrs Graham for all her love & kindness to me & mine. They will never be forgotten.

I will telegraph if anything occurs and I have jotted down particulars of affairs in my box to make things easy—What with

life assurance—	545
& House—	1550
Bank—Chiltern—	270
Yourself—	150
Savings bank—	35
Debts due here—	100
Shares—about—	450
	3000
My acct city Bank	35
	3035

Due on House
about 300

Affairs will not be so hopeless or so complicated as many other persons leave them.

This was a *frightful* morning but a change seems imminent. Could eat no dinner—but am going to try a little cold fowl. 4 PM.

Fond love to my darlings. I hope they will bring back rosy faces.

1/220

[169]

Chiltern
Saturday {24 February 1877}

My dearest Marie
I got yours of Wednesday this morning. I did not feel well enough to write until Wednesday, as I had frequent fits of giddiness which made

me reel like a drunken man, & I had to hold on to fences when out walking. There must be something wrong inside my head. You know I have complained of headache for some years ever since that sun stroke at Ball[ara]t I hope I am better now however. Judge Hackett called Friday, & asked me to dinner at the Star. Shortly after Espinass Martin came up & apologising for the shortness of the invitation, said he had asked the Judge to dinner that day, & would I go down to meet him: of course I thought Martin had arranged with the Judge & went. Judge of my astonishment when 7 o'clock arrived & no Hackett. Martin sent off to the Star & found that he *had dined* alone, Martin not making the case out clearly to him. He came sat at table would eat nothing & I thought treated them with great rudeness, at all events with want of politeness. Everything was splendid Fish, lamb, capital pudding, *splendid dessert* & all for nothing as it were! There is something behind the Martins.

In the midst of dinner in comes a note from Brooke Smith who arrives at the Star—We soon joined him & his language of the Martins was something dreadful. He said he *was a liar* & worse! but would give no explanations. I thought of going on to Beechworth today but am afraid of my giddiness & must keep quiet until you come back—one or two patients but poor people. The weather is sensibly cooler we had fine rain Thursday all night. No fear of the tank now. Nights & morning are cold. Mary is still all that can be desired. She has mended my socks for me. I hope this will find you at Queenscliffe & that my last will have comforted you & that you will have a better week with dear Mrs C. Give her my kind love & say I hope her health keeps good. How happy she & Mrs Graham ought to be with no cares on their minds for the future. The Archdeacon preaches March 11th morning & evening: but the place is gone so <u>completely</u> *to the bad* that I do not believe any other clergyman will get a living.

Brooke does not speak hopefully of any other place at present. He is nearly quite bald & lame still & denounces the world & things in general as usual. He seems to be harder worked than ever.

I do not think I could stand the 16 miles jolting in the coach.

Love to my darlings & much to your own dear self from

Your loving W.L.R.

1/217

[170]

Chiltern
Tuesday {27 February 1877}

My dearest Marie

Yours of Saturday came this morning. The weather is still awful Ther 90° to 100°.

Hope you will enjoy your Queenscliffe trip. Am thankful to say I am better. Hope you will get stronger before you return to this wretched place. I shall not even if we stay put in another Feb[ruar]y here. It would be as much as my life is worth.

I hope you got my letter posted here Thursday for Sorrento & one to Queenscliffe posted Saturday.

It was well I did not go to Beechworth as B.S. did not get home until Sunday night & I had a confinement Sunday night—

You must use your own judgement about a nursery governess—if *you wish it* I shall not oppose it—only do not make a long engagement for the practice is altogether gone—& will never return.[1] You will see the state when you come back—Of course if we moved she could go with us—The last tea was splendid & is still & I think another box would be good—I think a few pair of merino socks & a pair of driving gloves or two with some paper & envelopes from Purtons.

Mary is still all that could be desired. She cooks & washes well— makes me stews & curries & pastys.

It has been threatening rain all day but the wind changes round & carries all away—

Kind love to Mrs. C. & 100 to the darlings. How nice to have cold weather, it seems to be giving you Rheumatism.

No news from this vile place—Not a soul ever comes near the house & I see no one but Lloyd.

Your affect & attached
Husband
W.

1/219

[1]   A Miss Fenton was engaged, as one sees from Letter 187.

[171]

My dearest M.

Just as if we had not got enough troubles I have received notice from Mr Flower of Toorak who was joint security for Brooke Smith with me & Rutledge in 1871 that there is a sum of £60 still due—that he has forfeited his Life Policy & that we are looked to for payment. I have of course written & telegraphed to Brooke. Is it not scandalous?—

I do not see that we can incur expense of governess as my practice has quite gone—A few poor people with no money.

Then the mine is flooded & will require pumps & machinery & delay for 6 months.

I hope you will come home soon before I go quite mad for what with solitude & misfortunes I am very very put about—

Your affect Husband
Walter

I thought you had done all your shopping before you went to Sorrento. Don't buy anything for me.

1/207

[172]

Chiltern
Sunday {4 March 1877}

My dearest Marie

The weather is now delightful & the nights & the water cold. I wrote in great annoyance in consequence of the rascality of that un-principled fellow B[rooke] S[mith] I suppose I will have to pay it. I have received no reply to 2 letters & suppose he is as usual away from his home—I am still doing literally nothing—the Newingtons are going up & it is thought they will get the reef struck by the Patricks which has given 1 oz 18 100 wt to the ton for the first crushing.

If you like to venture on a governess you *can* try for 6 months to a year—

I think you might buy a nice reading lamp or a drawing one like Mrs. Martin's.

Also you had better get some paper & envelopes a[t] Purtons for I use a great deal—

I have a case of apples I told you I bought but I am afraid they won't last till you come back as they are too ripe. I cannot measure the collar of the shirt—you had better leave it—I have plenty to last me another 6 months.

Your boat sickness seems to have done you good, it is a pity you did not take more fishing excursions—

Arthur Green passed thro' to Wodonga & dined & took tea with me on Saturday. He is much improved—

Love to the Grahams—& to the darlings & write & say what day we are to expect you.

Your affect Husband
W.

I think it will be wet Wednesday.

1/208

[173]

My dearest Marie

I enclose Sarah's.

Thank dear Mrs Graham for her kind invitation. I must however think of the money & coming back first class with you—

I am sorry you found the sea too bleak—

No news here whatever.

The weather is pleasant & the nights cold—

You will see Sarah has got quite a lot of things & boots—

I am afraid your new dress & bonnett will be lost at Chiltern—The place is deserted & the streets empty.

Tell Dr G. that I found that rascal Gueria had sent me wine that was fermenting in the bottles & bursting—I wrote him at once & countermanded Dr Graham's order—I do not know if I was in time to stop it or not.

Your affect
Husband
W.

Be sure if you buy a lamp to get one of Rowatt's without inside chimney—

Just heard from B[rooke] S[mith] He says he is asking for time & will settle it by April 11—

1/218

PART 6
Queenscliff

1877

WALTER RICHARDSON LEFT Chiltern for the last time on 27 August 1877. After a few days staying in Melbourne with Dr Graham, he travelled to Queenscliff where he contemplated opening a practice. Another possibility was to go to Clunes, which appears to have been Mary's preference, but it would seem from Walter's earlier letter to the children that his heart was always set on Queenscliff. The sixteen letters sent to Mary from Queenscliff are in many ways a repetition of those from Chiltern: concern as to whether or not he could establish a successful practice; worries about finding a suitable house; advice to her about packing or selling their furniture and leasing the Chiltern house; requests for her to chase up unpaid bills.

This time Mary at least had the help of Mrs Graham, who was staying with her. Although initially resistant to Walter's remaining in Queenscliff and taking on another house she had never seen, the tone of Walter's letters of 6 and 7 September, with their accounts of continued poor health, mental as well as physical, evidently convinced her not to oppose him further. So she packed up his things, wrote to patients about their unpaid accounts and polished up the furniture for sale. In early October she and the children moved to Queenscliff to join Walter in their rented house in Mercer Street (now no. 26).

[174]

Melbourne
Monday {27 August 1877}

Dear Marie

I arrived safely after a long & weary journey as you know—I fell asleep—the carriage was full. I enjoyed your good things very much.

As I am convinced the wine does not agree with me I am going to make Dr. G. accept it—as it acts very injuriously on me and I am sure I am better without it—I left that book on the Port wine mark. I put it away carefully in my book case, so that I might have it in my hand & read it going but I forgot it. I think it fell down behind the books on the 2d shelf. I also forgot my testimonials addressed to Mr Shell. I think you might have it posted at Chiltern.

I hope all are well, & that Josephine keeps better.

I have not seen anyone as yet but post this early so that you can get it Tuesday midday—Love to Mrs. G. & all as well as to your own dear good self from

Your affect
Hub
W.L.R.

1/242

[175]

Melbourne
Tuesday {28 August 1877}

Dearest Wifey

I am not going to Queenscliffe before *Thursday* as I find I have matters to detain me here, & Graham is pressing that I should not hurry.

I feel better already, and had better night: what I suffered from the last night at *home* did not affect me thank God. I drank nothing but milk since I left you & there is splendid milk at Dr G's. I have written to Mr. Johnson telling him I wd not be there until Thursday. Dr. G prescribed some med[icin]e for me this morning which I must get made up. I hope you are all well & that Mrs G is getting good nights still—I saw Ham, he has asked £1700 to a Mr. Simmonds who went to look after it—Now Graham tells me he thinks Mr. Alsop may become a purchaser—Tell Mrs. G. I found Griffiths most obliging, & convenient. In fact I do not know what I should have done without his kind services in allowing my pile of luggage to remain there—Tell Mrs G. that Miss Rivers says all are well & good, & the way in which the youngsters play into a *huge* heaped plate of porridge shews that—

Of course the birds awoke me at daylight but I felt so well that I did not mind—I hope things will enable you to leave that horrid place before Nov[embe]r.

I will soon be strong as ever.

Dr G. tells me that Mrs G has £300 in City Bank. He thinks Jacques Martin[1] not so safe—as he has been *once* an inmate of Cremorne[2] —So I will *not* risk it, but will lodge the 3 hundred in the City Bank & when you draw the hundred at Chiltern Oct 31st you can lodge the £105. in Melbourne as well—

I am going out a drive with Dr. G. this afternoon & will go round by the house.

Kindest love to Mrs G. to Josephine to dear Ettie & my own Lillie. Tell them Willy & his brother want to go to Chiltern & beg me to take them & Miss Rivers. Your own hubby

WLR

1/241

[1] Thomas Jacques Martin (1839–96) was the manager of the Australasian Insurance Company, the founder of the Mutual Life Association of Australasia in 1869 and of Colonial Mutual Life Association in 1873.

[2] Cremorne Private Hospital, Richmond, where Walter was to be himself a patient a year later.

[176]

Melbourne
29 August {1877}

Dear Marie

I leave for Queenscliffe tomorrow mor[nin]g at 10 30. I am told we shall not get in before 5 or 6 o'clock so you need not expect any letter that day. I drove round with Dr. G. yesterday & called at our house. Mrs Tully insisted on my going all over & shewed me the improvements. They have distempered all the rooms & the lower ones green the upper blue & certainly it has added very much to the appearance; they have put up a little crib of a servant's room off the kitchen & she said I had allowed £15 & it had cost £18. She *had my letter*. She evidently *indulges*, for her face was like a peony & she was very pressing that I should have some ale or wine. Mr. Tully was away but she said she had sent the acc[oun]t. The house does not appear to have deteriorated on the outside—but the garden is untidy & the Camelias are gone—Stolen G. says. *They always are!*

I hope you are all keeping well & that I will get a letter at Queenscliffe. I got no sleep last night owing to the carriages coming home from the fancy ball, & the *birds* at daylight—I send Newspaper *Argus* with this & Dr G. says he sent a Warder with an interesting case of breach of promise.

Dr. G. says he makes £500 a year bad debts.

I do not feel quite so well today. I suppose it is the want of sleep. I see the Clunes are still advertising.[1] Dr G. says it will be too hard work for me.

I hope to get better by that time—Give my love to Mrs G. & to the darlings & write & tell me all the news if there is any which I don't expect. I am going to the picture gallery this day & shall leave tomorrow.

All well at Lyndoch.[2]

Your affect husband
—Walter—

We came in last evening to the Georgian Minstrels, but I was too poorly to enjoy it.[3]

1/240

¹   Refers to an opening for a doctor to take up private practice at Clunes.

²   The name of the Grahams' property in Melbourne.

³   The all-black Georgia Minstrels toured Australia from 1877 to 1880.

[177]

Off Queenscliffe
Thursday evening {30 August 1877}

My darling Wifey

I came off in the steamer this morning & judge of my surprise when a nice looking gentleman came up & spoke to me. It seems he is a Dr. Lovell who used to be in Geelong he has been unfortunate like myself & has had to resume practice. He said he had been staying at Queenscliffe all the week & had quite decided to settle there, but that as I had made arrangements to go there, he would make way for me and if I did not like it after a fair trial say of a month he would fulfil it himself. I told him of Chiltern & mentioned the house & Sale of furniture & told him there was a practice ready at hand, rather quiet just now, but certain to improve.

I told him my income for the year was over £600 & I stated that I was certain that he would do £400 & if so all I asked was a cheque for £50 at end of the year. He must make terms with you about the house: perhaps you could accomodate him with a room as he is a perfect gentleman. The only thing is he is too good for the people. I told him that loneliness & the climate drove us away. I am keeping pretty well but get very little sleep. I am sorry you sent the acc[oun]ts to Ham he has nothing to do with them & will only charge us for anything he does with them. I authorized Tully by letter for a joint expense of £15 each & I am very pleased with the improvements he has made. I have written to Ham to send them to me. I found I could not sell a single share. There was a perfect panic on all the time I was in Melb—All were sellers no buyers. I therefore paid in £50 only to your name which makes £250 & will put in the other £50 as soon as ever things mend.

Kindest love to Mrs G & so glad Josephine keeps well. Beg of Mrs G to stay. Dr G. will be so pleased & is so thankful to have quiet nights for Mrs G. Unfortunately I forgot to bring a hat from the Yorick Club. It was an old wide awake that I had sent there when I got a new one. I must try & get it down here—Lots of loves & kisses to all—& kind regards to Miss Fenton.

You will get this unexpectedly on Friday.

I am glad the people miss me, they will perhaps know better in future how to treat a gentleman & not to injure him because he does not drink with them in every pub. Love to the darlings.

I do not think there will be enough to do here & Graham does not think I could overtake the work at Clunes. I told Lovell about Clunes he said he would prefer Queenscliffe.

I do not know what to do for stamps this big portmanteau costs 1/– every time a man looks at it.

I had a capital dinner on board. Soup, two joints, two vegetables, capital plum puddings & tarts, & cheese & biscuits & all for 2/– Of course my appetite is ravenous as soon as I smell the sea air.

And now good bye. I hope the troubles of the house & furniture will not be too much for you & that the bills will come in—I am very thankful to get away from the bark huts & the 10 Publicans, & the ever lasting lake & the mill whistle.

So good bye Sweetheart. We shall soon meet again, both stronger to renew the battle of life. Your affect Hubby

W.

1/238

[178]

Queenscliffe
30 August {1877}

My darling Marie

Just arrived got yours at Graham's this morning & at this place 8 PM. We had a nice run down. I told you about Lovell. I explained to Mr Johnson who came to meet me & who before I explained was full of apologies & regrets that I had not come sooner, however I think it is all right now. I was obliged to come to Admans[1] until I can get apartments as Mrs Richardson where Johnsons stay could not accomodate me.

It is very kind of Mrs Martin & Mrs G to interest themselves so much. If you send Miss F. she can post the testimonials & they will think it music besides the Post Mistress does not gossip like Stevenson —*please don't* send them here.

There are a lot of unpaid bills. Riley is a scoundrel & uncertified insolvent. Your only chance would be to see Mrs R. but I'm afraid you will be insulted. Grundman is a contractor under the council & engaged now making the Barnawartha Road he lives close to the Wesleyan Chapel near Les. Martin. Smith has gone away, been long from work injured the bones of his foot, could not possibly pay as he was off work for weeks. Boyd Doma Indigo must only be charged 10/- Letchmere Farmers wife Indigo must be posted—Soule has been insolvent. Tomkins never pays any I got a pound out of him. Richards up near Williams on the Hill 7/6.

You can try & get the enclosed, they live up on the hill behind us. I think I am better my darling. Father Bleasedale[2] came in to the hotel & we had a long chat about Clunes. I got a tremendous fright on arriving I went up to my room & washed face & hands for tea—After I wanted to open my portmanteau & put my hands into my pockets for my keys. Gone! Oh the state I was in—I went out & asked for a blacksmith thinking I wd have to have them burst open. As I was asking the way a sudden light struck me that I had taken them out of my pocket in my bedroom. I came back—no light or servant visible, felt my way up to room & in the dark got them on the dressing table with my knife wh' I had taken out of my pocket. I certainly thought it was a great misfortune prevented. You will of course make a charge if Lovell wants accommodation. He is a perfect gentleman I have known him for years. I only hope he will go altho' a jolly sight too good for the place—do not put him against it. He will want a nice table & the charge at the Star is 30/- a week. He is living at present in 4 Victoria Parade in apartments next to Brownless—I will wait patiently here for a month without grumbling until October 9 when as you know I must be off to Beechworth. I don't think I have much to grumble about unpaid bills. Graham's loss is $\frac{1}{4}$ or 25 per cent of all—Mine was nothing like that—certainly not more than one twentieth or 5 *per cent* on the gross—about £30 out of £650.

I never expect to do anything like that here or elsewhere—So Lovell ought to know that they pay up—if they are looked after—I enclose acc[oun]t for £5.18s. You must put in the dates *7–18*. McCorrs of Shamrock Hotel his wife promised me repeatedly & he is earning good wages at the Tamar.

1/239

[1] Admans' Royal Hotel.

[2] Dr John Ignatius Bleasdale (1822–84), a Catholic clergyman who became a long-term friend of Walter. A science enthusiast, he was a foundation member of the Melbourne Microscopical Society, a Fellow of the Geographical and Linnean Societies and a prominent member of the Royal Society of Victoria.

[179]

Queenscliffe
Friday evening {31 August 1877}

My dearest Love

You cannot get this before Monday morning & I hope to get one from you before that. I sent you this morning a letter containing a lot of bills that I never could get in. I want you to copy out on rough paper *John* Tanner's acc[oun]t & I will make it out, & send it, he is earning wages now, & will doubtless pay. Can you give any news about the reef at Lamberts? ask Mr. Piper about Horne's reef—I hope you may get in the bad bills. With Rileys they would make another £12—I put up at Admans last night & went about this morning to look for apartments —the first 3 or 4 asked £2.2. but after a while I found one at 25— including my washing. The rooms were small & poorly furnished but Mr Johnson came & took me to a Mrs Keane where Father Bleasedale is staying—nice rooms clean & sweet & only 30/- per week including washing. So you see I am favored so far, lovely situation looking out on the Sea near the lighthouse. We had W. C. Smith[1] here today opening the public school & a feast for 280 children buns, sausage rolls, oranges, £20 collected: Wilkinson & the Scots parson spoke. Most people are introduced to me & they say they are glad to see me. Wilkinson says if I keep a horse & ride round the district & go over to Sorrento two or three times weekly there is about £400 a year to be done. Others tell me Dr Barker will not go out at night. He has the clubs & they *must* give him 3 mo[nth]s notice. There certainly are no poor people about, but there does not appear to be any sickness.

I suppose by waiting 6 *mo{nth}s*, matters would arrange themselves so as to give me a little settled income. Of course it would be an easy life, & we could take a house here, & perhaps fill it with boarders— that is to say if we _could get_ a house which I doubt. I will look about next week & see how the land lies & tell you more.

Of course we would decide on nothing hastily or before October end—Most medicos who come here, end by getting muddled with liquor, & one Dr. Roberts not only got drunk & neglected his patients but left heavily in debt paying _no one_. I suppose it is the solitude that drives them to alcohol. Don't forget to send me the Port wine book by post. Lee has gone to Bethanga.

You need not be afraid of the people knowing I am here.

I never got a wink of sleep till early morn from taking a cup of tea at Admans late on arrival. I have just opened the tin box, my darling & I have shewed the cakes to my landlady. I enjoyed your sandwiches going to Melb & now shall think of you at dinner. Will still hope to get a letter Saturday. Dr Bleasedale is a most interesting companion. W. C. Smith made a most *wretched* ungrammatical Speech.

Love to all. I hope the darlings are well & that Josephine keeps free—we only get our letters 5 P.M. & the mail leaves 9 P.M.—God bless you & keep you safe for

Your affect Husband WLR.

Send down the book by Mr Graham. Also get from Mr Wendt tobacconist 2 long sticks of Dr. Richardson's *own* tobacco. Cannot get it anywhere else & it suits me as it is so mild,

it is 2/– a stick & the two will last me 6 months—put them both in one parcel & Graham will leave them at the Yorick for me.

1/237

¹   William Collard Smith (1830–94), politician, was then Minister for Mines and Public Instruction.

[180]

Queenscliffe
Monday {3 September 1877}

My darling Marie

My telegrams doubtlessly surprised you. I have taken a splendid house in a fine high, dry, situation. It contains 8 rooms, kitchen, boiler, & washhouse with surgery, & side door. It belongs to Dr. Williams¹, he lived there. Everyone tells me I shall do £300 a year; our house money will give £100 & we can get £2.2 to £2.10 for boarders per week in the season. We can let three rooms & have a common table. Try & induce Mary to come & offer a rise of wages, say 15/– a week. Mrs Keane tells me they are difficult to be got. Of course we will require new carpets so you can arrange about the old *worn* ones. The drawing room about 18 × 15, the dining room about 16 × 15 & bedrooms of *tremendous size*. I must either have taken this, or smaller ones at *same price* & not near so good. I am told there is a tremendous rush here & I feared I could not get any house at all. This was the *only* one unfurnished.

Dr. Bleazedale has taken a great fancy to me, & he & Keane my landlord have been *running about* looking for a house, & I closed this morning from the 1st of October, or *sooner* if the house is ready & *you* are ready. The garden back & front is to be done up & other things done. It is in excellent repair inside, marble piece in drawing room, tank, boiler & wash house *safe old*—lawn in front & facing the East. I called on the parson & asked him if he knew anything *against* the house. He said I had got an excellent bargain. This will make a friend of Dr Williams & we will once more be among civilization, & away from bark huts *thank God!* everything happens for the best, & our fortune may improve, & this be the turning point. Of course you will bring as much as you can with you—Try & get Ned to arrange, or McCulloch's agent at Chiltern unfortunately that is 'Fred Nickless'—but he must *do if* you cannot find another; you had better send for Peter & the German carpenters, as Maclachlan is never at Chiltern: ask Frederickson his charge & you had better get them both father & son. If you are satisfied of course that our good things *which are worn* would fetch a *fair* price we might let them go. You could put a reserve on them, & if they did not *bring that* from which the expense of carriage should be deducted they should come. Say a reserve of £20 on the dining room, carrriage & packing £4—If they don't bring £16.0.0 they should not go. No furniture can be bought here. All must come down in the Steamer.

The Piano of course you will put reserve of £60.0.0, carriage £5.0.0. If it does not bring £60 or £55 you can bring it. Mrs G. will say if you can replace it in Melb or get a 'Aucher Freres' for £60 which the tuner told me is much *better suited for the climate* so I should put a reserve on it of only £55. Auchers stands the heat better!

I enclose letter from Lovell Dr. *this* decided me I should hardly think he will come *now*: I was delighted to hear of Dear Josephine. How nice it will [be] to have them here & for you to go to Sorrento. Send *immediately* about the accounts, for if the Chiltern people get wind about the auction, they *will never pay* a farthing—What terms with Porch?

I am much better since I came here—Eyes *quite right*, the other thing *gone*, free & open from pills; appetite good & yet no bathroom. Mrs Keane gives me a tub every morning & of course in summer I shall jump in to the Sea & the darlings can bathe. I have heard them say 'they love it'.

I am sure all this will be better than Clunes, a place of dust & dirt & poverty—there is no dust here, & *no* poor persons—Splendid turn out of children on Friday, 280 stuffed with buns, sausage rolls, & tea & oranges. It was the opening of the new State School by W. C. Smith, & a mess he made of his speech. Excuse the scribble but I am late for the post, & I am anxious you should get *this* Tuesday afternoon.

Love to Mrs G to the darlings, to Josephine, kind regards to Miss Fenton, & a thousand kisses to your dear self.

Won't you all be delighted to get away from that hole & its back-biting people. This good news ought to make you *strong & well* before you *meet* me; I know the change will tell on the darlings & yourself when you get peace of mind.

I returned the spectacles & paid in £2.10 to make up the £50. Did the Bank send you deposit receipt?

You had better sell the pig at *once*. I suppose the wood will be sold & all the things I got from Hancock. Pig trough—hen coop, rabbit hutch. There is an old large Col[onial] oven in the kitchen here—you must get the range in, or get Porch to agree exchange when he leaves. Give my kind love to Mrs Porch thank her for all her attention to you.

Find about Horne's Reef from Piper—I must forfeit my shares if no shew—write him a note & get a written answer or ask Mrs Horne. If you can bring the wine do so; drink Braines with the *red seal badly corked*—but save the other if any.

It is raining now, Monday and it has been wet & cold all yesterday, gales, but inclined to clear. Old Bleasedale is a fine old man, an enthusiast in all sciences, can preach a sermon on everything.

Won't the darlings enjoy the Cliff.

I left a pamphlet on *wines*—try & save it if you can—Also find my card plate & send it by Post to Purton. *This is important* as I want to put it in the Sorrento Hotels & Portsea & other places.

Your affect Husband
W.L.R.

Monday evening
I have just got yours my darling do not be so anxious or worry so much—things will all be right if you do not make yourself ill—*Offer the house to Porch for £35* for the remaining 10 months—That will be better than leaving it—Do not be in a hurry with the Sale, it will be better for

me here to *pay the October rent* for the house £4.4.0 than for you to leave £20 or *£30 of debts* behind you. You ought to be pleased that our prospects are brighter & that I am better. Do not mar our pleasure by making yourself ill—I have written to Graham. Altho' I had nothing to write about.

How could I answer chicks' letters better when I was ill & could say nothing definite about this place? I hope you are satisfied with what I recommend about Porch & the Sale & the debts write to them the best of them if not paid this week.

Love to all and for God's sake Cheer up Your affect

Hubby
Walter

1/228, 1/258, 1/250

¹ Dr David John Williams, the port Health Officer.

[181]

Queenscliffe
4 September 1877

My dear Marie
You did well with the dining room suite. You had better sell everything if you can get such prices.

The dining table ought to go; it is not an oval table & it cost £9. at Harrisons, look on the file. Then my book case cost £5.5. I should get the Fredericksons father & son & let them varnish the drawing room sofa.

Copy out John Tanner's acc[oun]t *the whole page* & I will select *his* acc[oun]t unpaid and I will recopy it & send it to you, he ought to pay as he is in work—The weather here is bleak and cold. Do not forget about my card plate and I also want my gate plate.

The earth closet nuisance is likely to turn up again, a man asked 5/– a week.

I hear that Jakins of Ball[ara]t is coming. A Wesleyan who preaches on Sunday—

This is rather hard after my taking the house, but I hardly believe it. I have been obliged to put an advertisement in the *Argus*.

I wrote to Lovell. The mining market is in a fearful state. I cannot get some scrip from Nixon. Thank God I cleared out of Patricks they are down to £2.10.0. Everything unsaleable!

The chemist says he will arrange about the closet for 2/6 a week— This & everything will be right if we can only get our house furnished: the Season & the rush begins on the 1st October and with 3 large Rooms & 4 middling ones it will be hard if you cannot get £10 a week during the Season: for if another doctor comes no dependance can be placed on practice. I hope you are sending out the accounts and that they are coming in better. You had better put an advertisement in the *Standard* I think—I find it very difficult to get to sleep.

I hope you do not lie awake. You had better pack me a box with my books—only send Braithwait[1] from 1869, leave the others. Also splints, bandages & instruments.

No word from Ham. I am afraid he will charge for his interference. I agreed for alterations up to £15 & I consider the house to be £50 better by them. Send my books & brass door plate & bring my card plate as soon as you can with comfort. I will tell you when the house is ready to receive anything. Of course there will have to be new carpets, but they need *not* be *the best* as the rooms are so huge—

druggetting or matting at the sides—Another reason for selling the table is that it is not large enough if we take boarders and it cost £9. at Harrisons. I should let my bookcase go—You never told me what you got from Porch for the 10 months to run—You had better arrange to stay at Mrs Gr[aham]'s a week & you can send on the furniture as you buy it in small lots. I believe the freight by steamer is 8/– per ton. So you see you save packing & the railway charges to Melbourne besides the wear & tear & get new furniture. Everyone takes boarders here & there is no disgrace.

Milk is 6d. quart.

The out mail from this closes 9 AM & 5 PM: only one comes in at 5.30 PM: just after the Melb mail leaves by the Steamer. I do not think I have anything else to say except that I hope Josephine keeps well & still does without medicine that the darlings are well & that you are not killing yourself with hard work. Your letters posted by the afternoon mail reach me by the Steamer next eve[nin]g & mine posted 5 PM get to you 2.30 PM—With much love to all. Your loving

Hubby W.

1/236, 1/254

¹   W & J Braithwaite, *Midwifery and Diseases of Women and Children*. Published by Simpkin semi-annually.

[182]

Queenscliffe
Wednesday {5 September 1877}

My darling Marie

Yours of Sunday came tonight. Have you got the medicine? I have cured many cases with it & among the rest my sister Lucinda who was very bad if you remember and who got relief very soon she was delighted. It has no taste & should be continued until looseness & pain come then & then *one* drop a dose ought to be stopped & 4 drops taken gradually dosing down to one drop but the case will be sure to be cured before that generally the 2d week does it—Of course Mr Wain paid I wrote it before. I did not put down accounts opposite the names in the day book but on the days they were paid you may be certain I would have put down Wain's name if it had not been paid.

All right you had better let the box go with the rest, I do not see that it will cost less however. I know nothing of the plates they may turn up in some corner perhaps when the house is cleaned. I must get a new one at Purtons. Saturday is the best day for the country beg of him to put up a flag & to have the bill man. You will be too worried to see about the glass. You had better get it packed as I wish & forwarded to Solomon & I will tell him to call at Spencer St. unless you are going with the luggage which you cannot do.

You know the luggage & all the things are likely to be 4 days or a week on the road unless they are all put into one van: the freight for packages across in the Steamer is 10/– per 40 feet cubic measure, it was £2. coming from England. You had better come over after sending the chicks to Mrs Graham. The boat leaves ½ past 10.

Let Mr Sammond see the enclosed—this was passed by the Chiltern Council in the *Standard* you sent me. The scoundrell owes us £1.0.0 for about 6 attendances on his wife & when I asked him he declared he could not pay—

Freer owes a guinea. I see Wheat is down & flour at Chiltern—this is what made Porch so savage.

It has been bitterly cold Sunday & Monday.

I had a good night for the first time.

Dr G. was to pay in £20 & £17 last week. I paid in the £2.10 for the glasses & made it up to £50 I thought as we were making a fresh start that I had better keep a little ready money in the Bank until we saw an income. Of course there is nothing yet but I expect to get the clubs by Xmas & the acting health officer's billet after young McFarlane leaves. Then there is sure to be sickness when the visitors arrive. I have not seen Dr. Williams yet. I called on Mrs W. but the house appears to be shut up. I told you milk was 6d Butter ¼ Beef 7d & 8d. Mutton by the side 3d Bread 8d.

Where did you put my ring with the stone loose? I cannot find it—

Give my best love to all.

I suppose the weather is getting hot and you ought to be getting some peas & beans & cabbages soon. Are the hens laying better?

The mirror as it is now is valueless but if repaired will be good as ever.

Your loving Husband W.

I have got a little giddiness come over me today.

1/229, 1/256

[183]

Thursday morning {6 September 1877}

I had written the letter Sept 4 before I got yours. Of course I have *declined* to sign the agree[ment] as you seemed to wish it!

I *again* think that I am *not* able for Clunes. Graham said so—My poor head will soon give way & having to provide for a substitute after 4 hours would simply be ruin—The attending on 400 men & half the number of women besides the average of 3 or 4 children, the night work, the exposure to the heat, the having to keep horse, man & buggy —are all serious questions. It is very easy to go there & attempt it & if I break down there there will be *no saving money*. I cannot do imposs- ibilities, & I feel that I am an old broken down man. Of course all were surprised, Dr. Bleasedale said I was wrong. It was *not* the Cliff that would support me it was the *entire* district; that a *competent* man had <u>never</u> settled here before & that it would soon become known.

Revd Wilkinson says there is a good population at Drysdale 5 or 6 miles off: Mrs Keane said I *need have no fear*, that numbers of visitors would much prefer a private family that there was sure to be sickness when the visitors came & would pay what you liked. That they *never* had a sober Med[ical] man & that I had only to wait a few months & I would find she was right. There is no doubt that Lovell will be here now & will *jump at it* & I consider your decision most unfortunate.

I have not [been] well at all for the few days the old pain & swelling & your letters keep me from sleeping. You must excuse my writing for some days as I don't feel able & my old *head*ache & giddiness. I feel that I should not have left home to fall sick among strangers—

I generally have to write my letters twice over owing to the mistakes, so do not expect so many. It was your writing that Porch wanted the house by the *24* that misled me, & to find now that nothing is going to come of it. I thought it better to have a place for you & the furniture & children at once & I made sure that Porch would have given you nearly the rent of the house here! I will reply to my little darling's letters in a few days.

I had written all about the Cliff & the Sea to Ettie, but it is no use now.

Yours
W.

I'll take no other house until you come yourself but sorry you did not see to the bad debts before, there will be little chance now if the good ones come in so slowly. I put an advertisement in the *Argus* by the advice of my landlord which you will see Thursday & 3 succeeding Saturdays. I thought it better to lose no time. It will be a *quiet* practice & there would be no risk of breaking down by over work as at Clunes: the one would lead to strength the other to the Benevolent Asylum—

Why don't you ask Mrs. Graham? I am getting quite stiff after sitting a little while my old enemy seems come back pain in one knee— after the late rain—

Another reason against Clunes, is that I am *not* well up in Surgery: I know no one there to *consult* with & that I should be all alone & have to pay for any consultations.

You had better telegraph on receipt of this if you wish this place sacrificed or not. If you want the house given up or not *Yes or No.*

1/232

[184]

Queenscliffe
6 September {1877}

Dear Marie

I have concluded that in spite of my debility I had better not con-clude about this place until I see if I get Clunes. If I do I had better go there alone for 3 months & if I find I cannot overtake the work I must give it up. This will be the best thing to do; we then can but come to Queenscliffe.

When did the Secretary say the election would take place? There are six lodges I see, he could not say how many members—

I have just been offered one lodge of 48 members 30/– each out of wh' 8/– goes to the druggist—This would just pay the rent. Embling told me he made in the one season £40. Old MacFarlane[1] & his son are still here & old Dr. Barker—I have not succeeded in meeting Dr. Williams. The Clunes is not so good for we could get no boarders & our expenses would therefore be much higher. Two horses, man & buggy— However I will say no more. I have not got Clunes yet & shall not build on it but can only try it alone for 3 months & then give it up if I find things not to answer.

I shall have to go to Beechworth Oct 10 & if Porch is *not* going to take your house I think it is a pity that you should have the Sale so soon. I did *not* know this when I telegraphed. I concluded by your letter that you had an *immediate offer*. Do not write so again. It would have been better if you had remained quiet till Oct 10 as we decided at first.

I should not have rushed away I see no chance *now* of *our meeting* again, nor indeed of *our saving any money*. I do not consider this as the main object of life—comfort & ease & a moderate income are better fitted to induce happiness—I had written letter to Ettie about this place I cannot send it now.

On thinking the matter over carefully it appears best that I should try Clunes *if I get it*. Therefore do not telegraph—

I will try Sea bathing as soon as ever the weather gets warmer love to all

Your own W.

1/234

¹ William Macfarlane studied in Edinburgh and registered in Victoria in 1855. He
was Honorary Medical Officer at Ballarat Hospital 1860–62.

[185]

Queenscliffe
7 September 1877

My darling Wifey

I am now quite reconciled to try Clunes; & if I do *not* get it will
think it very hard after waiting so long. There is a small living to be
made here if what every one says is true £50 from the lodges, £40 or
£50 from the office of acting health officer & some sickness in the
Season, besides Sorrento, Portsea & Drysdale. Of course it would be sup-
plemented by boarders & friends would have to be told that we did *not*
keep open house but could not pay our rent unless it was shared by visitors. I telegraphed this morning as I felt & indeed do feel now pretty
bad with the old pain & swelling. If it does [not] mend next week I certainly must go & see Graham again & perhaps come home. I wish I had
not come but stayed until the 10th October. The applications are to
be sent in by 15 of this month—do you remember *when* the election is
to take place? My head is bad. I am quite stupid at times. Young
MacFarlane who has been acting health officer for 6 weeks, tells me he
took during that time £2.2. & his father £4.4.0. Of course there is
nothing doing except in the Season.

Give my kindest love to Mrs Graham. I hope some of the accounts
are coming in.

Dr. Bleasdale is still here & as full of anecdote as ever. A young
fisherman was drowned crossing Swan bay & leaves wife & family. He
says I am certain to do well if I can only wait six months. I will therefore tell them all I am coming back. Dr. Lovell has declined to come
now & I do not suppose anyone will, & with young MacFarlane away I
shall hope to get the acting health officer's billet if we come here.

Give my dear love to the darlings

Your afft
Husband
WLR

1/233

[186]

Queenscliffe
Saturday morning {8 September 1877}

My dear Wifey

I think under the circumstances it will be the wisest thing for us to do to come here. I shall not sign the agreement until I have seen Dr. Williams & have his opinion. He is expected from quarantine on Monday. Our income will be small but you & dear ones will be much more comfortable even with a small income. Everything is not dearer. I told you I had written to Solomon about the mirror—Tell me when it is packed & sent off. Solomon & Co Furniture dealers Swanston St. I suppose I must wait patiently here.

I am a little better this morn[in]g. I am going to take nothing but porridge until the pain & swelling abate & go away. When is the sale to be? Has Porch taken the house? I am sorry the acc[oun]ts have not come in better—don't hurry away until you are compelled. Lovell is not coming now. This will be a comfortable home for you & the children if the income be small.

Everyone cannot be wrong & every[one] says there is a living to be made. Dr Barker is an awfully ignorant old man he doses the people with Calomel & orders most expensive medicines.

Young MacFarlane the assistant health officer is going away & his father is not much.

Love to all. You will I suppose stay in Melbourne for a week or two & arrange about the furniture coming if I decide after seeing Williams. You will I suppose store & get Ned to forward the things.

I will have the house ready as soon after I decide as I can.

Your affect Husb.
W.L.R.

I have told the people I shall not decide until after October 10th.

1/249, 1/257

[187]

Queenscliffe
Sunday {9 September 1877}

My dearest M

I am so grieved that you should be so annoyed & worried. What a good thing it is that Mrs. Graham is with you. You will have to write to the people in the country if they do not pay. Drop a line to O'Brien Schoolmaster Barnawartha Hunter. I should post a note to one every day. There will be a lot left behind if you don't.

I am sorry about the Porchs I don't believe they want the house after all.

You are quite right to sell all the furniture you can & save Railway fare. I can replace them in Melbourne. I hope it will be as good a sale as our two last.

I think this will be better than Clunes as more comfortable for all of us. Dr W comes ashore tomorrow & I shall see him & get his opinion. I have accepted the Club £55, they give a month's notice. Everybody says I will do well, that there has never been a sober man here before. Time will shew.

I am very sorry to hear about poor Josephine I thought her recovery was only temporary. I am very grieved to hear of Miss Fenton. It is a poor return for our selecting her from 20 others. Of course a little slap will not hurt anybody but it will only make them dislike her. She is too young & too well paid & has no control over them. She should not tell lies to her mother. Six month's engagement is too long. One month's notice is quite enough.

The most beautiful church in Victoria & capital choir here.

Please put on 2d stamp & post the city bank book. You had better get the door plate cleaned & taken down. I know the darlings will be delighted with the place if I can only make a living.

No word from Ham. I was very poorly indeed Thursday but am thankful to say better in every respect today. I am certain I would not be able for hard lodge work & night work. I hope dear you will not mind taking boarders; old Mr. Johnson says he will be changing soon, & gave a hint that he would like to be in a family. I think he pays 30/– a week but then he is permanent. Thank McLeery from me for his attention. I will not leave this my darling do not be uneasy. I must have been a little wrong in my head when I telegraphed. I did not telegraph on receipt, as I knew my letters would reach you & it would cause excitement.

I will have the house thor[ough]ly cleaned & washed out.

Did the N.N. Clunes div. come? If so send the cheque to me here. The city Bank is only one, we have two others—I keep that for the Building Society's acc[oun]t I think Dr. Bleasedale might come & live with us too. He pays 35/– & has been here some months.

Rain again last night & today. Have you had much? Make M. take off the upper part of the water pipe. I must see Dr. Williams as soon as he arrives & find out if he recommends the cliff as much as he did six months ago. If he does I think I may venture to sign the agreement. Be very careful to pack *all* my instruments. I have left my Hypodermic Syringe & speculum behind me. Bring the inkstands & ornaments & my card board & pasteboard.

Dr. Bleasedale enjoys my wine very much. He tells a nice story about the Baron.[1] It seems that some years ago a German under gardener named Wilheim sent home to England for a complete & expensive work on Botany & Horticulture. When it arrived the Baron insisted either that poor Wilheim should sell the book to the Baron or leave the service. He would not have his under gardener studying science. Ultimately the book was sold to the government & poor Wilheim got rid of. Dr Bleasedale's stories of the old Melb identities would fill a volume. He has given me receipts for driving bugs & fleas out of the house. The whole history of the Aspinal & Beaney case[2] & L. L. Smith's trial for murder[3]—He has taught how to test wine & there is no subject except Medicine on which he cannot deliver a lecture.

Frightful gales here. It is a cold place in winter altho' there is no frost. They will want all their warm things if this continues.

Love to all. It is blowing so hard that I do not think Dr. W. will be able to come across today. I am keeping better thank God.

Good bye dearest. Do not be so worried, all will I hope be well yet.

Your loving Hubby
W.

Rowe should be written to.

1/223–5

[1] Walter's old friend Baron Sir Ferdinand von Mueller (1825–96), Government Botanist and Director of the Melbourne Botanic Gardens.

² In 1866 there was an inquest into the death of barmaid Mary Lewis, who died after an abortion performed by a surgeon, James George Beaney (1828–91). The jury failed to agree, leading to a second trial at which Beaney's advocate, Butler Cole Aspinall (1830–75), succeeded in having him acquitted.

³ L. L. Smith (1830–1910), surgeon, known as Melbourne's leading abortionist, had also been acquitted of murder at a similar trial in 1858.

[188]

Queenscliffe
Monday {10 September 1877}

My darling Marie

I have seen Dr Williams. I said I thought of taking his house if I could make a living here. He said I could do £500 a year—that he was glad I had come—that I had lost £60 by not coming when he recommended me 4 months ago. The assistant health officer gets £2.2 a day—I am going to sign the agreement as I am now perfectly satisfied that we shall be comfortable & happy & as I said our luck is about to turn. I posted letter this morning to you. The mail leaves every morn[in]g at 9. The house is to be thoroughly cleaned, the garden done up & the kitchen range built anew—

Dr. Williams has lived on the Cliff for 20 years & he likes it better than [any] other place & would not exchange it. He asked after you. I am so happy & relieved of a great anxiety which has pressed on me since I came here. You will cheer up now, with our little we need have no fear, & we will add to them by degrees, living among nice people and once more within the bounds of civilization; What a blessing for our darlings too to have associates of refined manners. You can send me down my box the first opportunity & the glass to Solomons. You will want another large Mirror & some looking glasses for the bedrooms get the best of everything; it's cheapest in the long run. Try Harrisons, he is the best in Melb. You can *take his word* he always treated us well.

I will write to the Steamer as soon as you are able to tell me what you are going to bring. Anything by weight. Harrison must take the furniture to pieces & send a man here to put it together again—that will be the best way but I will enquire if there is anyone here who will undertake it. The boat leaves now at 7 in the morning—I am going to buy a goat as we have a splendid paddock & back orchard with grass

1 foot high. I see Ham is advertising the house in Saturday's *Argus* it is to be put up by auction Sept.

I shall chain the goat up and perhaps have 2.

We are getting fearful gales here.

Your affect Hubby
WLR

If you can do with £50 from me for the expenses of moving & new furniture, I think I can manage but if you get £35 from Porch & the sale brings £100 you won't want much.

I think you might send me a box with the splints bandages, paste board & card board Tow instruments & some books, any warm socks or flannels that I did not take with me as it is very cold here—Dr Williams has recommended me to open a little surgery at Sorrento & says it will be worth £200 a year. Try & send my card plate & door in the box. I will go over to Sorrento & Portsea the first fine day but we have had such frightful weather you might send me my very old greatcoat for if I have to board ships I am told we generally get wet thro'. I am going to get an oil skin coat—I hope you are keeping better & that the pain in the heart is better if you can pack all bottles I left on my chimney piece they will be of great use if I am to dispense medicine.

Your loving Hubby
W

1/235, 1/251

[189]

Queenscliffe
Thursday morning {13 September 1877}

My darling Polly

You will have had mine telling you that I had arranged to take the house from the 1st. of October. You will have lots of time between your auction & the 9th of October when I must be off to Beechworth.

I enclose the form of endorsement I have every confidence in Mr Sammond but I fear he will never get the accounts in. I hope you will be easier in your mind now dear & will not fret so much. It is all past &

done & you will soon be here now. Ham is offering on Thursday the 27 inst our house by auction. He told me he would put it up at £1700 & as he said £50 would cover all expenses I said I was prepared to take £1650. I hope you will sell all the furniture at good prices. I want a box packed with all my things—the books in a box by themselves, clothes & instruments &c, door plate, card plate, old ribbon box—Draper's 'Physiology'[1]—the comic book, the arm book, the little science books on Astronomy, Physiology. I never found my ring.

Mrs Keane brought in an old servant of hers to recommend her. Fancy she was in the family way a widow. Mrs K never noticed it until I told her of it afterwards.

Get Ned to manage the giving up the keys after you are ready to go. I shall not get the man to put things right until the last week of this month. I still intend to get a goat or two as there is splendid feed in the orchard & Dr Bleasedale advises me to get it cut into Hay—I am much better & can eat again without pain. Thank Mrs Graham for her kindness. I hope & trust she won't desert you until you are clear of the place. Hadn't Dr Bleasedale & I a laugh about the event recorded on the preceeding page. You had better order a lot of matting for the bedrooms & some of the sitting rooms as they are of immense size, we have it in the room I am sitting in. It can be taken up occasionally. If we get a house full we will require more than one [servant] 10/– a week is the regular thing—The Russians have had their first victories and a great and final battle is impending. I am afraid poor Turkey is going to be conquered at last and the Greek flag will have to be bought.

Did you read an account of the loss of the Great Queenslander ship that left Engl[and] in 1876 with 2 tons of O'Connor's powder on board 33 passengers & 16 crew, O'Connor's name being mentioned?[2] It seems there was ignorance & villainy in the manufacture of it & it was liable to explode at any moment owing to its being bad. There is no doubt that the ship exploded. Poor O'Connor the firm has smashed & is ruined. We had fine rain. I hope we will get into the house soon & that you will have a house full. We will try and get another servant.

I hope you will try & get better & not be awake all night—that does no good. There are very nice neighbours next to us—one takes borders & the other family is highly spoken of by Dr. Bleasedale who describes them as very nice. Does McLeerie think it is going to be a good sale?

I sent that letter to Melb by private hands on Saturday as there was no mail from this before Monday.

The Sandhurst lottery comes off tomorrow 13th. We have a bank here.

Love to all try to get better

Your affect Hubby
W.L.R

[1] J. W. Draper, *Human Physiology* (2nd edition, Low, 1860).

[2] The *Great Queensland*, an iron ship, went missing while on a voyage to Melbourne. The cause was believed to have been the spontaneous combustion of impure wood powder. The Patent Gunpowder Company and the ship's owners were blamed for the disaster.

[190]

Queenscliffe
Friday {14 September 1877}

My Dear Mary

Send Draper's Physiology & put it on the top of the box so that I can get at it easily.

On talking over the matter alluded to in my last with Mrs Keane I am inclined to think that I was wrong because 1st Mrs K noticed it when she was in her service 6 mo[nth]s ago & 2dy because she rode in on horseback from Drysdale, Dr. Bleasedale moreover gives her such an excellent character that I have written to her & asked her to call & see you the first week in October. Mrs Keane says she expects to get out often when her work is done. Wages 10/– a week, I suppose if we get boarders & she stays you would raise it in 6 months.

I thought of going over to Sorrento & Portsea but the weather is too rough.

It has been frightful all the time—This paper seems to be very greasy it will not carry the ink—Call at Purtons & get some ruled like this but better & 250 better envelopes better than this but *not* square.

The people still blow about the fine practice I will get but I had not a single patient except old Johnson which was gratuitous.

Mrs Martin should not be allowed to blow & I am afraid Williams is another. However I tell the people I came here for a rest—

Young McFarlane does not go before Monday—I am leaving my apartments: The man has been drinking for nearly a fortnight & his wife in spite of all my remonstrances will send out for drink for him.

I told her today I could stand it no longer & I have moved to a place where there will be nothing of that sort. I never in all my life felt anything like the continued blow of the equinochial gales all the week. The food here has been excellent but she only washed one shirt & that was dreadful do you remember how many shirts you put in? I hope truly this weather will not last for I had a twinge of my old evening Rheum[atism] today. I put on 2 flannel shirts my red one & 2 pair of flannel drawers I hope it will be warmer before you come or you will all be laid up—It blows all day & all night—No fishing, a wreck off the jetty—& raining constantly—

Love to all. Your loving hubby
W.L.R.

1/231

[191]

Queenscliffe
Thursday {20 September 1877}

My dear Marie

I find that my room is 11 feet × 8 Passage 4 feet. 1st. bedroom 10 × 8. 2d bedroom 10 × 11. 3d bedroom 14 × 13. Cupboard 4 feet in with shelves 5 rows all round. Dining room 18½ × 14½. 4th bedroom 18 × 12—Drawing room 18 × 14. They are all newly papered. The lady next door takes boarders & teaches children & I am told that a lady next between is from Ballarat & has opened a ladies school a month ago. I hope you are better & take your medicine.

Thursday the 27. is the day of the sale of the house at Ham's. If you think of coming here to see the house you had [better] wait at Mrs G. until over that & go to the sale or not just as you like. I may go —I have written to Ham to know if there have [been] any enquiries or likely buyers. We are getting the house done up & Dr. Williams says we can go in whenever we like. I hope the auction will not be too much for you. I hope you will drop me the enclosed postal card the last thing to say if the sale was good or bad or middling. We could try boarders for one season & get a young person to help the cook. I want you to send me the £20 I deposited in your name. I do not want to spend it, but I want to make up a cheque that I have to place in the auctioneer's hands at Stawell which will be returned to me when those 15 Newingtons are put up to auction. I have been trying to sell New North Clunes but cannot. I have got 40 Newingtons & they have gone up 10/– a share since I bought—the only bit of luck I have had for some time. They are likely to go very much higher & if I can hold them without selling I will make a good pile as they will get the great cross reef, but not until after Xmas. Ned & the children will have their fortune made. When [I] told you to buy they were only £2. Now they are £3.10. Send me the cheque like good girl by Friday's afternoon post. Love to all. We shall meet soon again.

I hope Josephine keeps better—Your loving Hubby

W.

Sign the cheque *yourself* & make it payable scratch out or bearer & write over *or order*. That is the safest way to send it—nobody can draw but me.

1/227

[192]

My dearest Wifey

Your nice letter made me much happier. How clever of you to polish up the furniture. It ought to bring good prices. I have written to Flower & asked him if it *is true* that he committed the breach of confidence to show my private letter to A.B.S. I don't believe it! You are very clever, and Mary is invaluable. I shook hands with her when I left. We shall never see her like again—so good and simple, so kind to the wee ones & such a capital learner from you.

I hope Sammond went to the people who had received such sums & who pleaded poverty to me. I had a 2d patient today. The man & myself have been at work in the garden all day & Williams spent an hour superintending. He tells me that I must be made a P.M. & said that nobody but good men sit on the bench at the Cliff—I had a most pleasant letter from Blair saying the Sorrento people had long been crying out for a doctor, that he had indeed been looking out for one to settle there but now that I had come he would give me all his influence. 'I shall be very glad to advance your interests in Sorrento in every way in my power. I had an application since I received your note about getting a medical man for the Sorrento side but now that I know you to be there my influence if any will be in your favor.'

So you see I _must_ go over there & stay a day at Portsea & another at Sorrento—I have now some nice cards by Purton.

Dr Richardson

Queenscliff.

I must spend a day or two at each hotel & ask them to put my placard in the window. Certainly buy the wine. I can get splendid & magnificent 7 year old here for 24/– doz but I am not taking anything but I hope you will go in with Mrs [G] & that she will get it bottled. The Bank Manager called & the Scotch parson. Everybody is so nice & pleasant & so agreable. The Bank Manager has got a splendid little place with a tiny bit of garden behind where he has the choicest flowers. I got some cuttings of magnificent Geraniums from him—His family are in Tasmania. I took a season ticket for bathing today. The place is much improved by the garden being done up. The old man who is a capital gardener & has worked for Williams for 20 years agrees to come every month for 5/– To my surprise the Secretary of the Foresters came to see me & told me that tho' they had been paying Dr Barker 30/– a year to include medicine they had to pay 5/– a year out of their own pockets & could not afford [it] & offered me 25/– I told them I would not accept it & they had better keep Dr Barker—He said he was going away. I said apply Dr. McFarlane: He would not attend anybody but his own personal friends—The man seemed uneasy—I said it would pay you better to give me £2. than Dr Barker 30/– We had a long talk & finally he begged me _not to mention it to anyone_ till after their next meeting—I took a firm stand & I know that I will get [it]. Fancy them trying such a trick—love to all & Mrs G. & good luck for the Sale.

Your loving husband
W.L.R

Remember I have promised [not] to speak about it to any person.

To Mr Holt
Contractor Chiltern Valley
Co Chiltern
Sir

Please pay Dr. Richardson amount of my account due to him and deduct same from wages due to me.

A Matzen

July 22 1877

This is Matzen's order on Mr Holt for my acc[oun]t you must make it out if necessary & send to Holt with this pinned to it—R.

It will serve them right if in a year Barker [is] gone & McFarlane still determined not to practise for me to raise my terms. That would be a good joke—

He said they had never given more than 24/– & 20/– before Dr Barker.

The accounts seem to come in a little better. Our tank here is down to 4 feet from the bottom. Dr W. says the water has been stolen that before he got in quarantine he measured it & it was 4 feet from the top. October rains will fill it he says. I hope so.

Thank dear Mrs G for the socks. I hope they will fit. I hope dear Ettie has not been reading too much & no London Journals or novels.

1/246, 1/259–60

Epilogue

As anticipated in his Queenscliff letters, Walter Richardson was appointed to the post of Acting Health Officer and, from early 1878, also to that of Acting Tide Surveyor, positions previously held by Dr Williams. The continued rapid deterioration in his mental health, however, led to him being relieved of these positions in June 1878. On 11 September he was admitted to Cremorne Private Hospital, Richmond, and two months later transferred to the public asylum at Yarra Bend. The diagnosis, incipient general paralysis of the insane, has been interpreted by modern medical scholars as the tertiary stage of syphilis. If this diagnosis is correct, Walter must presumably have been infected as a young man, either through sexual contact or, as Dorothy Green has argued, perhaps during his medical training and practice.

Mary, meanwhile, decided to train as a post mistress in order to support her family and in mid-September 1878 she and the girls moved to Koroit in the south-west of Victoria, where she would run the post and telegraph office until August 1880. On 24 February 1879, Walter was sent to Koroit 'on leave' from Yarra Bend, presumably so he could die at home. This he eventually did on 1 August 1879, at the age of fifty-three, and was buried in the Koroit Cemetery.

A year later Mary was promoted to the position of post mistress at Maldon, a much larger and less isolated town. It was from there that the young Ettie went in April 1883 to become a boarder at the Presbyterian Ladies' College, Melbourne. In January 1887, after Mary had been appointed to the Richmond South post office in Melbourne, Ettie became a day girl and Lil also now attended PLC. In May, with her daughters' school education almost completed, Mary felt financially secure enough to resign from her job at the post office. In the middle of 1888 the Hawthorn house was sold at last, for over £4000.

Mary used the proceeds to take her daughters to Europe for further musical training, sailing from Melbourne on 3 August 1888 on the RMS *Ormuz*; none of them was to return to Australia permanently. In her ship-board diary, Mary wrote on her wedding anniversary, 27 August, 'Sad day for me 33 years ago was my happiest'. Clearly her thoughts and love were still focused on Walter, despite all that had happened in those years.

After visiting various relations in England, including Mary's sister Grace and brother William, Mary and the girls travelled to Leipzig early in 1889. There Ettie studied piano with Johannes Weidenbach and Lil the violin. There also, Ettie met John George Robertson, whom she was eventually to marry on 30 December 1895. The wedding took place at the house of Mary's old friend Mrs Graham, now a widow and living in Clontarf, near Dublin.

Mary returned to Munich, where Lil was continuing her musical studies. Initially, Ettie and George also lived there, in their own apartment, but moved to Strassburg at the end of September 1896. Surviving letters show Mary sending her daughter many pages of domestic advice, including recipes. At the end of October she fell ill, apparently with some form of intestinal cancer, and died on 26 November 1896, at the age of sixty. As Henry Handel Richardson, Ettie wrote a story about her mother's last days, originally entitled 'Death', later renamed 'Mary Christina'.

Richardsons and Bailey family trees showing persons mentioned in Walter's and Mary's letters

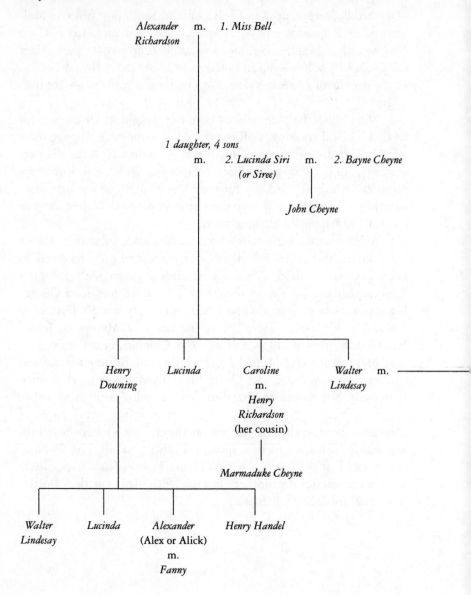

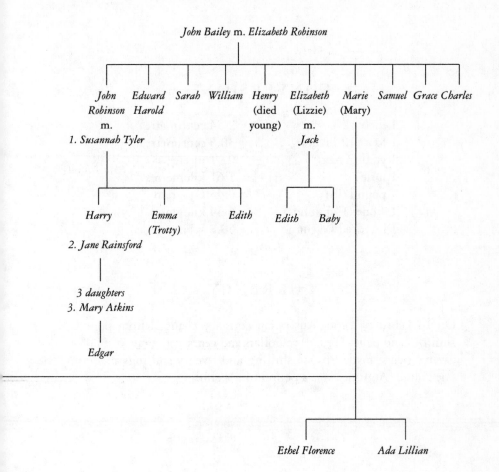

John Bailey m. Elizabeth Robinson

John Robinson m. 1. Susannah Tyler | Edward Harold | Sarah | William | Henry (died young) | Elizabeth (Lizzie) m. Jack | Marie (Mary) | Samuel | Grace | Charles

Harry   Emma (Trotty)   Edith

Edith   Baby

2. Jane Rainsford

3 daughters
3. Mary Atkins

Edgar

Ethel Florence   Ada Lillian

CONVERSIONS

1 inch	2.54 centimetres
1 foot (12 inches)	30.5 centimetres
1 yard (3 feet)	0.91 metre
1 mile	1.61 kilometres
1 pound (lb)	0.45 kilogram
1 stone (14 pounds)	6.34 kilograms
1 hundredweight	50.8 kilograms

CURRENCY

On 14 February 1966, Australian currency changed from pounds, shillings and pence (£, s, d) to dollars and cents at the rate of £1 = $2. Twelve pence made up one shilling and twenty shillings made up one pound. A guinea was a pound plus a shilling.

INDEX

Bailey, Mary Jane (Jeannie), 218
Bailey, Samuel (Sam), 2, 94, 96–100, 103–6, 109, 117, 119, 129, 153, 174–5, 180, 190, 195–6, 198, 203, 206, 218–20, 222–3, 226
Bailey, Sarah (Sara), 2, 50–2, 54, 57–8, 62, 65, 97, 113, 115, 152, 161, 168, 183, 187, 189, 191–2, 196, 201, 209–11, 232
Bailey, Susannah (Susan) (née Tyler), 48, 57–8, 60–2, 64–5, 68, 70, 72
Bailey, William Henry (Bill), 2, 12, 14–15, 19–22, 27–30, 32–3, 35–6, 41–2, 44, 50, 58, 68, 110, 117, 265
Baker, W., 89
Ballarat, 9–130 *passim*, 137, 167–70, 179, 186, 190, 193, 213, 220, 229, 246, 260
Ballarat Horticultural Society, 107
Ballarat Hospital, 101, 105, 252
Ballarat Star, 48, 58, 71, 87, 95, 100, 118, 122, 125
Ballarat Times, 94, 97
Bandmann, Daniel E., 169–70
Bank of New South Wales, 174, 221
Bannister, Henry (Harry), 13, 19, 47, 51
Barambogie, 4, 6
Barker, Dr, 242, 251, 253, 262–3
Barnawartha, 222
Barry, Mr and Mrs, 56, 59, 65, 68
Barwon Heads, 33, 34, 39
Batesford, 11, 77
Bath, Elizabeth *see* Hudson, Elizabeth
Beaney, James George, 255, 256
Beaufort House, 167, 171
Beechworth, 148, 162, 189, 198–9, 203, 224, 229–30, 241, 251, 257
Beer, Revd Joseph, 159, 160
Bell Post Hill, 2, 9–45 *passim*, 49–50, 52
Bellew, John Chippendall Montesquieu, 160
Benalla, 217
Benevolent Asylum, Ballarat, 90, 107
Bennetts Hotel, Geelong, 69
Bethanga, 242
Bingley, Dr, 127
Bird, Dr Samuel Dougan, 116, 117, 173

Black Hill, 121
Blair, Dr and Mrs, 173, 262
Blanche Terrace, 167, 171
Bleasdale, Dr John Ignatius, 241–5, 249, 252, 255, 258–9
Bonwick, James, 187, 203
Bonwick, W., 212
Botanic Gardens: Melbourne, 177; Sydney, 177
Botany Bay, 177
Boucicault, Dion, 125
Bradley, Mr, 204
Bradley, Mrs, 73
Bradshaw, Billy, 12
Bradshaw, Charles, 41
Bradshaw, Charles (Charley), 12, 22, 25
Bradshaw, Edward, 2, 15, 19, 22, 27, 29, 30, 32, 37, 41
Bradshaw, Harriet Matilda (Tilly), 2, 10–14, 20–2, 24, 27–8, 34, 37, 43, 49; marriage, 47, 51–2
Bradshaw, Maria, 2, 9–16, 18, 20–2, 24, 27, 29–34, 37–9, 44–5, 47, 49, 53, 57, 63–4
Bradshaw, Mrs William Jnr, 22, 48, 56–7
Bradshaw, Polly, 2, 11, 14, 20–2, 28, 32, 37–8, 43, 45, 49, 52–3; engagement to Brooke Smith, 10, 13, 16–17, 22, 25–8, 30–1, 33–4, 39, 45
Bradshaw, William Jnr, 2, 12, 22, 25, 35, 37, 41–2, 48, 56–7, 59
Bradshaw, William Snr, 2, 10, 12–14, 19, 27, 30–5, 39, 52–3
Bradshaw, Willie, 44
Bradshaw family, 2, 11, 20, 30–1, 48, 57, 64, 67, 69–70
Bradshaw Family Hotel, 2, 12, 30–1, 34, 47, 69–70
Bradshaw's Railway Guide, 134, 135, 154
Braithwaite, W. & J., 247, 248
Bramley, Mr and Mrs, 148, 150
Bresnan, Mrs, 203, 212, 216
Brighton, Victoria, 76, 113, 219
Brind, Mr, 128
British Prince (ship), 132
Broadford, 127
Brooke, G. V., 43